TYRWHITT OF THE HARWICH FORCE

The Life of Admiral of the Fleet Sir Reginald Tyrwhitt

TYRWHITT
OF THE HARWICH FORCE

The Life of Admiral of the Fleet
Sir Reginald Tyrwhitt

A. TEMPLE PATTERSON

MACDONALD · LONDON

First published in Great Britain in 1973 by
Macdonald and Jane's
49 Poland Street
London W 1
Printed in Great Britain by
Redwood Press Limited
Trowbridge, Wiltshire

ISBN 0 356 04530 7

'No finer Fleet Commander ever sailed....He earned by personal courage and example the love, respect and confidence of every man under his command'

(Commander C L A Woollard.)

CONTENTS

LIST OF ILLUSTRATIONS

Between pages 146 and 147

PREFACE AND ACKNOWLEDGEMENTS

Heroes of the old-fashioned and uncomplicated kind are now unfashionable; it is rather the anti-hero who commands the stage and attracts attention. Our navies, no longer far-called, are melting away; and on dune and headland sink the fires that once celebrated the heyday of a British Empire which is already, for weal or woe, on its way to become one with Nineveh and Tyre. But that is no reason for allowing the memory of one of the last heroic figures of the age when Britain could still be called great to fade into oblivion.

'Tyrwhitt of Harwich' – 'Com. (T)' to the whole Navy – was once a household name to the British public, scarcely less famous than Jellicoe and Beatty in the days of the first world war and the years that followed. But unlike them, he was an uncontroversial figure, a man about whose deeds and qualities there could be no two opinions. And to have been that kind of figure sometimes does disservice to the posthumous fame of even a great man; especially a great simple and modest man. The controversies that men stir up, or that others stir up about them, often live long after them; while plain undisputed valour and steadfastness, even when coupled with notable achievements, may fail to survive into the changed climate of another age.

The life of Sir Reginald Tyrwhitt, an Elizabethan or almost Nelsonic figure free from any taint of bombast or braggodocio, should have been written long before this. It is with this conviction and in the hope that this age is still not so unsympathetic to such men as to make it too late that I have attempted it. One reason, and possibly the main one, why it was not written by some earlier hand is that his modesty and distaste for the disputes that arose in the between-war years over the memoirs and biographies of so many of the naval and military leaders of 1914–18 combined to make him destroy a considerable part of his papers. Fortunately enough survived, taken in conjunction with the hundreds of letters which he wrote to his wife when (as so often) his service parted them, as well as to his brother and sisters, and with documents in the public records, to make the task possible. In two or three of the less eventful periods of his life, however, especially since at such times he was reunited with his wife and hence wrote her no letters, there is some paucity of materials, and these periods have therefore had to be treated relatively briefly.

For placing these letters and the surviving Tyrwhitt Papers temporarily in my keeping for the purpose of this biography, and for many helpful reminiscences, I am greatly indebted to the Admiral's elder daughter, Dame Mary Tyrwhitt; as also to Lord Keyes for granting me access to the papers of his father the late Admiral of the Fleet Lord Keyes, in the archives of Churchill College, Cambridge. My warm thanks are due likewise to Professor Arthur J. Marder and Captain Geoffrey Bennett, R.N., both of whom suggested to me that I should write Sir Reginald Tyrwhitt's life; to Professor Paul G. Halpern of Florida University for helpful correspondence and discussion; to the late Admiral Sir Barry Domvile and Vice-Admiral B.C. Watson, once the Flag-Captain and Commander of his flagship respectively, both of whom placed their diaries at my disposal and aided me by their personal recollections, as also did Captain Neville Hardy, R.N., who also served in his flagship in Harwich days; to Admiral Sir Alan Scott-Moncrieff for similar recollections of service as his flag-lieutenant in the Coast of Scotland Command; to Admiral Sir Charles Madden and the late Vice-Admiral Clifford Caslon for their reminiscences of the China Command under him; to Captain P.L. Gunn, R.N., the President of the Harwich Naval Force Association, who sent me particulars and papers of the Association; to Commander F.W. Lipscomb for details of his connection with the Ex-Services Mental Welfare Society; to Mr. A.W.H. Pearsall the Keeper of

Manuscripts in the National Maritime Museum, who greatly facilitated my study of the diaries of Admirals Sir Louis Hamilton and Sir William Tennant and other papers deposited there; and to Dr. Edwin Welch the former Archivist of Churchill College, Cambridge, who did the like to my work on the admirable and growing collection of sources for modern British naval history which Captain S.W. Roskill has built up there with his assistance.

A.T.P.
Stoughton, Sussex, 1972.

THE NARROW SEAS

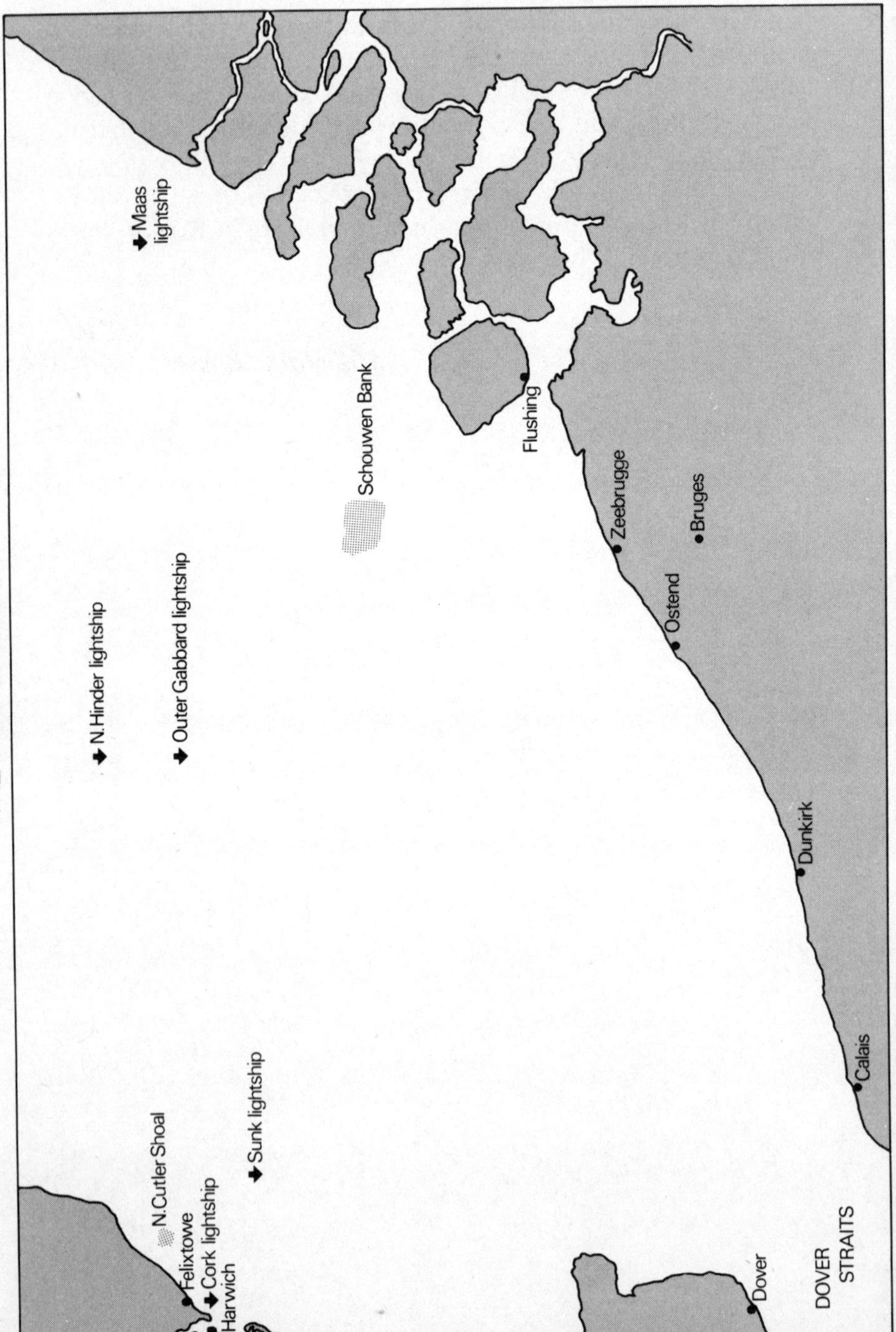

CHAPTER ONE

THE FIRST HALF OF THE JOURNEY

'If it was thought there was the least chance of war in the next two years', wrote the First Lord of the Admiralty's Naval Secretary to Sir Roger Keyes in 1930, apropos of the command of the Mediterranean Fleet, 'I feel sure everyone would be in favour of Admiral Tyrwhitt...but as it seems very unlikely it is felt that the appointment ought to go to a younger man.'[1] A strange anomaly this – a man too old to command in peace but young enough for war – and yet natural enough in the case of perhaps the greatest fighting-man who ever held the highest rank in the modern British Navy. Known to his officers and men throughout his command of the then famous Harwich Force in the first world war, and to many for all the rest of his life, as 'Com. (T)' from the rank of commodore of (Torpedo-boat) destroyers in which he began that war, he was the *beau idéal* of a 'salt horse', as the Navy calls officers who seek and repeatedly hold commands at sea rather than administrative positions ashore. He also came during the war to be nicknamed, at least by the Press, 'the stormy petrel of the Navy', from his knack of being not only in the midst of almost every scrap with the enemy but often responsible for starting it. Indeed, it came to be said of him that whenever gunfire was heard in the North Sea he was sure to be somewhere about. To this there was one sad exception. Through no fault of his own and in spite of his efforts to get there almost in defiance of orders, he was not at Jutland; had he been so, it was (and still is) the opinion of many that that battle might have had a very different outcome.

Like Nelson, Reginald Tyrwhitt was the son – and like

him the fifth son – of an English parsonage. His family was of Lincolnshire and more remotely of Northumbrian origin. Far up among the grey-green fells of Coquetdale on the northern border lie the twin hamlets of High and Nether Trewhitt from which its various branches trace their name though in an altered spelling. From the morrow of the Norman Conquest onwards occasional documents give us glimpses, dim at first, of knights and landholders bearing that name. In the early fourteenth century they are found possessed of lands in Lincolnshire as well as of their Border patrimony, and in the middle of that century a younger son took these Lincolnshire lands at Ketelby as his portion, while his elder brother's stock stayed in Northumberland and in due course died out. These Tyrwhitts of Ketelby included a knight of the body to Henry V who fought at Agincourt, another stalwart warrior knighted by Henry VII on the victorious field of Stoke, and an early Tudor vice-admiral. Then in their turn they too became extinct in the direct male line during the seventeenth century and Ketelby passed to other hands, though Reginald's father preserved or resurrected its memory in the name he gave to the house which he built in Banbury Road, Oxford, and in which Reginald himself was born and brought up.

An Elizabethan younger grandson of the vice-admiral, however, had in the meantime acquired or inherited other lands at Scotter in the same county, to which his son added the manor of Cameringham. Four generations later again the senior branch of this line likewise came to an end with a Thomas Tyrwhitt, 'a genial and careless person' who alternated between spending a month at his manor-house consuming a pipe of port in entertaining his neighbours and a year of travel. Eventually he sold Cameringham to the then Duke of Marlborough and died unmarried at Paris in 1755.

From his younger brother Robert, however – a cleric of some eminence, a canon of Windsor, a canon residentiary of St. Paul's and Rector of St. James's Westminster, as well as of Kensington – there descended a numerous progeny of clergymen, scholars and naval and military officers; in particular from his fifth son John, who entered the Navy and was Reginald's great-great-grandfather. John's eldest son Thomas (1765–1811) acquired a baronetcy and estates in Shropshire and Derbyshire, and from him were descended in the third generation the brothers Raymond, Hugh and Leonard of whom a little more will be heard hereafter. His third son Richard had as the eldest of his seven sons Robert, a barrister and magistrate who married a lady of the eminent St. John family and in consequence called his own two elder sons Richard St. John and Beauchamp St. John respectively.[2]

With this latter Richard, who in 1858 became Vicar of St. Mary Magdalene at Oxford, we come to the substantial parsonage where twelve years later Reginald Tyrwhitt was born. The Rev. Richard was a clergyman of broad and cultured outlook, possessing both literary gifts and outdoor tastes. It was these last which descended in marked degree to his youngest son, while the others were distributed among his older children. By his first marriage, with a Yorkshire country gentleman's daughter who died fifteen months later in childbirth, he had one son, Walter, who became a painter of some distinction. Two years later he married again, choosing a friend of his first wife, Caroline, the youngest daughter of John Yorke of Bewerly Hall in the West Riding. By her he had four sons and two daughters: Cecil, who entered the Church, spent three years as a missionary at Zanzibar, returned home and in 1911 became Rector of Barton Westwood in Oxfordshire; Alice Catherine ('Kitty') who became a Roman Catholic in 1900 and entered the convent of St. Mary's Priory at Princethorpe near Rugby three years later; Hugh, who emigrated to Australia at the age of eighteen and became a sheep-farmer; Beauchamp, who became an Oxford solicitor, and a twin sister Frances Mary ('Polly'); and finally Reginald Yorke, born on 10 May 1870.[3]

There could in fact hardly have been a more typically English ancestry than this for a naval officer destined to rise to the top of the tree – a junior branch of an ancient family, landed and professional but never ennobled, contributing its sons to the Church, the Law, the Services and the universities; and more immediately, the comfortable and cultured vicarage of a well-connected clergyman.

According to his sister Polly,[4] the boy was much beloved by all the household – nurse, cook (for whom he would sometimes carry buckets of coal to the kitchen in the basement), groom and housemaids as well as by his brothers and sisters. In those days the neighbouring Port Meadow was often flooded and Reggie liked to row on the floods, sometimes taking the maids or the cook or the nursemaid with him as passengers. On one such excursion they met a boy who touched his cap and explained to the maids that he had recently pulled Reggie out of deep water into which he had tumbled, whereupon Reggie, seizing the opportunity to reward him in what to his childish mind seemed a munificent manner, borrowed sixpence from one of them for the purpose.

In due course he was sent to an Oxford preparatory school which later developed into the now well-known Dragon School. Here his fondness for the water involved him in another misadventure, when a bathing-place was opened in the Cherwell at the foot of the school playing-fields and he undertook (or according to his sister was invited by the Headmaster) to open it by taking the first header. Unfortunately sufficient care had not been taken to ascertain the depth, and Reggie, going in with the same boldness and dash with which he was afterwards to lead on wider waters, struck the bottom with some force and came up scraped and bleeding.

Full of spirits, and fond of outdoor sports and pastimes such as swimming, boating and birds'-nesting, he was well liked by his fellows and a leader in the school, but (in his own later words) 'not a great success academically'. Strong-willed and quick-tempered, he was in fact a rather difficult boy to handle; and when at the age of twelve he was removed to a naval crammer's his headmaster, who was perhaps not the most perceptive and understanding of men but may also have been somewhat sorely tried, wrote to his father forecasting little success in life for him. In later days when he had become famous, Tyrwhitt took an understandable pleasure in retailing gleefully this wildly wrong assessment, but it is unlikely that the letter was quite so terse and blunt as the form in which he reproduced it from memory more than fifty years later, in a brief autobiographical fragment[5] which his family and friends finally managed to goad him into writing:

'Dear Mr. Tyrwhitt,
Your son Reggie is no good and will come to a bad end.'

Whatever the precise wording may have been, his father, who had a keen sense of humour and perhaps better judgement than the exasperated headmaster, merely laughed heartily.

The crammer to whose establishment Reggie then went was the celebrated Rev. E. Burney of Gosport, and after a year in his charge he succeeded at the second attempt in passing into the training-ship *Britannia* at Dartmouth, last but one of his term of thirty-four.[6]

The *Britannia* was a wooden three-decker of the old type, laid down in 1848, launched in 1860 as the *Prince of Wales*, and renamed when in 1869 she replaced an older *Britannia* as the cadet training ship. She was connected by a covered-in bridge to a two-decker, the *Hindostan*, which provided additional accommodation. Here cadets were given a two-year course in seamanship, navigation and a few miscellaneous subjects such as elementary French before being sent to sea. There had latterly been a good deal of criticism of this course and some stiffening-up, though a new commanding officer who took over at the same time as Reggie joined recorded afterwards that at that time:

> 'In the so-called seamanship instruction too much time was still taken up with masts, square yards and rigging, which were fast becoming obsolete, whereas there were

> no machine-shops for the cadets' instruction nor any vessel with engines of modern construction. On the other hand there was a sailing yacht and plenty of boats for the boys to handle under oars and sail...and the instructors were all zealous in performing their duties.'

In 1884, however, half-way through Reggie's course, a small barque-rigged vessel of 300 tons and 250 horse-power was added in order to provide some instruction in steam; and since in any case his early interest in boats was now finding its full outlet and he would have been the last to complain that the curriculum was overloaded in that direction at the expense of classroom work, he spent two very happy years here. In July 1885 he passed out twenty-first in the term of which he was afterwards to be the most distinguished member (though it contained the future Admirals Sir Hubert Brand and Sir Richard Webb).[7] It is significant that his only first class was in seamanship and that although he won no prizes he had been a cadet captain. His conduct was recorded as very good, though it did not attain the highest grade, of 'exemplary'.[8]

In the following month he was appointed as a naval cadet to the *Alexandra*, the flagship of the Mediterranean Fleet, along with Webb and four others of his term-mates. At that time she was flying the flag of Admiral Lord John Hay, though he was shortly afterwards relieved as Commander-in-Chief by Queen Victoria's second son, the Duke of Edinburgh.

Six months after Tyrwhitt joined her he was followed, as he had been at the same interval in the *Britannia*, by the young David Beatty, with whom his name was to be linked in later years by the plaudits of the British people. Beatty, socially popular and well connected, soon became friendly with the family of the royal C-in-C., with whose daughters he shared a devotion to riding. Small and rather slightly built, he was described afterwards by Webb as 'always very quiet in the gunroom and certainly not in the least of a ragging disposition', such as in due course brought the high-spirited Reggie also to the Duke's notice.[9] They may not at that time have had a very great deal in common, though Beatty certainly knew him well enough to call him – later at least – by his nickname of 'Peewit', given him because his surname was said to be a synonym for that bird.

In December Tyrwhitt passed his examination for midshipman, and in all spent three years in *Alexandra*. This was still the time when the Navy was making its transition from masts and yards to heavy armour and steam; and the Mediterranean flagship was a compromise typical of the age. A vessel of 8,000 tons, she was fully ship-rigged and had side-armour of malleable iron; one of the last battleships to be armed with muzzle-loaders, she was also the first to carry torpedoes. Her two eleven-inch and ten ten-inch guns were arranged in broadsides on two decks in a central citadel, but she was then considered one of the finest and most up-to-date battleships in the world.

Just at that juncture a period of complacency about Britain's naval strength was giving place in governmental and Admiralty circles to uneasiness about our position *vis-à-vis* our chief rivals, France and Russia. Life in the Navy was nevertheless not taken so seriously as it was to be fifteen or twenty years later. The influence of the age of sail remained strong; the smartest ship was the one which could cross royal yards or make plain sail in the shortest time, and gunnery was still merely a necessary but regrettable evil. Target practice had to be carried out once in every quarter of a year, but few except gunnery lieutenants took any interest in the results. Polo, pony-racing and other sports mattered more than gun-drill; not that midshipmen normally took part in the polo or the racing, but they followed the exploits of the senior officers of their respective ships with keen interest and pride.

The yearly routine rarely changed in a world that was at peace. The Mediterranean Fleet made three cruises every year, which were seldom interfered with by any outside events, and in the course of his three years Midshipman Tyrwhitt visited almost every port in that sea and enjoyed himself hugely in spite of a very limited cash allowance. A long letter to his sister Polly in October 1887 gave a boyish account of the Fleet's autumn visit to the east coast of the Adriatic. At Zara (now Zadar in Yugoslavia but then part of Austria-Hungary)

> 'the people were awfully enthusiastic about the Fleet and were very nice to us. The first night they illuminated the town, fired any amount of rockets and fireworks, and sent three different bands in three steamboats and they steamed round the Fleet for about one and a half hours and then went ashore to play on the landing-place. They invited everybody off; it was great fun. The next night they gave a ball but I could not go.'

At Cattaro, which was next visited, the inhabitants were equally welcoming, letting off more rockets and fireworks and also setting fire to 'a lot of furze bushes on top of the mountains, a fire which naturally spread and ended in a tremendous blaze'. The Fleet then went on to the Ionian island of Cephalonia, where it carried out manoeuvres for a week.

Tyrwhitt and three other midshipmen were detatched to the torpedo depot ship *Hecla*, a former merchant vessel which had been converted into the parent ship of half-a-dozen small torpedo-boats and carried supplies of torpedoes and mines. The plan of operations was that the battleship *Colossus* and she, with the torpedo-boats, were to defend the harbour of Cephalonia against the rest of the Fleet. The torpedo-boats patrolled the approaches; 'pretty hard work and one did not get much sleep', wrote Tyrwhitt, adding 'It is awfully hard to keep one's eyes open the whole night.' 'Torpedo-boat work at night is awfully dangerous,' he went on importantly, and proceeded to give chapter and verse:

'...at 2.30 a.m. we were run into by another friendly torpedo-boat which made a nasty hole in our bows [and] we had to steam back to the ship full speed to prevent sinking.' Less fortunate was yet another of the defending boats, which was cut clean in two by one of its 'enemy' opposite numbers and sank in four minutes with the loss of two stokers. Yet although 'it was a very hard and rough life [he] liked it very much' and 'enjoyed [himself] awfully the fortnight he was away [from the *Alexandra*].[10]

On another of these cruising visits Tyrwhitt was able to take advantage of his father's cloth to secure a temporary easing of his limited finances. The Fleet was due to call at Jaffa, and it was announced beforehand that officers would be given facilities to visit Jerusalem from there at their own expense, the arrangements for horses and accommodation being made by the already well-established pioneer travel agency of Thomas Cook and Son at a cost of five pounds apiece. For such a pilgrimage Mr. Tyrwhitt could hardly refuse the necessary 'fiver' and Reggie, mounted on an old fleabitten grey, was therefore one of the eighty officers who set off on a perfect evening to ride the forty miles to the Holy City. Stopping only for dinner at Ramleh, they continued through the night and arrived rather saddle-sore (in his case and many others) to spend three days in seeing the sights of Jerusalem.

When the time came to return he discovered that someone had appropriated his horse and after trying in vain to get another he found himself as darkness was coming on horseless and alone forty miles from Jaffa, virtually penniless and unable either to speak a word of the local languages or find anybody who spoke English.

Starting off on foot, he fortunately had no difficulty in following the correct route and had walked about four miles without meeting a soul when he saw a dim light and heard voices and the sounds of horses. Approaching cautiously, he found that the light and the voices came from an inn outside which about fifteen horses were tethered. Selecting one which was somewhat separated from the rest, he untied it, led it for about 200 yards, and then mounted and rode as if the devil himself was after him, without drawing rein for an hour or more, after which he could hear no sounds of pursuit. By this time the moon was up and he had no difficulty in keeping on course, so that he was not long in catching up the rearguard of the party of officers, who in due course stopped at Ramleh for a pre-arranged light breakfast before going on to Jaffa which was about sixteen miles further.

Young Tyrwhitt's troubles were not yet over, however, for being tired he sought a quiet corner in the Ramleh inn and settled down for a nap while awaiting breakfast. Nobody roused him and he awoke to a deathly silence with apparently not a soul about. Eventually he found another midshipman, also asleep, but when they searched for horses the only two they could discover proved to be both dead lame. There was nothing for it but to walk; the Fleet was sailing at twelve-thirty, and they arrived at the landing-stage just as the last boat was leaving, in charge of an officer who had been sent ashore to leave their descriptions with the British vice-consul in case of the worst.

On board they were received by a very angry Commander who promptly stopped their leave for the rest of the cruise. A *deus ex machina* was at hand, however, in the person of the Commander-in-Chief, the Duke of Edinburgh, who happened to be walking on the poop and noticed the Commander berating the unhappy pair. Beckoning Tyrwhitt to him, he asked the reason of this wrath, to which Reggie replied: 'We are late, Sir; we had to walk from Ramleh.' 'Do you mean to say', the Duke exclaimed, 'that you boys walked from Ramleh?', whereupon Reggie volunteered that he had nearly had to walk the whole way from Jerusalem. Much intrigued and amused, the Commander-in-Chief then invited the pair to dinner that evening in order to hear their adventures. After an excellent dinner Reggie recited his story, and when he arrived at his theft of a horse the Duke began to roar with laughter and burst out: 'So you're the rascal who stole the horse belonging to the commander of my Turkish cavalry escort!' (with which the local authorities had provided him). Greatly tickled and rather impressed by Reggie's resource, the Duke then rescinded the punishment the pair had received.

Another adventure during one of these cruises goes far to explain why the royal C.-in-C. was adored by every gunroom in the Fleet and perhaps casts a little retrospective light on the reasons why Reggie's late headmaster had taken a poor view of him.

The Fleet had anchored in Aranchi Bay in Sardinia, and the midshipmen were spending their spare time in bathing picnics on the many uninhabited islands in this bay. During one of these picnics Reggie discovered a herd of moufflon led by a magnificent ram, and arranged with three of his closest friends to slaughter it in order to augment the gunroom diet. Setting off ostensibly for another picnic, they smuggled their guns aboard their skiff, loaded them with cartridges specially cut in a manner known to Reggie, landed on the island, stalked the luckless ram, and fired two salvoes into it which almost tore it to pieces. Dragging the mangled carcase down to their boat, they loaded it on board; but by this time they were beginning to have belated but disturbing doubts whether the herd of supposedly wild moufflon might not after all be private property. They therefore decided that it would be better to smuggle the carcase aboard the flagship and for that reason did not return to it till after dark.

Arriving with their crime undetected and enlisting the ready aid of the rest of the gunroom, who produced a rope, they hauled the gory evidence into it through the torpedo port. After that things began to go wrong. The gunroom steward refused to cook the meat since it was full of lead, and the midshipmen decided to cut off the head and keep it as a trophy, but stuff the carcase with coal and sink it unobtrusively overboard. This was done and the sick-berth steward stuffed the head, but on the following morning the captain of the side reported to the Commander that the 'young gentlemen' had been spilling what seemed to be red lead under the torpedo port in the gunroom. Even so, nothing happened for a few days until Reggie was suddenly sent for by the C.-in-C., who was entertaining a large party of local notables and evidently had a pretty good idea of who was the leading spirit in the gunroom of his flagship. Entering the cabin with a slight sinking feeling in his stomach, Reggie was invited to sit down beside the Duke, who poured him out a glass of port and then asked him: 'Have you been shooting any moufflon lately?' Knowing that one of the guests was a local landowner, Reggie realised that all was up and replied, 'Yes, Sir,' whereupon he was commanded to 'Tell me all about it.'

Amid a deathly silence he recounted the whole story. When he ended the Duke said: 'I see. By the way, where did you learn that trick of cutting the cartridges?' 'Oh, my father told me about that, Sir; he once shot a stag that way in the Highlands.' 'H'mm. Was your father a poacher?' 'No, Sir, he's a parson.' Another moment of silence followed this rejoinder, and then the whole cabin, including the landowner whose prized ram had been shot and who understood English well enough, burst into laughter and the episode ended better than the 'young gentlemen' probably deserved.

The C.-in-C's indulgence may well have been partly due to the fact that Tyrwhitt, despite an occasional and very human propensity to pranks, was looked on by his superiors as a promising young officer.[11] Towards the end of this term of service in the Mediterranean he was detached for a spell of three months (May–July 1888 inclusive) in H.M.S. *Cruiser*, a sailing barque used for training midshipmen and seamen in sail. During this course the midshipmen were allowed to keep watch and given frequent opportunities of handling the ship, which Tyrwhitt greatly enjoyed and of which he availed himself with credit, earning from the captain the report that he could 'work the ship under canvas very well'.[12] On one occasion, however, his career was nearly brought to an abrupt end through no fault of his own, when as midshipman of the main top he was nearly knocked out of the top by the main topsail being allowed to fall on his head, dashing him on to the forks of the mainstay with every bit of breath battered out of his body. Fortunately the captain of the main top who was on the main yard caught hold of him and hauled him back, earning thereby many a later bottle of beer at Tyrwhitt's expense.

After returning to the *Alexandra* till September to complete his three years' service, Tyrwhitt was ordered home, along with three other midshipmen, to join the Training Squadron. On the day before his departure the Fleet Regatta was held, and he rowed in the winning boat in both the officers' and the gunroom races. In the evening Prince George, the future King George V, who was then a watch-keeping lieutenant in his uncle's flagship, invited him to a dinner which was naturally rather hilarious in view of the ship's successes in the regatta. Afterwards he rejoined his friends in the gunroom for further celebrations and was eventually rowed by them across to the gunboat *Cockatrice* shortly before midnight, at which hour the *Cockatrice* was due to leave with the homegoing midshipmen. Having, as he put it afterwards, 'done himself well', he went straight to his hammock without reporting himself and immediately fell asleep. No one had seen him come on board, and it was not till after the captain of the *Cockatrice* had signalled that he was ready to proceed but was one midshipman short and a general signal had been made to the Fleet: 'Is Midshipman Tyrwhitt on board? If so he is to be sent to H.M.S. *Cockatrice* immediately' that he was discovered, shaken into wakefulness and told that the captain wanted him. Naturally he was not very popular with that officer for a time, but was presently forgiven.

After six weeks' leave at home Tyrwhitt then joined the *Calypso*, one of the four corvettes composing the Training Squadron. Here he found life very different from that in the *Alexandra*. The captain was a martinet of the first order;

punishments for the officers and men were very severe and usually unjust; and the food was bad, consisting mainly of unadulterated salt tack, since the squadron was constantly at sea under sail, carrying out the annual manoeuvres in conjunction with the rest of the Fleet. When in the course of these manoeuvres 'war' was declared the captain assembled the ship's company and announced that during the period of 'hostilities' all punishments would be doubled. 'In these days', wrote Tyrwhitt nearly sixty years later, 'no one would believe what went on in that ship.' In spite of everything, however, the gunroom managed to be happy and even proud of their ship, which was the smartest in the squadron; and Tyrwhitt left it in December 1889 with a good report as 'a reliable young officer.'[13] During part of this time he had been detached for service in the *Australia*, whose commanding officer was rather more expansive, reporting that he had 'taken much interest in his work and shown himself a zealous and capable young officer, ready and willing'.[14]

Having passed his examination in seamanship, he then went through the sub-lieutenants' courses at the Royal Naval College, Greenwich, and in H.M.S. *Excellent*, the gunnery school at Portsmouth, without particular distinction and was appointed in that rank to the armoured cruiser *Aurora* in October 1891. From her he passed, after a brief month in the first-class cruiser *Blake*, to the brig *Pilot*, one of six sailing-tenders attached to the training-cruiser *Impregnable*;

Each of these brigs had a complement of a lieutenant in command, a sub-lieutenant, a boatswain, a nucleus of petty officers and able seamen and a hundred boys for training, and cruised continuously except at week-ends. Hard work though this was, Tyrwhitt enjoyed it thoroughly; but he did not see the training season through, for on July 1 he was appointed for a short spell to the royal yacht *Victoria and Albert*, where he again found David Beatty, now a lieutenant, among his brother-officers.

'Swinging round a buoy' at Cowes was a very different life from that of a training brig, and although he found it very interesting to have the opportunity of meeting most of the members of the royal family he was perhaps not altogether sorry when after his promotion to lieutenant he was appointed on 21 September to the corvette *Cleopatra* for service in the North American and West Indies Fleet. The *Cleopatra* was commanded by Captain the Hon. Assheton Curzon Howe, a strict disciplinarian, a fine seaman and a good friend. His officers both feared and loved him, and Tyrwhitt always regarded the three years (1892–5) he served under his command as the happiest commission of his life. Since Captain Howe was Senior Officer of the Fishery Squadron in Newfoundland waters during this time, the *Cleopatra* spent each summer there from May to November and each winter in the West Indies, after which she paid a brief visit to Bermuda for her annual refit.

It was during the winter cruise of 1893–4 in the West Indies that Tyrwhitt was given an opportunity of special service of which he availed himself with credit. This arose from an outbreak of trouble in the Central American republic of Nicaragua. Nearly the whole coastline of this little republic was known as the Mosquito Coast and inhabited by a tribe consequently called the Mosquito Indians. Here a complicated situation had developed in which the chief ingredients were: the settlement of foreigners along the coast, at first chiefly British woodcutters but more latterly Americans intent on prospecting for gold or on growing bananas; the rather waning interest of the British government, which at one time had amounted to a virtual protectorate of the Mosquitos; the growing interest of the United States now that the project of a canal across the isthmus of Central America was developing, and their consequent suspicion of any British interference; the existence of a treaty made in 1860 and interpreted further by an arbitration award in 1880, making Nicaraguan sovereignty over the region merely nominal, protecting the Mosquitos' autonomy, and practically giving Britain a right of intervention on their behalf; and finally the wish of the Nicaraguan government to establish effective rule over them.

The only seaport on the coast was Bluefields, developed by foreigners and particularly by recent American settlers. In 1893 a war had broken out between Nicaragua and the neighbouring republic of Honduras, and the Nicaraguans now took advantage of rumours of a Honduran invasion of the coast to descend upon it themselves. At the beginning of 1894 Bluefields was surprised and seized in the middle of the night by a force of about 200 of them under a General Corbezo, who immediately proclaimed martial law. The Americans appealed to the United States government, and a warship, the U.S.S. *Kearsage*, was sent down but struck a reef and was lost. The British North American Fleet was then lying at Barbados, and the *Cleopatra* was despatched to take the *Kearsage*'s place.

Bluefields was not actually on the coast but separated from it by a lagoon about six miles square, and Captain Curzon Howe on arriving and gathering the general outlines of the situation decided to return to the nearest telegraph station, 350 miles away at Colon on the Caribbean coast of Panama, in order to get instructions from the British government. In the meantime he left a landing-party of about fifty men under his first lieutenant and Tyrwhitt to maintain order and if necessary protect the inhabitants from violence at the hands of the Nicaraguans.

In spite of Britain's rather rusty right of intervention under the award of 1880, and in view of the touchiness of the United States, it was felt that a landing under arms might need considerable justification, and the party was ordered not to take up its quarters in the town except in case of an emergency, but to camp on an island in the lagoon. During the next few days, however, Tyrwhitt went into the town more than once to have a look round and size up the Nicaraguan 'troops', whom he described as about the poorest and most starved-looking set of scoundrels he had ever seen, without uniforms or boots or in a few cases even trousers. Meanwhile the landing-party amused themselves by fishing for the sharks and alligators which swarmed in the lagoon until at the end of a week the *Cleopatra* returned with instructions that the Nicaraguans were to be disarmed and disbanded, without bloodshed if possible. This Captain Curzon Howe managed to effect, except that about fifty disappeared with their arms into the surrounding forest and Corbezo begged successfully to be allowed to keep another twenty-five as a bodyguard.

The *Cleopatra* then sailed off again with the remaining 125 for Greytown, the republic's only other port. No sooner had she gone than the fifty who had taken refuge in the forest emerged again, and at night a canoe came over from the town to the camp with an imploring appeal from the foreign residents to the British to come and take charge, since violence had broken out. Some of the Nicaraguan troops had tried to arrest an American, and this had led to a shooting affray in which two soldiers were killed and an old woman lying in bed was wounded. The British responded with alacrity and as soon as they had landed everyone else disappeared from the streets, which they patrolled till daylight. Afterwards they continued to police the town, closing all liquor shops and forbidding anyone except themselves to carry arms.

The patrolling which they kept up day and night was a heavy task, though it was somewhat lightened when the ship came back again and the landing-party was doubled. Tyrwhitt had meanwhile disarmed the rest of the Nicaraguan troops, who submitted without a murmur, but many rifles and a good deal of ammunition were believed to have been hidden in the neighbourhood and searches for them proved fruitless. Tyrwhitt carried out several of these searches, chiefly at night, and was at least able to round up a few more Nicaraguan 'soldiers' who were still at large in the bush. One of them, who took to flight, he ran down and overpowered after a long chase which left his men, who were in heavy marching order, far behind. Eventually all the Nicaraguans were allowed to depart inland, after some alarm had been caused when two of them (whom Tyrwhitt afterwards imprisoned) were caught putting arsenic into one of the water-supply tanks.

Shortly afterwards the *Cleopatra*, whose engines needed repair and which was due for a spell in dry dock, was relieved by the *Canada* and sailed for Jamaica. Throughout, the American inhabitants of Bluefields had shown much appreciation of the timely intervention of the British and had done all they could to make them comfortable. 'I must say', wrote Tyrwhitt to his brother Beauchamp, 'my opinion of the Yankee has gone up very much.'[15]

Negotiations followed in which the British government repeatedly assured the United States that it had no intention of establishing or resurrecting a protectorate over the Mosquito Indians and that its forces had been landed simply for the protection of life and property. The *Canada* was withdrawn in its turn, the American warship *San Francisco* arrived, and the ultimate outcome was that with Britain tiring of the difficult and equivocal position in which her relations with the Mosquitos were placing her and refusing to support their wish for autonomy any further, while the Nicaraguans for their part began to treat them a little more tactfully, the republic's control of the coast was established and recognised.[16]

Meanwhile the *Cleopatra* had gone north again with the rest of the squadron; and Tyrwhitt, whose energy was almost boundless and who had a vast capacity for enjoying most sides of his service and a particular love of fishing, was soon revelling in the wonderful opportunities for this which the rivers of Newfoundland gave him and his brother officers. All the rivers were free and they were even exempt from the fishing tax, in addition to which they were in a position to fish waters which in those days were accessible only from the sea, since there were no roads in the greater part of the country.

This lack of roads and the resultant difficulty of communication were forcibly brought home to Tyrwhitt at the start of his first independent command. This was a very small torpedo-boat, *TB 78*, sixty-nine feet long and eight feet in beam, which carried a crew of eight and was commissioned each summer to patrol the west coast of Newfoundland between May and October. Of this he was placed in charge in 1895.

On his initial trip, from St. George's Bay to Port Saunders, he put in for the night at a harbour of which he had no chart and on entering which *TB 78* struck a rock, breaking her propeller shaft. Tyrwhitt recovered the broken shaft and propeller by diving for them, although the temperature of the water was very little above freezing-point; but he had no means of communication with his senior officer, who was then in the harbour of St. John's. The nearest telegraph station, at Cow Head, was fortunately only thirty miles away as the crow flies, but there was not even a track through the intervening country and all intercourse was normally carried out by sea. At Rocky Harbour (as it was appropriately called) where *TB 78* was effectively stranded, there were three or four huts occupied by hardy fishermen whom he tried in vain to induce to carry a telegram to Cow Head. The journey there and back would take a week, they told him, since ten miles a day was the recognised rate of travel in that part of the country and one full day would be needed for rest at Cow Head before starting back.

Somewhat nettled and in a spirit of bravado Tyrwhitt replied that he would take the telegram himself, starting at daylight next morning and returning on the following evening. This they informed him was a flat impossibility and a very dangerous thing to attempt, since three fairly big rivers had to be swum or waded and in any case he would probably lose himself in the woods.

Undeterred, he started at early dawn next day and was not long in realising what he had let himself in for. There was not a sign of a track and he was compelled to keep close to the coast in order not to lose his direction; but he struggled on for fifteen hours almost without stopping, pushing his way through thick forest and wading up to his waist through bogs and rivers. At half-past eight that night, very tired in spite of his strength and fitness, he reached Cow Head to find the telegraphist as helpful and co-operative as the fishermen had been the opposite. Having sent off the telegram, he fed Tyrwhitt well, insisted on giving him his bed, called him at 4 a.m. next morning and sent him off in good shape on his return journey. Despite the same difficulties as before Tyrwhitt managed to complete it by 9 p.m., desperately tired but kept going by his determination to show the Newfoundlanders that they had no monopoly of the walking powers on which they habitually prided themselves.

After an interval of three weeks the sloop *Pelican* to which the torpedo-boat was attached arrived with a new shaft which was duly fitted and *TB 78* resumed her service.

The headquarters for this was Port Saunders, a fishing village of thirty or forty inhabitants, most of whom worked in a canning factory and the oldest of whom had lived there all his life without ever having seen a horse. Here, when they were not actually cruising, the patrol found accommodation in a wooden hut derisively christened Admiralty House and containing a cubby-hole which Tyrwhitt occupied and one large room which the crew used as both living and sleeping quarters.

His duties included keeping a register of all the recognised canning establishments along a stretch of about 150 miles of coast and practically unsurveyed waters, which he was supposed to patrol once a week in each direction. He also acted as a magistrate, settling the numerous disputes between the Newfoundlanders and the French fishermen who frequented this coast. Despite an inability to master the French language which had already hindered him in examinations, he met with no difficulty in doing this, all parties accepting his decisions peaceably. The weather was by no means pleasant, but he considered that he and his crew were in clover, since he was able to hire a cow which provided them with milk and butter, fish was plentiful, and every six weeks or so the commissariat was restocked by one of the fishing vessels, which also landed mail and newspapers. In addition he had brought with him a collapsible canvas canoe in which he made frequent visits to a fine salmon river called the Torrent, where he enjoyed excellent sport and sometimes spent the night in a shelter he had built.

The little crew had nevertheless one very unpleasant adventure while on patrol. Returning from one of their weekly cruises, they were rounding Point Rich, a 200-foot cliff to which Tyrwhitt was giving a wide berth, in a heavy sea and a strong westerly wind, when the engines broke down and they began drifting towards the cliff. Outwardly unperturbed, the engine-room artificer and his two stokers set to work on repairs, though the little ship was rolling so much that it was difficult to keep one's feet. Nearer and nearer to the cliffs she drifted until she was actually being kept off them only by the backwash of the heavy seas that pounded them. In this situation she lay for nearly two hours until the devoted E.R.A. and his tiny staff had temporarily made good the repairs and she was able to go ahead very slowly, rounding Point Rich and running with a fair wind into Port Saunders nine miles beyond, the crew helping the engines by making sail with every blanket they could find. Tyrwhitt duly reported the cool and competent conduct of his engine-room staff, who received a letter of commendation from the Admiralty. Neither their behaviour nor this appreciation of it, however, alters the fact that *TB 78* was quite inadequate for the service on which she had been employed for several years. Tyrwhitt himself also received a similar letter from the Admiralty, whose attention had been directed by the vice-admiral commanding the North American station to his services while engaged in this fishery patrol.[17]

At the close of the fishery season he returned to St. George's Bay and rejoined the *Cleopatra*, whose commission was at an end and which now proceeded home under sail (being a fully-rigged vessel), making a quick passage with a following gale for most of the way and arriving in Plymouth Sound early in December. For Tyrwhitt this proved a sad homecoming, however, for his father died on the day after he reached Oxford.

After a few weeks' leave and through the recommendation of Captain Curzon Howe (who had reported on him warmly as 'a most capable, zealous and trustworthy officer')[18] he found himself to his delight appointed to command one of the earliest of a new class of ship, the destroyer *Hart*, thus making his first acquaintance with the arm of the Service in which he and after him his son were both to become famous in war.

It was the evolution of the torpedo and then the torpedo-boat which had brought the torpedo-boat-destroyer into being. France was still regarded as Britain's potential enemy and British naval policy was still based on the strategy of close blockade in the event of war. Immediately on the outbreak of war, that is, all French ports and naval bases were to be closely blockaded by flotillas of light craft with cruisers in support and a superior battlefleet in reserve. But with the development of the torpedo the French in particular were building torpedo-boats with the hope of making close blockade impossible. To these the first destroyers were the British reply; originally their purpose was to checkmate torpedo-boats and so enable close blockade to continue. It was only afterwards that they also took over the torpedo-boat's function of attacking with the torpedo.

The *Hart* was one of a flotilla of six which with two cruisers and two battleships constituted a new Particular Service Squadron under Rear-Admiral Dale. Since the Admiral believed in trying out these new-fangled craft, not perhaps in all weathers, but at least in some pretty rough seas, life in these early destroyers was apt to be exciting. In a letter to his sister Kitty in March Tyrwhitt described a full-speed trial which the flotilla held in the form of a race from Queenstown to Berehaven. In this the *Hart* came in second, averaging just under 23 knots, which was considered quite good under the circumstances.

> 'At times [he wrote] I think we were absolutely under water fore and aft. A good deal of damage was done; half the bridge was washed away – luckily I was standing on the other half – and a good many stanchions, etc., were broken...I got washed off my feet and was banged against an iron stanchion which knocked the stuffing out of me. My left thigh is about twice its proper size and I am in bed...I think nearly everyone was seasick, especially the stokers. I am lucky in that respect.'[19]

After the trials were completed the squadron was sent out to reinforce the Mediterranean Fleet and its destroyers became instructional ships spending their time in training personnel, and especially stokers, for the numerous destroyers which were now being turned out. Tyrwhitt found this a very pleasant life, since it meant that the captains were their own masters and so long as they put in the requisite number of hours under way no one seemed to care where they went or what they did.

After four months in command of the *Hart* and a further six in charge of another destroyer, the *Ranger*, he was appointed in November 1896 first lieutenant (and therefore executive officer) of the *Surprise*, the despatch vessel of the Mediterranean Fleet, which was commanded by his distant cousin – of the Shropshire branch – the Hon. Hugh Tyrwhitt, who afterwards became private secretary to the First Lord of the Admiralty in 1902. Commander Tyrwhitt reported on his young kinsman as 'a very good executive officer' who possessed 'tact and judgement' – praise which was repeated by Commander Hervey, who took over the ship in October 1898.[20] In the *Surprise* Tyrwhitt spent three more very happy years in the Mediterranean. To all intents and purposes she was the Commander-in-Chief's yacht, accompanying the fleet on all its cruises and frequently embarking him in order that he could visit ports that he could not have entered in a battleship.

Life in the 'Med' was still much the same as in Tyrwhitt's first commission there, but with the important exception that thanks mainly to the enterprise and inventions of Captain Percy Scott the Navy was just beginning to wake up again to the fact that its guns had been supplied to it for the purpose of hitting an enemy as often and as hard as possible. Scott's own ship had achieved what was then the remarkable feat of scoring 80 per cent of hits in the annual gunlayers' test, with a very high rate of fire, in contrast to the 20 per cent to 40 per cent usually attained. To effect this he had invented a device called a 'dotter', with which all ships were afterwards equipped. This was a machine which moved a cardboard target up and down a short distance from a gun. By following this target with his gun-sight a gunlayer could perfect himself in 'following the roll' and keeping continually on the target ready to fire the instant the gun was reported loaded – a marked improvement on the old method of waiting for the sights to roll on with the ship's motion. Moreover by pressing the gunfiring key the layer actuated an electrically controlled panel which marked the target and recorded his exact aim. As the result of this and other improvements prize firing had been instituted, and was having the effect of stimulating competition amongst all classes of ships, so that gunnery now began to take a more and more prominent place in inter-ship rivalry, though firing practice was still normally carried out at a range of no more than 2,000 yards at the most.

A good deal of Tyrwhitt's spare time on this commission was devoted to polo, of which he had become very fond, though he never excelled at it. This was also the heyday of bicycles, which were in great demand in Malta, where bicycle-parties and bicycle-picnics were very popular, and he not only cycled all over the island but invariably took his machine to sea with him in order to have the opportunity of riding inland from the ports he visited.

One such ride, from Beyrout to Damascus and back, on which he was accompanied by two friends, lingered long in his memory. The road cut across the Lebanon Mountains and then the Anti-Lebanons, each range 6,000 feet high, with a plain between them. Having visited the impressive ruins of Baalbek and crossed the Lebanons, the three friends spent the night at an inn on the nearest side of the plain and rose at early dawn to ride on across it. Here they were objects of much interest to the many shepherds who were watching their flocks and had perhaps never seen a bicycle before. Reaching the top of the Anti-Lebanons rather exhausted about 10 a.m., they rested for a time and then set off downhill towards Damascus about twenty-five miles away. The road was good but steep, and one of Tyrwhitt's companions took a nasty toss, dislocating his shoulder and bruising himself badly, as well as 'writing off' his bicycle. Fortunately the third member of the party happened to be a doctor, and after Tyrwhitt and he had made a sort of four-wheeled carriage of the two remaining cycles, on which they conveyed the injured man till they came to a small but hospitable farm, he was able to set the dislocated shoulder and make his patient reasonably comfortable on the only bed the farmhouse possessed, until a conveyance could be sent back for him from Damascus.

During this spell in the Mediterranean Tyrwhitt also came into contact again with the genial Duke of Edinburgh, who had by now become the Duke of Saxe-Coburg, though in naval circles he continued to be thought of and known by his former title. The Duke was now very ill and the *Surprise* was suddenly ordered to Venice to take him to Alexandria for a rest-cure at Helonan. In the skilful hands of the *Surprise*'s surgeon, Bankhart (afterwards Surgeon-Admiral Sir Reginald Bankhart), he made so much progress that when the ship arrived at Alexandria it was instructed to wait there and take him for a cruise during his convalescence. Among the places that were then visited were Monte Carlo, where the Prince of Wales came on board to visit his brother, and Nice, where

Queen Victoria – wheeled up the gangway by her attendant John Brown – also visited him. But although the Duke seemed to have regained his health when he left the *Surprise* soon afterwards his cure proved to be merely temporary, and the only time Tyrwhitt saw him again was when he called on him not long before his death in 1900. As he entered the sick-room where the Duke lay propped up with many pillows the dying man, who had always retained a soft spot for the young officer whose mischievous exploits as a midshipman he remembered, pointed at him, said "Moufflon" and burst out laughing.

Near the end of the *Surprise*'s commission the Fashoda crisis of 1899 threatened war with France. Every fighting ship in Malta was immediately made ready for active service, among them being the *Orion*, an elderly coast-defence vessel armed with four eleven-inch muzzle-loading guns, to which the crews of the *Surprise* and the training-ship *Cruiser* were turned over. She had been laid up at Malta for ten years and was not in seagoing order, but within a fortnight she left harbour for a steam trial and reported ready for sea, after which she was inspected by the new Commander-in-Chief in the Mediterranean, Sir John ('Jacky') Fisher. Sir John was quite complimentary, but as he went over the side his parting order was 'Get your torpedo-net defence out tomorrow.' Since this had been stowed in the head room for ten years getting it into position would involve no mean effort, and many bets were laid in the Club about how long it would actually take, three days being the favoured time. By backing his own opinion that it could be done in half of that, Tyrwhitt made what he described as 'a nice little packet', since the net defence was completed by noon on the second day; though most of his winnings went on the beer he had promised the ship's company if they achieved this.

After the *Orion* was paid off he returned overland to England and within a few days was appointed in December 1899 first lieutenant of the light cruiser *Indefatigable*. As before in the *Surprise* this meant that he was the ship's executive officer. Having coaled at Bermuda the *Indefatigable* joined the North American Fleet in time for its annual cruise in the West Indies in 1900 and afterwards remained on the station. From a personal point of view this proved to be the most important commission in Tyrwhitt's life, for at Trinidad early in 1902 he met at the house of the Governor, Sir Alfred Moloney, a young friend of Lady Moloney's who was staying there, a Miss Angela Corbally, daughter of Matthew Corbally of Rathbeale Hall in County Dublin. They fell in love with each other at once, and within a comparatively few days Tyrwhitt was nerved by the imminence of his departure for a long cruise, from which the *Indefatigable* would not return to Trinidad until after Miss Corbally had left, to propose and was accepted; though a separation of nearly a year followed before they could be reunited in Britain.[21]

It was when the *Indefatigable* had returned to Trinidad and was lying in harbour there at the beginning of May that the terrible eruption of Mont Pelée in the island of Martinique took place. This volcano had long been thought to be extinct, but at the end of April it came to life again and on 8 May erupted with such violence that the town of St. Pierre which lay at its foot was completely destroyed in a disaster rivalling that of Pompeii in ancient times. The neighbouring British island of St. Vincent also suffered severely from an eruption at the same time, about 1,600 people being killed, others injured and many rendered homeless.

The *Indefatigable* at once set out thither with a huge cargo of provisions and other necessities, and after delivering them brought a second cargo from Barbados, to which she immediately returned to take on board yet another for Martinique. She had just arrived there and was lying off the ruins of St. Pierre and about to land a party, when without the slightest warning another eruption took place.

> 'We were in the act of lowering a boat [wrote Tyrwhitt to his sisters] when suddenly there was a clap of

> thunder and a huge upheaval of what looked like mud, steam and muck, which shot up like a column and then opened out and spread with frightful rapidity but luckily not our way. In less than five minutes there was a tremendous explosion on the beach about a mile from us. This was caused by the lava running into the sea. The effect of it running into the water was beyond description. Hugh clouds of steam rose, the water appeared to be boiling and the row was awful. I have often heard the expression "boiling sea" used and now I've seen it and don't want to do so again...We cleared out for Fort de France [another port a few miles down the coast] at full speed, as it was much too close to be pleasant.'

Having unloaded her cargo, the *Indefatigable* was preparing on the following day to leave Fort de France and Tyrwhitt was superintending the much-needed scrubbing of decks when still another eruption took place that far surpassed the previous day's. The ship was then lying about fifteen miles from the peak of the volcano and it was a perfectly calm and clear morning, when suddenly an enormous mushroom-shaped cloud shot upward from the crater and spread rapidly. Tyrwhitt ordered the crew to their fire stations, furled awnings and drenched the upper deck; while at the same time most of the population of the town rushed into the waterfront and within a very few minutes scores of crowded canoes and hundreds of swimming natives were making for the *Indefatigable*. Twenty minutes later there was 'standing-room only' on her upper deck, and about forty-five minutes after the eruption the contents of what was by now the vast umbrella-shaped cloud began to fall like a hailstorm. 'I must say', wrote Tyrwhitt, 'I was never in such a funk in my life myself.' But by the time the lava reached the ship it was comparatively cool, though since it covered the deck to a depth of several inches it was as well that the hoses had been kept going. Half-an-hour later the lava shower ceased as abruptly as it had begun, the sun came out again and all was peace except for the excited chattering of the natives. By now the land was completely covered by grey ash and not a single leaf was left on the trees, though beyond this no further harm had been done. A few of the bolder natives now returned to the shore, and when they had reported that all was comparatively safe the remainder took to their boats and went back to their ash-covered homes, leaving the *Indefatigable*'s ship's company to spend the rest of the day shovelling ash overboard and cleaning up once more before departing.[22]

There followed a summer cruise in North American waters, with visits to Halifax (from which Tyrwhitt travelled 300 miles for three days' fishing – always his favourite sport) and Quebec in July (from which he slipped away again for another three days' sport on a tributary of the Saguenay river, catching eight salmon, the largest being seventeen pounds, and having 'a ripping time'). From Quebec the *Indefatigable* went to the Bay of Islands in Newfoundland for a few days, thence to Halifax again, and afterwards returned up the St. Lawrence in September with the intention of going up to Montreal.

Here, however, something near to disaster overtook her. The river, sometimes difficult below Quebec, was narrow and dangerous above it, and the ship was in charge of a pilot who on a very dark night with a strong tide managed to run her on to some rocks while she was steaming at ten knots. Although the ship's bottom was sheathed with three-inch teak planking covered with copper it was pierced right through, and if the stokehold fires had not been drawn very quickly the boilers might have burst. As it was the ship made water fast and the stokers were working up to their waists in it for some time, but fortunately the pumps were in good order. From 2.30 a.m. when she struck until 8 a.m. the crew were labouring to get her off, and when they eventually succeeded they found themselves confronted by the problem of lightening her sufficiently to get her over the sill of the dock at Quebec. Long hours of further toil followed, shifting everything moveable from aft forward, including heavy guns, and getting out 150 tons of coal. This cruel task was not finished until nine o'clock on the following morning, after which she was just able to get into dock, where she was temporarily repaired sufficiently to allow her to reach the naval dockyard at Halifax. As this was merely a small yard there was some fear that even its resources might prove inadequate and she might have to return to England, but this was not necessary and at the end of the autumn she was able to go south to the West Indies again in the course of her normal routine.[23]

As the end of the year approached and the three years of the *Indefatigable*'s commission drew towards their close Tyrwhitt was hoping to return home for his marriage by Christmas or early in the new year. He was also hoping for promotion to commander, though with intervals of pessimism. 'You know I am not particularly ambitious', he wrote to Miss Corbally, 'but I do want to get one step higher at least.'

At this point a crisis developed in and over Venezuela. That republic had defaulted on her debts to bond holders; and Britain and Germany, though their naval rivalry was already beginning, decided to co-operate in forcing a settlement by naval pressure. The *Indefatigable*, which was at Trinidad, was ordered to La Guayra, the port of Caracas, the capital of the republic. There she found two German warships already lying, and was presently joined by the light cruiser *Retribution* from Bermuda and afterwards by other British vessels.

While negotiations with President Castro of Venezuela were proceeding, Tyrwhitt was not long in making friends with a couple of German officers who spoke English very well and whom he pronounced to be "very nice fellows". Having spent a pleasant evening with them aboard their ship, he confessed to Miss Corbally that they had all drunk a great deal of whisky and had parted vowing eternal friendship.

When the negotiations produced no result the Germans took the lead in presenting an ultimatum. President Castro already had a rebellion on his hands, but he apparently thought – wrongly – that he might be able to quash it by calling for a common front against the foreigners and accordingly struck warlike attitudes and imprisoned some British and German subjects. Others, including the ministers of the two countries, sought refuge aboard the British warships, the German vessels being temporarily absent. The German Minister, a most genial old gentleman with a vast beard who spoke fluent English, took up his quarters aboard the *Indefatigable*, where he was very popular and spent much of his time learning to play bridge, which Tyrwhitt had also taken up just at this time. Meanwhile, since the ultimatum had expired, an Anglo-German blockade had been imposed and two Venezuelan 'so-called gunboats' (as Tyrwhitt put it) and a torpedo-boat were seized by the Germans after they had been prudently abandoned by their crews, and were then towed out to sea and sunk. The few other small vessels which constituted the Venezuelan navy were also rounded up rapidly and bloodlessly. The two forts at La Guayra, crammed with rather tatterdemalion troops, trained their guns on the British warships, which replied in like fashion and ordered their crews to sleep by their guns at night; but no shot was fired here, much to Tyrwhitt's disappointment.

> 'Don't be alarmed, my dear [he wrote to his *fiancée*]. I am sorry to say there is not the slightest chance of our being even shot at. I only wish there was. It has always been my fate to be out of all that sort of thing and I suppose my bad luck will continue.'

Few prognostications can have been wider of the mark than this was in the long run, but as far as the immediate future was concerned he was correct.

At Puerto Cabello, however, about a hundred miles westward along the coast, the Venezuelans seized a British collier which was discharging coal and imprisoned the crew, whereupon the German and British commodores (the latter having just arrived in the light cruiser *Charybdis*) both proceeded thither to demand their release. The outcome of this was a bombardment of the forts, apparently on the German commodore's initiative. A period of tension followed, during which the blockade continued and the *Indefatigable* was sent to cruise in the neighbourhood of the port of Guanta, where she captured a number of Venezuelan schooners and other small craft, whose crews were set ashore with a promise that their vessels would be restored to them when things returned to normal.[24]

Under this pressure Castro, who also still had the rebels to cope with, released his British and German prisoners and the situation began to ease as far as Venezuela was concerned. But now new complications had arisen. However much camaraderie Tyrwhitt and his brother officers might feel towards individuals among their German counterparts or towards the jovial German Minister who almost broke down when he took leave of them, their superiors in Britain considered that the Germans had taken too aggressive and violent a line, both in the imposition of the blockade and the bombardment of the forts. The Admiralty, moreover, was irritated by their action in sinking the gunboats they had taken and was most anxious to avoid exciting American feeling. Britain's complaisance in going along with Germany as far as she had already done had encouraged the latter country to commit what the United States regarded as a breach of the Monroe Doctrine, and President Theodore Roosevelt was now 'shaking the big stick' so vigorously that there was even a possibility of a German-American war, into which Britain had no wish to be dragged on the German side. Eventually Germany reluctantly, and Britain readily, consented to the Venezuelan issue being submitted to arbitration. The ultimate result of this affair as far as these two countries were concerned, however, was to worsen their relations, and Germany's behaviour was held up in the British press as another example of the aggressive purposes for which the new German Navy was allegedly being built.

Before this, however, Tyrwhitt's promotion to commander had come through at the end of the year, and in January 1903 he left the *Indefatigable*, which her captain reported as being 'in a high state of efficiency' as the result of the industry, zeal, tact and ability with which he had carried out his duties as executive officer.[25]

Returning home by passenger steamer, he was married to Miss Corbally on February 24. Throughout their long married life of nearly fifty years hundreds of his letters to her breathe his deep and abiding devotion, and reflect hers to him, though her letters have not survived. When absent from her, he wrote to her almost every day; and if at sea, would sit down at the end of the day to write, breaking off to resume on the morrow or (if, as sometimes happened, that was a day packed to the last moment with action) at the next opportunity. On December 27 of the same year their first child, Mary Joan Caroline, was born.

After a few weeks' leave he was appointed for a second time to the *Aurora*, now a training-ship for cadets. He remained in her for less than a year, however, since he had developed a great liking for the comparatively new destroyer service and was hankering after more experience of it. From early in 1904 he spent several years in command of various destroyers; though in the summer of that year he had an unfortunate misadventure while in command of one which might conceivably have prejudiced his career. During the manoeuvres of that year night operations were carried out without lights for the first time, the better to reproduce the conditions of actual warfare. Tyrwhitt in the *Arun*, one of the new 'River' class capable of the then high speed of 25½ knots, together with two older and slower destroyers, the *Decoy* and the *Sturgeon*, was scouting ahead of the Blue battlefleet in a high wind, a boisterous sea and pitch darkness. The three destroyers were steaming in single line at high speed between the Scilly Isles and the Wolf Rock lighthouse, when the *Decoy* crossed the *Arun*'s bows and was run down. Her plates were torn asunder, exposing her engine-room, into which the water began to pour, enveloping her in a dense cloud of steam. She immediately began to settle down and buckled in the middle, whereupon orders were given to the men to save themselves and many jumped overboard. The *Arun* and the *Sturgeon* lowered their boats and put on their searchlights, and in spite of the heavy sea managed to rescue all but one of the *Decoy*'s crew; the captain and chief engineer, who were the last to remain aboard, being taken off when the vessel's decks were already awash and the seas breaking over her.

The resultant court-martial acquitted Tyrwhitt of neglect but found him guilty of 'hazarding' his ship and her victim. Both in the Navy and in the Press there was much sympathy for him. The *St. James's Gazette* quoted with strong approval the last sentence of his defence before the court, in which he had appealed to it 'not only on his own behalf, but also on behalf of the large number of officers who were ever willing and able to incur the great risks and responsibilities inseparable from and necessary to the good and efficient development of the torpedo-boat service', and added that though he had indeed hazarded his ship it had been his duty to do so. *The Globe* was even more emphatic, holding that such a verdict could 'be productive of nothing but harm to the Service' and going on:

> 'The fact that the manoeuvres were being carried out, by order, without lights necessarily rendered the position of every vessel in the flotilla "hazardous" in the extreme, and although the disaster is to be regretted, it should have been treated as merely the outcome of the unavoidably dangerous conditions of mimic warfare. The sentence cannot fail to act as a most unfortunate check on the dash and enterprise of the officers of our destroyer flotillas.'

Tyrwhitt himself made this last point with characteristic vehemence in a letter to his sister Polly, in which he complained that there was not a man on the court who had ever served in a destroyer, or had any sympathy with or knowledge of what he was already calling 'our service'. 'They have dealt the latter a very severe blow', he continued, 'as no-one will care to take any risk now, knowing that if they come to grief they will be tried by court-martial and jumped on.'[26]

That he was nevertheless not held to be very culpable appears, however, from the fact that on the very day of the court-martial he was appointed to a brand-new destroyer, the *Waveney* (also of the 'River' class). Unfortunately it is at this point that the materials on which this biography is based dry up almost completely for nearly a decade, leaving only the bare framework of his career until the first world war is reached. The autobiographical fragment which in his old age he was persuaded with much difficulty to begin breaks down here into a few jejune sentences. No letters to his wife survive for these years, perhaps because his service was such that they were together or in close touch for a good part of the time, and also possibly since it was not such a period of peril for him and anxiety for her as caused her after the outbreak of war in 1914 to cherish every line and even every telegram from him. Nor do more than a very occasional letter from or to other people remain.[27]

It was during his command of the *Waveney* that on 18 April 1905 his second child and only son, St. John Reginald Joseph, was born. At that time and for several years about then the family was living in Plym Villa at Plympton in south Devon. St. John, a delightful and otherwise healthy boy, grew up with at first an eye defect which to his parents' chagrin and anxiety threatened to prevent the naval career to which they and he looked forward. To their delight, however, it yielded to two operations with a year's interval between them, in 1915 and 1916 respectively, and he was able to go to Osborne and Dartmouth and afterwards have a career of great distinction which but for his relatively early death might have reached heights some of which even his father never scaled. In 1913 came another daughter, Patricia Angela Mary. Their father's joy in and deep love for 'the brats and Patsy' breathe forth constantly from his letters to his wife.

Meanwhile he had gone from the *Waveney* at the beginning of 1906 to a new scout, the *Attentive*, in which he remained a year before being transferred to the *Skirmisher*, another scout. In June 1908 he was promoted captain and given as his first command in that rank his old acquaintance the *Hecla*, still serving as the parent ship of a number of destroyers and torpedo-boats. These, according at least to Tyrwhitt's recollection many years later, had previously spent most of their time in a basin in Portsmouth Harbour; but on his suggesting to Admiral Sir Arthur Fanshawe (who was then Commander-in-Chief at Portsmouth and had been his captain for a brief space during his first spell of service in the *Aurora*), that this was a poor way of training destroyers a 'trot' was laid down in Fareham Creek which improved things considerably. The rather miscellaneous collection of craft of which he had become the foster-parent very soon became a sea-going flotilla, the Fourth, which he commanded from the flotilla leader *Topaze*, and he was instrumental in training and turning out a number of very useful destroyer officers. After two years with this flotilla and a short period of study at the War College[28] he became flag-captain to Rear-Admiral Sir Douglas Gamble, who commanded the Fourth Cruiser Squadron in the Mediterranean Fleet and flew his flag first in the *Bacchante* and then after February 1912 in the *Good Hope*.[29] From the Mediterranean Tyrwhitt returned in August 1912 to the destroyer service as Captain (D) of the Second Flotilla in the Home Fleet, which he led from the light cruiser *Bellona*. On 1 December 1913 he was promoted Commodore (Second Class) in command of all the flotillas of the Home Fleet. These were based on Portsmouth, and he flew his broad pendant in the light cruiser *Amethyst*, in which he still was at the outbreak of war in 1914.

During his absence in the Mediterranean his family had not followed him thither, but had lived in rented houses in

Fareham, Southsea and Bedhampton. Shortly before his return Mrs. Tyrwhitt had bought and made ready what has been described as a hideous but very comfortable modern villa, which he called 'Ketelby' after his boyhood home, at Waterlooville a few miles north of Portsmouth on the London road beyond the brow of Portsdown Hill. In spite of its name, which betrays its comparatively modern development around a public-house called 'The Heroes of Waterloo', this was then a not unpleasant country village in the days when motor-cars were still few – though the Tyrwhitts possessed an Austin of early vintage, which in his absence was sometimes sedately driven by Sanders,[30] their gardener and man-of-all-work. The house possessed four acres of garden and orchards, which Sanders tended with the aid of 'one overgrown boy', as well as a full-sized croquet lawn which was later turned into two very good lawn tennis courts. Here Mary – or Bobby as she was always called to distinguish her from a maid of the same Christian name – and St. John played, or wandered on the gentle slopes of the hill whose mild outline was then scarcely broken by the low silhouettes of the inland-looking forts; here Patricia was born, and here their mother developed that interest and skill in gardening which enabled her to leave her mark on the garden of every house in which they lived thereafter.

CHAPTER TWO

THE BATTLE OF THE BIGHT

One result of the almost complete lack of materials for the story of Tyrwhitt's life during the nine years before the first world war is that we are left to guess, or at best to deduce, his reactions to the growth of Anglo-German naval rivalry and the possibility or prospects of war with Germany. Since he was a plain patriotic Englishman, however, this is not a very difficult task. As a junior officer he had liked well enough some of the German naval officers and other Germans he had met, and when his letters reappear on the eve of the war they do not suggest undue belligerence or a positive thirst to decide that rivalry by the test of battle. But it is a reasonable assumption that as a keen naval officer he was both very well aware of the increasing likelihood of a collision – indeed there could hardly have been a naval officer who was not – and anxious to fit both himself and the men under his command for the struggle. Like his brother-officers, he must have regarded war as probable and he was ready for it.

For the Navy *was* ready; as ready, that is, as it could be in view of its material limitations: inadequate protection of its bases against submarines; inferior shells, torpedoes and mines; and capital ships that proved less well protected and more vulnerable than their opponents. But these limitations were as yet unrealised or in some cases realised by only a few, and some of them – the last-mentioned at any rate – did not affect Tyrwhitt's command. Meanwhile in October 1913 Winston Churchill, the First Lord of the Admiralty, had suggested to Prince Louis of Battenberg, the First Sea Lord, that in the summer of 1914 a test mobilisation should take the place of the annual manoeuvres, and Battenberg had agreed.

When the time came, a fortnight after the assassination of the Archduke Franz Ferdinand of Austria which provided the flashpoint for war, this mobilisation proved of even greater value than had originally been expected. It had been intended as a rehearsal; it turned out to be the real thing. On July 10 the orders were issued. On the 13th and the subsequent days the Atlantic, Home and Reserve (or Third) Fleets assembled at Spithead. On the 17th and 18th they were reviewed by the King, passing the royal yacht in single line ahead, including Tyrwhitt's destroyers – which were much admired, as he wrote proudly to his wife, who had watched them equally proudly from H.M.S. *Doris* in the company of her two elder children and his brother Beauchamp who had come down to Waterlooville for the week-end. That night he was among the senior officers who dined aboard the fleet flagship with the King, who, he reported, 'was very nice' to him.[1] Several days of tactical exercises followed, ending at Portland on the evening of the 22nd. On the following day the fleets and flotillas were due to disperse again, and the ships of the Third Fleet did indeed begin to return to their home ports. Tyrwhitt's command returned to Portsmouth to refit and for leave, though he himself was one of five commodores who were required, along with thirty-two admirals commanding in home waters, to attend a conference at the Admiralty at which the official summons proclaimed that 'a variety of subjects dealing with naval war' would be discussed.[2]

So far the European situation, worsening in reality but still outwardly calm, had not only offered no valid excuse for postponing the dispersal, but might even have been damaged further by such a postponement. But now everything began to darken. It was on the 23rd that Austria presented her peremptory forty-eight hours' ultimatum to Serbia. Even then no immediate steps were taken to halt the dispersal, though the flag-officers' conference was postponed first for one day and then indefinitely. On the 25th the ultimatum expired and the Austrian ambassador left the Serbian capital; but the reservists were nevertheless disbanded, the nucleus crews of the ships of the Third Fleet were sent on leave by watches, and officers who like Tyrwhitt lived near at hand were also given leave. The advantage Britain had almost accidentally gained by her test mobilisation was beginning to slip away. Meanwhile Goodwood Race Week was at hand and on Saturday July 26th Tyrwhitt after going home went to a pre-Goodwood dance at a neighbouring country-house. Among the other guests was Commodore Roger Keyes, who was in charge of the submarine service and in immediate command of the Eighth or Overseas Flotilla of our most up-to-date submarines of the D and E class. His command and Tyrwhitt's had exercised together constantly for the past year and expected to operate together in the event of war; his headquarters were at Fort Blockhouse on the Gosport side of Portsmouth Harbour (though he had an office at the Admiralty); he lived nearby at Fareham; and the two men were warm friends.[3]

This dance has sometimes been called a miniature version of the Duchess of Richmond's ball on the eve of Waterloo. Austria had now rejected the Serbian reply to her ultimatum, the Admiralty had received news that the German High Seas Fleet had been ordered to concentrate off the Norwegian coast, and Battenberg on his own responsibility had cancelled the dispersal of the fleets – not Churchill, as so often said, who merely endorsed the step. At the dance some officers therefore received orders to rejoin their ships at once. Tyrwhitt was handed a telegram ordering him to go to Portland as soon as possible for further instructions. When he got there he was also given a sealed packet of war orders for Keyes, to whom he telegraphed to take it over from him at Fareham on his way back to Portsmouth on Monday the 27th.[4] On Tuesday Austria declared war on Serbia and the Fleet was placed 'on a preparatory and precautionary basis'. On Wednesday the First Fleet – henceforth to be called the Grand Fleet – left Portsmouth for Scapa Flow in the

Orkneys, taking with it the Second and Fourth Destroyer Flotillas, but dropping the First and Third off under Tyrwhitt's command to assume their war station at Harwich on July 30. Each of these flotillas was led by a small light cruiser, Captain W. Blunt in the *Fearless* leading the First Flotilla of twenty destroyers and Captain C.H. Fox in the *Amphion* leading the Third of nineteen.[5] In addition there was the *Amethyst*, in which Tyrwhitt himself was still flying his broad pendant and which he condemned as 'damned slow'.[6] In due course additional light cruisers were added to the force and formed into a separate light cruiser squadron, the Fifth, which eventually became seven strong, in the course of 1915.

On the evening of his arrival at Harwich, Tyrwhitt wrote to his brother Beauchamp that he wished he had a better ship; and on the following day, by which time he had realised that with war imminent the Admiralty had suddenly become much more amenable to his requests, he confided to his wife that if he did not 'get the newest and best thing in light cruisers' out of them he would eat his hat.[7] This, however, was a gastronomical promise that he did not have to keep. The functions of the Harwich Force, as it came to be called, were declared to be to patrol the waters between 52° and 54° N., acting offensively against enemy destroyers and minelayers that might be operating in this area; to assist in the Grand Fleet's sweeps, and to join the Channel Fleet (the other main British force in home waters, based on Portland) if it moved north. The Force was to be supported, theoretically at least, by Rear-Admiral H.H. Campbell's Seventh Cruiser Squadron, consisting of the four obsolete cruisers *Bacchante* (as flagship), *Cressy*, *Aboukir* and *Hogue*, manned mainly by pensioners and reservists and soon to be grimly nicknamed 'the live-bait squadron'. Of this Tyrwhitt, who knew Admiral Campbell from the days when the latter had been captain of the *Aurora* during his own second spell of service in her and of course knew the *Bacchante* from the more recent time when he had been her flag-captain, wrote:

> 'Henry Campbell is the admiral in command of the squadron that I fall back on if things get too bad. I would prefer it was someone else, as I don't think he has had much experience. The old *Bacchante*, is his flagship! Not much of a reed to fall back on, but better than nothing.'[8]

As one of his destroyer captains put it: 'We realised that it was only a question of time before these vessels would be bagged [by the enemy].'[9]

While Tyrwhitt and his command were on their way to Harwich, Keyes had by some misunderstanding been ordered to the Humber instead with his Eighth Flotilla of ten submarines, their depôt ships *Adamant* and *Maidstone* (in which last he was flying his pendant), and two very fast destroyers, the *Lurcher* (in which he flew it henceforward whenever he went to sea) and the *Firedrake*. He lost not a moment, however, in getting leave to transfer at once to Harwich, where he arrived a day later than Tyrwhitt, on July 31. This meant that there were now three commands there, all practically independent of each other (though Keyes was the senior ranking officer), for Captain (later Commodore) Cuthbert Cayley, who commanded H.M.S. *Ganges*, the training ship for boys at Shotley, also administered the port and was to give invaluable help to the two separate but closely co-operating forces which used it as their base.[10]

Another arrival on the 31st, coming from Chatham to join the First Flotilla, was the destroyer *Lizard*, whose second-in-command Lieutenant William Tennant[11] described in his brand-new diary the string of signals which the *Fearless* was now sending out – 'Prepare for war', 'Paint out all bright-work on upper deck and all funnel bands', 'Land any spare gear, woodwork, etc.' In obedience to this last order all officers packed up their more respectable plain clothes which (as he put it) 'might not be improved by lyddite' and dumped them in two vast jumble heaps, one at Shotley Barracks and the other in a shed at Parkeston Quay. These preparations looked like real business, but what impressed many of the younger destroyer officers more than anything else was to be issued with a hypodermic needle and a supply of morphia apiece. A destroyer carried hardly any surgical supplies beyond what were in the first-aid kits, and the purpose of this issue was to enable officers when in action to give morphia injections to men who were so severely wounded that the sight of their injuries or the sound of their cries or groans might distract their comrades from their duties. Soon most of those who had been thus provided were practising on each other with injections of water or saline solutions.[12] The ships also filled the ammunition racks at their guns, each keeping a gun manned at night, and 'exercised action' daily during the short period of strained waiting which followed and which Tyrwhitt described as 'awful'.

> 'I don't think [he wrote on August 1] that I shall mind a bit once we are started, but I shall never want to go through this period of anxiety and waiting again. I had a visit from Roger Keyes and Cayley this afternoon which helped to pass the time, as I have not very much to do now...Roger and I get on well and he is a great comfort to me, as he approves of my arrangements and I of his. Perhaps we are a mutual admiration society, which is just as well as we have much in common just now.'[13]

By August 2 all leave had been stopped; the ships were at three hours' notice and were coaling, since waiting with steam up was running away with a lot of coal; and Tyrwhitt, possibly remembering Sir Richard Grenville,[14] had quietly made arrangements for the *Amethyst* to be blown up if she should ever be reduced to such a condition that she could fight no more.[15] On the 3rd. they were brought to two hours' notice and warned by signal to be prepared against a possible sudden attack without declaration of war. Captains were instructed to open secret packet A, which notified them that on its outbreak the Germans might be expected to lay

26,000 mines in the North Sea and the Channel. They were also ordered to communicate to their officers the plan of campaign, which was that when war began the force would leave Harwich next morning in order to guard against enemy minelayers or other small craft that might try to operate in the southern part of the North Sea. For that purpose, on reaching the Outer Gabbard (a lightship twenty miles east of Orford Ness) it would sweep out across the sea in the direction of Terschelling and then patrol from there south-westward by day and back along the northern Dutch coast and nearly up to Borkum by night.[16]

It was now Bank Holiday Monday and Tyrwhitt found it

> 'so funny to see the Bank Holiday people all playing round as if nothing was happening...I want it to come now [he wrote to his wife] as the only thing that can keep us out is our Government not standing by France.'[17]

To his sister Kitty he enlarged somewhat on this:

> 'I was interested in the demeanour of the men. They looked on it all as a joke at first, but when they saw the officers' private effects being landed, also armchairs and comforts and such like, they realised that something was up...It seemed dreadful to think of it at first, but now I am only longing for this desperate *waiting* to be over and to begin business.'

The letter ended:

> 'I am sorry for the smudges, but they are made by a kitten which has attached itself to me. Give my kindest regards to the 'ship's company' and tell the Reverend Mother we shall appreciate their prayers.'[18]

Tyrwhitt had been very fond of cats ever since he had adopted a starving stray when he was a small boy, and this (black) kitten to which he referred grew up to go all through the war with him, producing a family which was distributed to various friends, including (it is said) Winston Churchill, though one offspring was kept and in due course succeeded its mother as Admiral's Cat during his later sea-service. The 'ship's company' was the nickname which had been adopted by or which he had given to the community of nuns to which Kitty belonged, who were intensely patriotic, sent sacred medals to Tyrwhitt, Keyes and some of their officers (even plucking up courage to ask Tyrwhitt to send one on to the Commander-in-Chief, Sir John Jellicoe, which he did), knitted comforts for their men, and prayed constantly for them all.[19]

On August 4 he wrote to his wife at noon that he and his force were 'still here, but it seems impossible that we can be here much longer.' He was right, for it was on that day that German troops invaded Belgium and Britain sent Germany an ultimatum demanding their withdrawal. In the afternoon all officers commanding ships were told of the ultimatum and that it would expire at midnight, but that they must be prepared for the Germans to begin hostilities before then. The possibility that they might even attack Harwich was considered, and instructions were issued for the eventuality of a fight in the harbour itself. Unless some such attack was made, however, Tyrwhitt intended as soon as war began to carry out a sweep with all his available forces from the Outer Gabbard Light Vessel towards Terschelling. Late in the evening he wrote to his brother Beauchamp:

> 'Please look after Angey if she wants anything...War is going to be declared at midnight and I sail at 4 a.m.'

Soon after midnight, when the Admiralty's signal 'Commence hostilities against Germany' had been received, he made a signal himself – 'The Commodore (T) wishes the officers and men of the First Fleet Flotillas the best of luck in defending their country,' and then another – 'Raise steam for fifteen knots at 6.30 a.m. Steam for full speed when clear of harbour.'[20]

When the flotillas left the harbour the next morning it presented a strange spectacle, for everything that had been jettisoned, from the straw hats that were then the fashionable plain-clothes wear to wardroom chairs, was still floating around in it. Despite the early hour the *Ganges* and the pier and foreshore of Shotley were crowded with boys who cheered themselves hoarse as each ship passed. Further out they met a steamer returning from the Hook of Holland crammed with Britons hurrying back from the Continent, who also cheered frantically on seeing the two light cruisers and nearly forty destroyers, with a couple of Keyes's submarines in tow, going out to meet the enemy.[21] Nor was it long before they did so, for a wireless message was intercepted – 'Trawler reports that liner has been seen dropping things overboard presumably mines.' This was in fact no liner but the German minelayer *Königin Luise*, which had intended to pass as a Hook-to-Harwich boat and lay mines off Harwich but on sighting Tyrwhitt's force now turned north, dropping her mines as fast as possible in the open sea. To Tyrwhitt's mortification, for he longed to fire the first shot of the war, this took her away from the *Amethyst* and nearer to the Third Flotilla. Hence, knowing that Fox would take the necessary action, he was obliged to leave him to do so and continue in the direction of Terschelling and Borkum according to the pre-arranged plan. After Fox had hoisted the cheery signal 'Good hunting!' the *Amphion* and some of her flotilla duly sank the *Königin Luise*, the honour of firing the first shot falling to the *Lance*. In the *Amphion* the guns' crews on the disengaged side so far forgot themselves in the excitement of being in action for the first time as to crowd over in order to watch and cheer on their comrades' shooting, which caused Fox as soon as the brief engagement was over to harangue them sternly on the heinousness of leaving their posts when an enemy submarine or other hostile vessel might at any moment have manifested itself within the area on which their attention should have been fixed. Some twenty-odd German survivors were picked up, but the minelayer soon had a posthumous revenge, for when the *Amphion* turned back for Harwich with her prisoners she struck one of the mines which had been laid and sank with the loss of one officer and 147 men, about half of her complement. All but two of the Germans she had on board, who happened to have been stowed in a compartment forward just where the explosion occurred, were also killed; and those two suffered the same fate when she struck a second mine just before she went down. Captain Fox, though wounded, survived to fight very effectively another day. One result of her loss was that for more than two months the *Arethusa* had to be flotilla leader as well as flagship.[22]

When the flotilla, after picking up the *Amphion*'s survivors, resumed its return to Harwich it was startled to meet a steamer flying a large German flag. This was in fact another Hook of Holland packet carrying the German Ambassador and his staff from England. (Keyes, incidentally had asked the Marine Superintendent of the port to order the captain to steer as if he were passing through intricate channels in a minefield, which he did very realistically, to the great interest of the German naval *attaché*, who was on board). The destroyers' commanders, having seen the *Amphion* go down with half her crew, were naturally out for blood and promptly opened fire, but fortunately realised their mistake in time.[23]

Meanwhile Tyrwhitt in the *Amethyst* and the *Fearless* with the First Flotilla had continued on their way to the patrol area, slipping the two submarines they were towing when they were off Terschelling and letting them proceed independently into the Heligoland Bight to seek the enemy. When Tyrwhitt's force was about thirty miles from Borkum at 9 p.m. on the 5th, it turned and patrolled back south-westward near the Dutch coast. This patrolling continued during the 6th, and on the 7th the Third Flotilla came out again and relieved the First, though Tyrwhitt remained at sea. At 5 p.m. on the 8th the First Flotilla put out again to take over the patrol once more, but four hours later it was recalled, since the British Expeditionary Force was about to begin crossing to France next day and the flotillas were needed to play their part in protecting it against any German attempt in force to intercept it. Tyrwhitt then returned with the Third Flotilla, never having caught sight of a German after his distant glimpse of the *Königin Luise*,[24] and was immediately summoned to the Admiralty.

This was the result of a change in the arrangement of the higher commands. Before and at the start of the war Tyrwhitt's flotillas had been considered an integral part of the Grand Fleet, and when they were stationed at Harwich it was at first intended that they should join it at sea, if possible, should a fleet action be imminent. Admiral Jellicoe had found communication with the southern area of the North Sea so difficult, however, that on August 8 he had asked the Admiralty to take over its direction. This it did by issuing orders direct to Tyrwhitt and sending for him forthwith for this purpose. Orders were also issued direct to Keyes and Admiral Campbell. The system was afterwards regularised by constituting the three commands an independent Southern Force under Rear-Admiral A.H. Christian, who flew his flag in the *Euryalus*, a cruiser of the *Bacchante* class.[25]

His sudden summons to the Admiralty proved something of a sartorial embarrassment for Tyrwhitt, since the peacetime habit of wearing plain clothes for shore occasions had not yet been abandoned, and as he had rather naïvely assumed that he was not likely to go to London during the war, still less to the Admiralty,[26] he had put all his more presentable plain clothes ashore in the general clear-out of a few days earlier. However, even if 'they were rather surprised at [his] get-up', he 'found everybody very nice' and seized the opportunity to press for a better ship than the *Amethyst*, humorously but exaggeratedly describing his concern at finding himself, after the loss of the *Amphion*, alone within a few miles of the German coast in a craft with a maximum speed of eighteen knots. In reply he was promised the first of the new oil-driven cruisers.[27]

On getting back to Harwich he found that one of the two submarines had also returned, her captain reporting that 'game was scarce and shy' in the Bight and that he had had no luck. A couple of days later the other also came in with a similar report. By that time Tyrwhitt had gone off again with the Third Flotilla to relieve the First, which on the previous day had begun the new patrol for the protection of the British Expeditionary Force during its crossing to France.

The general idea of this patrol was that a watch should be kept during the dark hours and especially at daybreak on a line from Heligoland to the mouth of the Ems and then out to the Terschelling Light Vessel, in order to report any German forces proceeding to sea that were likely to interfere with the passage of our troops to the Continent. One flotilla was always on patrol at a time, leaving Harwich between 3 and 4.30 a.m. and crossing to the Broad Fourteens off the Dutch coast in order to rendezvous with the incoming flotilla, then continuing northwards to round the Terschelling lightship about 11 p.m. and spreading out so as to be in position before daybreak. On the third day out it was relieved and returned to base by about 1.30 p.m. This patrol, which involved 66 hours at sea and 30 in harbour in every four days, was kept up more or less continuously till the middle of November. Almost at the beginning it was arranged that when a flotilla came in for its brief spell of rest as many as possible of the destroyers should lie alongside Parkeston Quay instead of at buoys in the river. This saved endless boatwork, provided somewhere to walk about during short intervals of spare time, and since the depôt ship was lying there it also greatly facilitated the task of obtaining supplies and stores. There were always some ships, however, which could not obtain these 'plum billets' and had to remain content with a buoy. Meanwhile even after a mere ten days of war Harwich harbour was beginning to show great signs of alteration and transformation as a naval base. Sheds were being built on the Quay, extra buoys laid, a boom defence was being put down at the approaches to the harbour and a seaplane base beginning to be constructed at Felixstowe on the opposite side.[28]

When Tyrwhitt returned to Harwich on August 13 from his second spell at sea he was again called to the Admiralty. There he was shown up to the Operations Room, where he found Churchill, Prince Louis and the Chief of the Naval War Staff, Vice-Admiral Doveton Sturdee. Churchill, who was probably delighted to find a man after his own heart in this stalwart and strong-jawed officer straight from the North Sea, was (as Tyrwhitt reported afterwards) 'very much on the warpath and seeing very red'. They showed him a scheme for a drive towards Heligoland which he was to carry out in two days' time and discussed it with him. When they had finished it was one o'clock in the morning, and he had planned to weigh from Harwich with the Third Flotilla at half-past three, though he had left instructions that he was to be waited for if he did not get back in time. Fortunately he had asked on arriving at the Admiralty to be provided with a car for the return journey and was driven down in what he described to his wife, with obvious and boyish pleasure, as 'a magnificent landaulette'. His enjoyment was mixed with some exasperation, however, for though the car was fast and the driver skilful the country was very spy-conscious in those opening days of the war, and they were stopped several times by police or troops. Since Tyrwhitt was again wearing plain clothes that were not of the smartest, he had some difficulty in convincing them of his identity and the urgency of his journey, in spite – or perhaps because – of the strong language he used. Nevertheless he arrived not much more than half-an-hour late and was under way by 4.25 a.m. on the 14th. Next day he was joined by the First Flotilla and the united force duly drove up towards Borkum and the Bight without any result until about ten on the following morning, after which Tyrwhitt took the Third Flotilla back to

Harwich, beginning to feel 'rather bored at looking for nothing', while the First patrolled back and forth until evening and then went on the patrol for the protection of the B.E.F. again, 'beginning to give up hope of getting at the Germans for some time' but 'still very cheerful'.[29]

Before Tyrwhitt came out again after exactly twenty-four hours in harbour, a chance had been missed in his absence. About 5 a.m. on August 18, when the First Flotilla was patrolling in sub-divisions two miles apart, of two boats each, the *Lizard* sighted a four-funnelled cruiser on the horizon coming full speed for her and opened fire. Unhappily the flotilla-leader *Fearless*, the only British ship present with an armament capable of dealing with the enemy, mistook the oncoming German, which was the *Karlsruhe* armed with four-inch guns like herself, for the much more powerful eight-inch-gun cruiser *Yorck* and ordered a withdrawal. The *Karlsruhe*, evidently concluding that the only possible explanation for this behaviour was that an attempt was being made to draw her on to something heavier, put about as soon as she saw that the British destroyers were closing on their leader and that any chance of catching one or two of them in isolation was gone. The *Lizard* and the *Goshawk* (Commander the Hon. Herbert Meade[30]) now signalled *Fearless*, submitting that the enemy was only a four-inch light cruiser, and the order was belatedly given to chase, but after about an hour the pursuit had to be given up. When the flotilla returned to Harwich with this sorry tale, depression prevailed at a golden opportunity having been let slip after nearly a fortnight of blank days.[31]

Meanwhile on the one hand the original four divisions of the British Expeditionary Force had crossed to France, and on the other the Belgian troops had evacuated Ostend and it was feared that if it fell into German hands the arrangements for covering the B.E.F's lines of supply might be prejudiced. In the hope of at least delaying its capture Admiral Christian was ordered to make a demonstration off the port with a light cruiser and two divisions of destroyers from Harwich, supported by two *Bacchantes* outside the shoals. Between the 20th and 22nd Christian and Tyrwhitt therefore carried out this demonstration. The destroyers *Lapwing* and *Lizard* were ordered to join some small craft which were preparing to bombard the advancing German troops over the sandhills, while the *Hind* was sent into Ostend harbour to find and report whether the enemy were already in occupation of the city. They were in fact still nineteen miles away, but the population had begun to panic and two large mobs of people who wanted to get across to England but found that peacetime formalities were still being observed were besieging the customs officials and the American consulate respectively (the British Consul not being available). Two Belgian cross-Channel steamers were moored alongside the jetty, but for some unaccountable reason they had not raised steam. The captain of the *Hind* ordered them to do so immediately, threatening to put an armed guard and some of his own stokers aboard if they refused to obey his orders; and although he was unable to persuade the Consulate to cut red tape and dispense with the signing of passports he managed to get most of the refugees on to the steamers within an hour. By now Admiral Christian had arrived in his barge and approved what the captain had done, and shortly afterwards the burgomaster came aboard the *Hind* almost in tears and begged that she should leave the harbour, explaining that it had been decided not to defend the place. 'If you remain and fire on the enemy', he pleaded, 'you will make them very angry. They will kill me and burn my house!' Admiral Christian thereupon referred back to the Admiralty for further instructions and was ordered to withdraw the whole force, much to Tyrwhitt's satisfaction.

'I have been here two days [he wrote to his wife on the 22nd] and feel just like a madman as things are humming in the North Sea...However I am off in two hours and I hope I shall not have to come back again for ages.'[3 2]

It was not so much that things were humming as that Keyes and Tyrwhitt had determined to make them hum. The reconnaissances of the Heligoland Bight carried out by Keyes's submarines had established that though it was patrolled day and night by relays of enemy destroyers the system by which they relieved each other was such that he believed a well-timed drive before dawn from inshore close to the German coast would inflict heavy loss on the returning night patrols. As soon as Tyrwhitt got back from Ostend, Keyes discussed the plan with him and went up to the Admiralty on the same afternoon (the 23rd), authorised by Tyrwhitt to say that he completely concurred in it, 'in order to try to pilot it through the proper channels'. However he 'found the Staff too fully occupied with the daily task to give the matter much attention'; but fortunately he managed to get speech with Churchill, as a result of which an order was wirelessed to Tyrwhitt – who in the meantime had gone to sea again with the First Flotilla and received it only at 9.30 on the following morning when he was a hundred miles out from Harwich – to bring the flotilla back and be at the Admiralty by three o'clock that afternoon. Jumping into a destroyer, he tore back, but did not manage to arrive until five.

At a meeting presided over by Churchill and attended by Prince Louis, Vice-Admiral Sir Frederick Hamilton the Second Sea Lord, Sturdee, Keyes and himself the plan was considered and slightly modified. Instead of beginning a sweep from inshore westward at or before dawn it was decided to make an inshore run from north to south first, starting at 4 a.m., and then to turn and sweep westwards at 8 a.m., when although the night patrols would be back in port the day patrols would be well out to seaward and could be fallen upon. The Harwich flotillas were to carry out the sweep while Keyes's submarines lay concealed close off the German harbours to intercept vessels coming out or returning. Support would be needed, however, and Tyrwhitt and Keyes felt that even if the nearest heavy ships, the battle cruisers *Invincible* and *New Zealand* which were in the Humber, were added to Campbell's cruisers, this would not be enough if the German battle cruisers came out in force. Keyes therefore asked whether the First Light Cruiser Squadron and the remainder of Sir David Beatty's battle cruisers from the Grand Fleet could be made available, but Sturdee said that this was not feasible and Keyes and Tyrwhitt let the matter drop. Nevertheless when Jellicoe was subsequently informed of what was afoot he was told that the battle cruisers might support the sweep if he wished, whereupon he promptly sent not only them but Commodore Goodenough's light cruiser squadron as well. But before the Admiralty learnt of this Tyrwhitt and Keyes were well on their way to the Bight, beyond the range of the destroyer wireless wave-length by which the Admiralty Communication Staff attempted to pass the message to them, and apparently nobody troubled to ascertain whether they had received it.[33]

To Tyrwhitt's delight, however, he was given the brand-new light cruiser he had been promised, the *Arethusa*, which was the first of her class to carry six-inch guns and was just leaving the builders' hands. He turned over to her at Harwich at nine o'clock on the morning of the 26th, took her to sea four hours later to exercise her guns, and sailed in her 'on business' at 5 a.m. on the following morning. 'From the oldest and slowest to the newest and fastest light cruiser', he had written to his brother Beauchamp when he took her over: 'She's a regular flyer and a ripper but I have had no time to get her into fighting trim;'

> 'I am of course *de*lighted at getting such a splendid new ship, but it is rather a trial having a new ship's company and new guns. Everything new – officers, guns, ship and men. I expect we shall soon get into order, but I would like to have had a week to do it in.'[34]

Just before Tyrwhitt left Harwich in the early hours of the morning of the 27th with the two flotilla leaders, sixteen destroyers of the First Flotilla and fifteen of the Third, Keyes had preceded him with his two destroyers, *Lurcher* and *Firedrake*, and nine submarines, making separately for the position assigned to them.[35] At 3.30 on the morning of August 28 Tyrwhitt sighted Commodore Goodenough's six light cruisers, which he had no reason to suspect were in his vicinity, took them for Germans and was on the point of attacking them, but fortunately challenged them first and so learnt their identity. To his enquiry, 'Are you taking part in the operation?' he received the reply, 'Yes, I know your course and will support you. Beatty is behind us.' Punctually at 4 a.m., therefore, he began his inshore run from north to south with the Third Flotilla in cruising order – that is, in divisions in line ahead, disposed abeam to port, the columns being five cables apart. Two miles astern was Captain Blunt in the *Fearless*, leading the First Flotilla similarly disposed. Eight miles further astern came the light cruisers, with the five battle-cruisers thirty miles away on the starboard quarter.

For nearly three hours the force proceeded in this order until the prearranged plan was disrupted by contact being made with the enemy earlier than had been expected. The Germans had got wind that something in the way of a destroyer attack was afoot, and had made their own plans to turn the tables, sending out destroyers and torpedo-boats only far enough to act as bait to draw the British destroyers deeper into the Bight, and disposing light cruisers and more destroyers to counter-attack them. Their patrols were spread in two concentric arcs with Heligoland as the centre, extending from the north to the south-west of it; the outer patrol consisting of ten destroyers at about twenty-five miles from the island, and the inner one of ten torpedo-boats at a distance of twelve miles. Shortly before seven o'clock a German destroyer was sighted about three and a half miles to the south-eastward of the Third Flotilla, and immediately made off into the Bight. Without altering course himself Tyrwhitt detached the nearest division of that flotilla in chase. His run at that moment was taking him through the outer arc of the German patrols and on towards the inner.

The chasing division soon made out other German destroyers, which it continued to pursue, engaging them at long range. The division thus began to draw so far away from the Commodore that he could not see what was happening, and as on the other hand the firing was increasing he decided he must go to their support, though he had just sighted more enemy destroyers to the south-south-west. Turning four points to port, in a few minutes he made out ten German destroyers with which his own were engaged. At 7.40, therefore, he altered another two points to port and settled down to a stern chase in line abreast with the *Fearless* and her flotilla following on astern.

For nearly half an hour the chase continued at full speed into the Bight, but the range was too great for effective firing, nor could his utmost speed reduce it. Two German light cruisers, the *Stettin* and the *Frauenlob*, now came out to support their fleeing destroyers, and for a time the *Arethusa* was heavily engaged with both at once. Her flotilla gave her all the support they could, but as a newly-commissioned ship taken straight into battle she was badly handicapped; and indeed really in no case to fight an action at all. Her only target practice had been carried out after leaving Harwich on the previous day, and had had to be discontinued since her four-inch semi-automatic guns constantly jammed. They were now continuing to jam and she began to suffer rather severely, one shell from the *Frauenlob* exploding some cordite charges and setting fire to her deck, causing a short but terrific blaze which was extinguished through the resourcefulness of a chief petty officer. Relief arrived, however, when the *Fearless* and her flotilla came up and engaged the *Stettin*. She soon made off south-eastward with them in chase, leaving the *Arethusa* to continue the action with the *Frauenlob* alone, since some of her destroyers were firing on an unfortunate Norwegian steamer which they had mistaken for a German minelayer (and whose crew promptly took to their boats), while others were engaged in smashing up a small torpedo-boat. This they eventually believed they had sunk but it was actually taken into port in a badly battered state. By now Tyrwhitt's force was becoming scattered and also getting too near Heligoland, so he made the signal for the drive to the westward to begin. The *Fearless* and the First Flotilla obeyed it at once, leaving the *Stettin* to vanish in the mist; but Tyrwhitt himself still held on, fighting it out with the *Frauenlob* until by 8.25 he had only one gun, a six-inch, left in action and both torpedo-tubes smashed. This last gun, however, now scored a bull's eye on the *Frauenlob*'s fore bridge, causing thirty-seven casualties, with the result that she sheered off and made for the protection of the Heligoland batteries, whereupon Tyrwhitt reformed his flotilla and also began the westerly sweep.

The first phase of the action was now over, but it had hardly ended before the second began. The *Fearless* and her destroyers as they swept westward caught and sank the German destroyer *V 187*, which went down with her flag flying and her after gun still firing. A little later the two flotillas, which for a time had lost touch with each other, were able to join up again, and Tyrwhitt re-formed cruising order and held on to the westward according to plan. Goodenough's light cruisers, having reached their final position west-south-west of Heligoland by 8.30, had also turned to the westward, but for the time being were not in touch with the flotillas and were now mistaken for Germans by Keyes's two destroyers, which after escorting their submarines to their position were making for the sound of the guns. Keyes, still unaware that any Grand Fleet units were involved in the operation, signalled at 9.45 to Tyrwhitt that he was being chased by enemy cruisers. Shortly afterwards he began to suspect that they were British and ventured to make the challenge, which Goodenough's flagship the *Southampton* answered. In the meantime Tyrwhitt had immediately stopped his westerly course and turned back eastward to his aid; but finding that the damaged *Arethusa* could steam only ten knots, feeling that he was getting too close to Heligoland again, and coming to the correct conclusion that what Keyes had reported was really Goodenough's squadron, he turned back again and then stopped at 10.20 to effect temporary repairs, signalling the *Fearless* and the First Flotilla to remain with him while the Third Flotilla carried on to the westward. About 10.45, having made these repairs and got all *Arethusa*'s guns except two four-inch into working order again, he resumed his westerly course.

The second phase of the operations was now at an end, and it might have seemed that the whole affair was over with disappointing results. But within little more than ten minutes another German light cruiser, the *Strassburg*, was sighted coming up from the south-east. She at once opened fire on the *Arethusa*, which was now able to reply but was at a disadvantage in view of her still semi-crippled condition. Salvo after salvo fell right alongside her, and although none hit her Tyrwhitt had to call on the *Fearless* for relief. The whole First Flotilla turned with *Fearless* upon the enemy, and in face of this overwhelming force the *Strassburg* sheered off again. Scenting a snare to lure his ships back towards Heligoland, Tyrwhitt then called off the chase and signalled them to carry on to the westward. The Third Flotilla, which at the first sound of the guns had turned sixteen points towards the fight, also reversed course once more when it saw them coming up. At this point the *Arethusa* and the *Fearless* sighted the *Stettin* further to the eastward again, which opened fire on them, and both turned round to engage her. A sharp action followed between the cruisers only, the flotillas – the Third having turned back yet again – being at first forbidden to take part.

Now, however, the First Flotilla sighted another enemy light cruiser, the *Mainz*, to the west-south-west on its port bow and heading northerly across its course. She had apparently been lying at Borkum when the action began and had been ordered to come to the aid of her sisters. Three divisions of the flotilla now engaged her for about twenty minutes, after which she suddenly turned sixteen points and began to make off. The explanation appeared at that moment in the shape of Goodenough's light cruisers, coming down from the north towards the sound of the guns and opening up on her. Meanwhile the *Stettin* had been driven off again, but now the *Strassburg* had reappeared and engaged the crippled *Arethusa* so hotly that although she was not hit Tyrwhitt sent urgent signals to Beatty for assistance, having in the misty conditions then prevailing taken the *Strassburg* for something much more formidable than she was. He also ordered the destroyers that were with him to attack her with torpedoes, and though none of the several that were fired hit her they caused her to turn away and disappear. During this attack the spare hands of the *Hind*, in spite of having been ordered to stay under cover out of the way of shell splinters, sat on a rail watching the show and singing at the top of their voices a popular music-hall ditty of the day, 'Get Out and Get Under'.[36] The destroyers then rejoined the *Arethusa* and *Fearless*, and all were once more resuming the westward course in cruising order when shortly after noon the *Mainz* loomed up ahead, running from Goodenough's fire which left her no option but to cross Tyrwhitt's bows.

The *Arethusa*, at 5000 yards, and the *Fearless* engaged her hotly; and Tyrwhitt, not knowing that Goodenough's light cruisers were pursuing her, ordered the five divisions of destroyers that he had in company to attack her. This attack she repulsed brilliantly with splendidly-aimed fire, damaging the *Laurel*, *Liberty* and *Laertes*, and then fled on into the mist, on fire fore and aft but still fighting. One of her shells which hit the *Laurel* burst in the engine-room, doing much damage and killing four men; another struck near the foremost gun and killed three more; while a third, bursting aft, detonated the lyddite shell in the ready racks on the upper deck, put the after gun out of action and practically demolished the after funnel. The *Laurel*'s captain, Commander F.F. Rose, was badly wounded in both legs but remained on the bridge directing operations till he lapsed into insensibility, after which the youthful Lieutenant

C.R. Peploe continued to fight the ship. In spite of her damaged engines, boilers and funnel, and thanks to the efforts of her engineer officer, Engineer-Lieutenant-Commander H.T. Meeson, she was eventually able to limp away, though she afterwards had to be towed home. The *Liberty* was hit on the bridge by a shell which killed her commanding officer, Lieutenant-Commander N. Barttelot; and the *Laertes* was struck by four shells of one salvo, which killed two men and wounded six, severely damaged her boilers, and so brought her to a complete standstill. Thanks to her engineer, Engineer-Lieutenant-Commander A. Hill, however, she was got under way again and, more fortunate than the *Laurel*, was eventually able to proceed unaided.

For Tyrwhitt the situation at this point still seemed critical. It was clear that a concentration of German cruisers was taking place to the north of him. The *Strassburg* had returned to the attack, and the *Arethusa*, glimpsing her for a moment through a break in the mist, gave her a salvo. The *Fearless*, running down across the *Arethusa*'s wake to help the damaged destroyers, became engaged not only with the *Stettin* once more but also with a sister ship, the *Köln*; while coming up astern of them was a fourth cruiser, the *Ariadne*. The *Mainz*, however, was near her end. Attacked by more destroyers and turning away to avoid them, she came within decisive range of the two British light cruisers and was brought to a stop and practically silenced. Leaving her to be finished off by Goodenough, whose squadron now appeared out of the mist, and knowing that the German cruisers to the northward could still turn the fortunes of the day, Tyrwhitt signalled to his destroyers to re-form cruising order yet again and resumed his retirement westward. Then at 12.37, out of the haze in that quarter loomed up the shadowy form of a very large ship coming on at high speed – and another – and another – and another – and another. These were Beatty's battle-cruisers.

Beatty had not taken long, after receiving Tyrwhitt's signal, to make a decision which was nevertheless difficult.

On the one hand the Bight was not a healthy place into which to take great ships. He did not know whether the enemy had laid mines there, or whether their submarines were in action, and he had to consider the possibility that they might now be getting a considerable force to sea. On the other hand he discounted this last risk on the calculation that nothing short of a squadron of battleships could stop him and if he was quick there would not be time for one to appear. Moreover none of these considerations outweighed in his mind the duty of coming to the aid of the flotillas, which on account of the constant irruptions of the enemy had made only ten miles westward since 8 a.m. and were still only twenty-six miles from Heligoland. Accordingly he led away eastward at full speed towards the position Tyrwhitt had given and in little more than an hour had reached the scene of action in time to rescue the *Fearless* from her unequal fight with the *Stettin* and the *Köln*. These two fled at his approach but, pursuing them, he destroyed the *Köln* and set the *Stettin* on fire, though she managed to escape. The unlucky *Ariadne*, which ran straight into range of his flagship the *Lion*, was also sunk; and at 1.10, half-an-hour after he had fired his first shot, he made the general signal 'Retire'.

Even now the *Arethusa*, limping homeward more and more slowly, was not out of the wood. She struggled on until seven o'clock in the evening, when her engines stopped altogether and Tyrwhitt had to wireless for assistance. Darkness had fallen before it arrived, and when about 9 p.m. the bulk of a large ship loomed up close at hand there was a moment of anxious uncertainty whether she was friend or foe. All doubts were settled, however, by a hail in a voice well-known to Tyrwhitt, that of his old friend Captain Wilmot Nicholson of the cruiser *Hogue*. According to his own later version of this episode, the words of the hail were: 'Is that you, Reggie?' 'I never was so glad to see him before,' he wrote afterwards. The *Hogue* quickly took *Arethusa* in tow and brought her safely back to Sheerness in the morning. As the two ships neared the Nore they were overtaken by a crowded

Margate steamer, which passed them quite close and whose passengers evidently concluded that the British cruiser was bringing in a captured German prize. While overtaking the *Arethusa* they stared in silence and some awe at her holed and battered side, but when they came abreast of the *Hogue* they broke into enthusiastic cheering and yelling which they kept up till they were out of hearing. Tyrwhitt signalled to Nicholson 'They evidently think you have a prize in tow,' to which his ready-witted friend replied 'And so I have, but not the sort they think.' From the Nore onwards however, *Arethusa*, whose fame had soared overnight to rival that of her first namesake[37] was recognised and received a great reception, being cheered practically the whole way. At Sheerness Churchill came aboard her in a great state of enthusiasm and (as Tyrwhitt put it) 'fairly slobbered' over him, continuing up to Chatham with him, making him fight the battle all over again, and promising him any ship he liked in place of *Arethusa*, which of course had to go into dock for repairs. Seizing the first moment to write to his wife, Tyrwhitt told her some of what he had presumably already told the First Lord:

> 'It really was awfully fine and not half so unpleasant as I expected. I was so surprised that so many projectiles could fall all round one and burst in all directions and yet so few people were killed. We lost eleven killed, including poor Westmacott [his signals officer of forty-eight hours' standing] who was killed at my side on the bridge, and about sixteen wounded, all in the first action with the two cruisers. We had fifteen direct hits on the side and waterline and many in board, besides hundreds of shrapnel holes.'

To his sister Kitty three days later he enlarged a little, writing of the engagement with the *Stettin* and the *Frauenlob*:

'I can only wonder that everyone on the upper deck was not killed. The air seemed thick with bursting shells and the sea was alive with splashes from shell and splinters... My signal officer was the only man killed on the bridge, such a nice boy. He was talking to me at the time and had just pointed out that we were on fire. The fire was extinguished. I could not say exactly what my feelings were all the time, but I don't think I ever thought of the danger[38] nor do I think anyone on board did. I was very agreeably surprised as I was under the impression that the first time, everyone bobbed their heads when shells flew over them, etc., but it was not the case.'

The British losses as a whole were very light, though more than a third of them occurred in the *Arethusa*. She and the three destroyers already mentioned were the only ships to suffer severely, and the total casualties for all ships engaged were thirty-five killed and about forty wounded. The Germans on the other hand had lost three light cruisers and a destroyer, 781 officers and men killed and 381 prisoners. In itself the victory was no great naval feat, since through Beatty's intervention the British had been latterly in overwhelming force, but since it had been won under the noses of the High Seas Fleet it had a considerable effect in both countries. The British had shown their old ascendancy at sea and – thanks above all to Tyrwhitt and the *Arethusa* – their will to seek out every opportunity of engaging the enemy even at his very front door. The moral effect upon the Germans could not be measured with equal certainty, but in the opinion of competent judges at the time it was at least as important as their material losses, and contributed to the reluctance to venture their ships beyond their base defences which they were showing and continued to show for at least some time. On the other hand the Admiralty Naval Staff had bungled the planning and arrangements for the operation and – worse still – remained complacently unaware how badly they had performed. Tyrwhitt for his part became famous overnight, and his name a household word, while from the day of the battle his command became nicknamed the Harwich Striking Force.[39] He was made a Companion of the Order of the Bath, and congratulations showered in from every side. Among those which he found specially pleasing were a letter from his kinsman Sir Raymond Tyrwhitt of the Shropshire branch of the family, whom he had never met, and who rather charmingly wrote that whereas he used to say that the Commodore was his cousin he now said that he was the Commodore's cousin; a message from 2081 Johannesburg miners who had each subscribed one penny to send it; and another from the boys of the training ship *Arethusa* who sent their respects and hearty congratulations on the success of their ship's namesake. To this last he replied: 'Very many thanks. I hope the young in the old *Arethusa* will have the same good fortune as the old in the young *Arethusa*' – commenting afterwards to his wife, 'Rather drivel, but you know I never can think of the right thing at the right time.'[40] She for her part wrote proudly to his sister Polly after seeing him briefly in London during his next visit to the Admiralty: 'He is just as fit and lighthearted as ever, and also as humble...It's all so glorious to think Reggie...did such splendid work, but I shall be terrified when I know he is out for blood again.'[41]

CHAPTER THREE

KEEPING THE NARROW SEAS

Tyrwhitt and Keyes were indeed soon out for blood again. Tyrwhitt had been given the *Lowestoft*, one of Goodenough's light cruisers, as his temporary flagship while the *Arethusa* was being repaired –

> 'a size larger [he wrote] than the *Arethusa*, but slower and rather too big for my job. I shall be glad to get back to *A*. as it is very unsatisfactory always hunting one's hounds with new horses and new hunt servants [a metaphor which, though he had hunted a little, he may have picked up from Keyes, who was a keen hunting man]. We destroyer folk have ways and customs which are quite unknown to the big ships.'[1]

Before taking her over, however, he spent several days shuttling to and fro between Chatham, the Admiralty and Harwich, while Keyes and he were concocting their next scheme. They decided that as soon as they could get some definite information about the German dispositions, which they felt might have been altered after the British attack, they would plan and propose another assault.

Keyes had sent seven submarines into the Bight on August 31, and when they reported that the German destroyer patrols were being maintained as before Tyrwhitt and he went up to the Admiralty to recommend another drive, based on their experiences of 28 August and these reports. Prince Louis approved, and in a conference attended also by Churchill and Sturdee they unfolded fuller details and were instructed to put them forthwith into the form of a draft scheme. This they did, Keyes drafting the general idea and Tyrwhitt the part to be played by the destroyers.

It was decided that the two flotillas should not leave Harwich together, in case the enemy received intelligence of this and deduced that an attack was imminent. The Third Flotilla therefore put to sea on September 8 and patrolled off the Dutch coast as usual, the First coming out and taking over from them next day; but both remained out for the projected operation on the 10th. The plan of this was that Tyrwhitt with the Third Flotilla should carry out a sweep in the Bight as before, supported this time not only by Goodenough, with Campbell and Beatty in the offing, but also more remotely by the whole Grand Fleet, which Jellicoe brought south to within a hundred miles of Heligoland in case the High Seas Fleet should come out. Meanwhile the First Flotilla and the submarines were to lie off the mouth of the Ems river in the hope of catching the German night patrol on its way back to Emden about 4 a.m. The main object of the exercise however, as stated by the Admiralty Orders, was 'to tempt the larger ships of the enemy, and possibly their main fleet, to come out and protect the vessels attacked', but the result was completely negative. In Tyrwhitt's own words, written that evening:

> 'We "bit the Bight"...this morning at 4 a.m. in a thunderstorm, which came on at just the wrong time, as it reduced the visibility considerably. We never sighted a ship or destroyer of any sort or description, which was most disappointing, especially as we were expecting so much. We did it a slightly different way to last time and again acted as the bait, but I suppose they either were not out or else they did not wish to meet us.'

What had actually happened was that the German night patrol had not been sent out on the night of the 9th–10th, while the day patrol on the 10th went out too late to be caught by the destroyer sweep. Keyes, who to his intense disgust had been forbidden by the Admiralty to go (as he put it) 'barging about in the Bight' again in a destroyer, and who had asked in vain for a light cruiser, claimed that as he was a kind of 'lucky joss' or mascot the fiasco was due to his absence.[2]

Among the destroyers which took part in this unproductive operation was the *Miranda*, which had arrived at Harwich from Yarrow's shipyard on the Clyde on August 29, just too late for the Battle of the Bight. She was the first of the new 'M' class, the fastest destroyers yet built, capable of thirty-four or thirty-five knots and armed with three four-inch guns and four torpedo tubes apiece. These 'Ms' continued to arrive in driblets from then on and were formed into a separate flotilla, the Tenth. The captain of the *Miranda* was Commander Barry Domvile,[3] an old friend of Tyrwhitt's who had become assistant to Colonel Maurice Hankey the Secretary to the Committee of Imperial Defence, but on the outbreak of war had begged successfully for a sea command.[4]

On September 14 Tyrwhitt and Keyes were directed by the Admiralty to hold themselves ready to accompany Churchill and Sturdee to a conference to be held on the 17th on board Jellicoe's flagship, the *Iron Duke*, which was then lying with the rest of the Grand Fleet at Loch Ewe on the west coast of Scotland – Scapa Flow having been thought too unsafe an anchorage till it was better protected against enemy submarines. They went up to London on the 15th and joined the party, which also included the Director of Naval Intelligence (Rear-Admiral Oliver) and the Naval Secretary (Rear-Admiral the Hon. Horace Hood), in a special train at King's Cross. Much of what followed may perhaps best be given in Tyrwhitt's own words:

> 'If anyone had suggested two months ago that I should shortly be travelling by special train with Winston Churchill and the War Staff to attend a Council of War "somewhere" in the North of Scotland, they would have been locked up. It is extraordinary how the

> pendulum has gone up and I only hope that I shall not be found out too soon! Winston Churchill is extremely nice to me, and I like him for himself very much. He is just a boy and a born fighter. [It presumably never struck him that Winston liked *him* for very much the same reasons]. I am not much of a talker but he won't leave me alone about the *Arethusa* fight. I know he'd do anything to see a naval fight. Barring his political views[5] I like him immensely.'[6]

After breakfast the next morning the train drew up at a little station on the line between Dingwall and Kyle, and the party drove across the moors to Loch Ewe. Churchill, Keyes and Tyrwhitt sat together in the roomy back seat of a very old-fashioned high-backed car, and the two friends – 'in stout alliance' (though one suspects that Keyes did most of the talking) – gave the First Lord their views on many service matters.[7]

At the conference, which was attended by all the squadron-commanders of the Grand Fleet, the first item on the agenda was the question of an attempt to capture Heligoland, which was presumably the reason why Tyrwhitt and Keyes had been summoned. Jellicoe's official report to the Admiralty on the conference later stated that

> 'naval opinion was unanimous that the reduction of Heligoland would involve far more serious losses in capital ships than would compensate for any advantage gained, and that the difficulties in the way of a successful bombardment would be very great. [It was] decided that in the present phase of the war no enterprise of this nature should be attempted.'[8]

There was less than complete unanimity, however, over the next item, the possibility of operations in the Baltic, for when Tyrwhitt records that he

> 'threw cold water on the proposals of two very distinguished admirals whose proposals were the equivalent of the death-warrant of a very large number of officers and men, besides being impossible and displaying considerable ignorance of the defences of Germany!',

adding:

> 'It was not pleasant, nor is it easy, nor entirely diplomatic, to entirely disagree with people who are old enough to be one's father, but at the same time I was not going to agree to murdering half my command, and what is more I carried my point,'[9]

he was presumably referring to the proposal of the fire-eating Vice-Admiral Sir Lewis Bayly, who was then commanding the First Battle Squadron, that an attack should be made on Kiel by light cruisers and destroyers.[10] This episode should suffice to dispose of any idea that his courage was mere bull-at-a-gate bravery.

On the way back from the conference there occurred an adventure which Tyrwhitt described to his sister Kitty and which has also been narrated by Churchill in his *Thoughts and Adventures.*[11] While driving to Loch Ewe they had passed a large house with a high tower on the top of which Tyrwhitt noticed a searchlight to which he drew the First Lord's attention. Since the house was in the middle of a deer forest none of the party could suggest any reasonable or innocent explanation for this, though they racked their brains for the rest of the journey. On the other hand, as Oliver and Churchill pointed out, it would be possible for a spy to signal the Fleet's presence in Loch Ewe by searchlight to a Zeppelin which could then relay the information to the German submarines from which – not to put a fine point on it – it was hiding. At lunch during the conference Churchill related what they had seen to Jellicoe, who replied after reflection that there might be something in their suspicions since there had been 'bad rumours' about the place and it was said that there were a number of foreigners there; also an aeroplane had been reported in the neighbourhood, after which it had not been traced. The party therefore resolved to examine it on the way back and armed themselves with revolvers for the purpose. Arriving at the house in pitch darkness and pouring rain at 11 p.m., they rang the front-door bell, which was answered by a portly and respectable butler who admitted them to the hall, where they were joined by the owner, a rubicund and grey-haired gentleman. Oliver, who as Churchill had pointed out was as Director of Naval Intelligence a properly constituted authority under the Defence of the Realm Act, questioned him about the searchlight, backed up by the First Lord, and after a pause he replied that it was used to locate game on the hillsides. 'From the tower', he added, 'we can see several of the beats, and the searchlight gleams on the eyes of the deer and shows us where they are lying, so we know where to send the stalkers in the morning'. He went on to say that it was possible to distinguish the eyes of deer from those of cattle in the searchlight's beam, which seemed to his hearers merely an attempt to add verisimilitude to an otherwise bald and unconvincing story, and confirmed their deepest suspicions.

'We wish to see the searchlight,' said Churchill. 'We wish you to show us it yourself.'

'Certainly,' replied their unwilling host, 'but you will have to climb up the spiral staircase of the tower'.

'Lead the way,' was the order, and after posting Hood at the foot of the stairs the others followed the old gentleman up their winding course, emerging on to a broad square platform with low battlements, in the middle of which was the searchlight, bolted strongly into the roof.

'Do you expect us to believe this story of yours?' Churchill asked.

'Well, it is quite true, whatever you think.'

'You will have to give these explanations to the proper

authorities. For the present we are going to dismantle your searchlight, so that it cannot be used.'

'You can do what you choose,' he replied very indignantly; and they proceeded accordingly, carrying various parts of the mechanism away with them when they left after sullen adieux. 'I don't think our plans were altogether dignified,' wrote Tyrwhitt afterwards, 'but it was impossible to choke Churchill off. He was just a boy and delighted at the possibilities of a scrap.'[12] Subsequently, however, the most searching investigations of the authorities discovered no grounds whatever for suspicion. The owner of the house was a gentleman of unblemished reputation and impeccable patriotism, and his unlikely story was perfectly true. The searchlight had been put up four years earlier and *had* indeed been used for sweeping the hillsides, though it had not been so used, according to overwhelming testimony, since the war began. It was not, in fact, in a state to have been used at the moment when Churchill and his party saw it. There were no foreigners in the house or on the estate, and no confirmation could be obtained of the rumour which Jellicoe had reported of an unaccountable aircraft having been seen in the neighbourhood. The whole thing had been a mare's nest..

Tyrwhitt and Keyes had seized the opportunity of the conference to express their views – with which Jellicoe concurred – about the unwisdom of keeping the old armoured cruisers of the 'live bait squadron' operating in the Narrow Seas any longer. These *Bacchantes* were not really fit for the work of co-operation with the Harwich flotillas, but in default of more suitable ships they had had to be assigned to it when war began. Now, however, that more light cruisers of the new *Arethusa* class were coming forward it would be possible for these to take their places.

By this time two patrol areas had been established for the flotillas – one off the Dogger Bank and one in the Broad Fourteens. As a rule the bulk of the cruisers were to the northward supporting the Dogger patrol, but at critical junctures such as the crossing of the Expeditionary Force they had been concentrated in the Broad Fourteens. For some days before the autumnal equinox, however, gales had prevented the flotillas from getting out at all; and on September 19 the Admiralty decided to suspend the Dogger patrol altogether and maintain only the other. Tyrwhitt was therefore instructed to re-establish the Broad Fourteens patrol next morning, if possible, by which time the cruisers would have arrived to support it. The sea was so high, however, that although the *Fearless* started to bring out the patrol she was forced to take it back to Harwich. The *Bacchante* was at Chatham having her condenser repaired; the *Euryalus* had had her wireless disabled in the gale and since she was due for coaling in any case Admiral Christian (unable to shift his flag because no boat could be lowered) parted company and took her back to port; and the *Aboukir*, *Cressy* and *Hogue* were left to maintain the watch without any flotilla support.

The area they were patrolling was particularly dangerous, since it lay between the Dutch coast and a German minefield and thus left little room for variations of course. Churchill, however, thanks to the urgent representations which Keyes and Tyrwhitt had made to him both at Loch Ewe and on the return journey, was in the very act of making arrangements to bring this suicide patrol to an end; and in the meantime it was thought that if the best destroyers could not make head against the weather submarines would not be able to operate offensively. Moreover the moment it began to abate on the night of the 21st–22nd Tyrwhitt set out for the Broad Fourteens with the *Lowestoft* and twelve destroyers of the Third Flotilla.

In spite of his prompt departure he was still well over fifty miles away when a single German submarine, the U9, torpedoed all three cruisers in quick succession early on the morning of the 22nd.[13]

> 'At 7 a.m. [he wrote later to his sister Kitty] we received a wirelesss "*Aboukir*, and *Hogue* sunk".

Knowing where they were supposed to be I dashed off at full speed and a few minutes later we received their position from the *Cressy* and part of a signal which ended abruptly and then there was no more. I knew too well what had happened and what was probably in store for us, but I could not think of 2 100 men drowning without giving them all the assistance in my power. We arrived about two hours after the disaster and there was no sign of the ships, but various boats, trawlers and two steamers, all very much spread over the sea and all very much crammed with men. We first went up to a small English trawler which was loaded with men. They looked just like rows and rows of swallows on telegraph lines, all huddled up together to keep themselves warm; they were all naked or nearly so as they had been overboard and were very cold. No sooner did we get close to them than we received three warnings of submarines from various sources...I made the destroyers steam in a circle round us while we got the men on board, which was a very long job as there was a heavy sea running and we had only two boats. In wartime we only carry two boats as they are shot to bits as soon as action commences. We took 280 men out of this trawler...Other destroyers picked up another 200 and eventually we collected 581. My friend Captain Nicholson was picked up by a Dutch steamer [the *Flora*, which showed a fine disregard of danger] with 170 of his crew and taken to Ymuiden where he charmed the inhabitants.[14] I was dreadfully sorry not to have picked him up myself but he would not wait as they had a number of injured men who required medical assistance ...Nicholson's ship, the *Hogue,* capsized in seven minutes. He of course was the last to leave the ship. As she turned over he walked from the bridge down her side and on to her bottom...[and] was...picked up by the mercy of Providence. I fancy he did not try to save himself as the boats were crammed and he would have

> been the last man in the world to jeopardise anyone for his own personal safety. One of his own men told me this and they said when they saw him standing by himself on the bottom of the ship they cheered him for all they were worth...We brought them back to Harwich. They were all very cheerful and landed about 8 p.m. and were made much of on shore.'[15]

In all 60 officers and 777 men were saved, which meant that as many officers and nearly 1400 men were drowned. When a fortnight later the First Flotilla patrolled these waters, which had come to be known as 'the Cemetery', Lieutenant Tennant recorded that the sea had given up the dead from the sunken cruisers and they too were keeping their last patrol there, six hours one way and then six hours the other, with the wind and the tide.[16]

At 11.05 a.m. Tyrwhitt had signalled to Harwich 'Loss due to submarine. Send destroyers to cut submarine off Terschelling.' Keyes, who received this as well as Captain Blunt of the *Fearless*, telephoned the Admiralty and with some difficulty got leave to go out with him as a passenger when the *Fearless* left with seventeen of the First Flotilla at 11.36 a.m. Shortly afterwards he managed to get in touch with his own second-in-command Captain Waistell, who was in the *Firedrake*, and instructed him to meet him with the *Lurcher* off Terschelling, where he would be at 6 p.m. with the First Flotilla. What he had in mind was a larger measure of revenge than merely the interception of the German submarine, for he then told Blunt that as soon as they met the *Lurcher* and *Firedrake* he would hoist his broad pendant in the former, take him and his destroyers under his own command, and proceed to make an attempt to mop up the German destroyer patrols entering or leaving the Ems. Blunt replied that he was quite ready to put himself under Keyes's orders straight away, provided that the latter would take all responsibility, which of course he was delighted to do. Keyes next informed Jellicoe by signal of what he proposed and in due course received a somewhat guarded approval coupled with a warning that in view of the short notice the only support that could be provided was a couple of cruisers which would be thirty miles north of Terschelling at 5 a.m. next day.

By that time, however, Keyes had received a peremptory order from the Admiralty, which even he could not disregard, to return to Harwich.[17] According to Tyrwhitt, who went up to London next day to report, Their Lordships '*were* in a state', one outcome of which was that they forbade him to take his two light cruisers to sea with the flotillas in future. His solution to this was to go out in a destroyer on the next occasion, and then submit on his return that he considered this dangerous, whereupon the Admiralty gave way and rescinded its prohibition.[18] But it is quite understandable that it should have been in a state of what is today called 'flap', since this was by far the most striking success that either the torpedo or the submarine had achieved since their invention and it was clear that in conjunction they represented a menace which would require new methods if it was to be coped with.

Tyrwhitt was all the more anxious to get the Admiralty's leave to resume going to sea in a cruiser since the *Arethusa*'s repairs were finished and she was fit for service again. On the 28th he went to Chatham to get her and brought her back to Harwich next day. To Kitty he wrote:

> 'Getting back to one's own ship is nearly as good as getting home. We had a full-powered trial on our way here and managed twenty-eight knots without the least trouble, so I am sure we shall get thirty the first time we chase a German. As you can imagine we are all longing to wipe out the cruiser disaster, but I am afraid there is nothing doing at present.'

On his way to Chatham he had lunched with Winston and Mrs. Churchill at the Admiralty, and of this he wrote in the same letter:

> 'He has been exceedingly pleasant to me ever since I took on my present job. Mrs. W. is very nice and most attractive. I like him and admire him intensely except for his politics, but he is nice about them and allows that we don't like them. I always say I have none.'[19]

To his wife he wrote:

> 'He is always nice to me and seemed to go out of his way to be extra nice.'[20]

At the beginning of October the operations of the flotillas were for a second time governed by the needs of the Army. After the German invasion of France had been checked at the Marne and the invaders thrown back to the Aisne the Allied counter-attack was also checked there in its turn and the battle-front became stabilized down to the Swiss frontier. Attention was then turned to the other flank which was still open, and what came to be called the race for the sea developed, as each army in turn tried to outflank the other on that side, with the result that the lines spread rapidly northward in the direction of the coast. It was now decided to remove the British Expeditionary Force from where it had become embedded in the French forces to its natural position on the sea flank. This involved new lines of communication to Dunkirk and (it soon transpired) Ostend, which the Navy would have to protect. Moreover reinforcements in the shape of another infantry division (the Seventh) and the Third Cavalry Division were now ready in England to take the field, and these could also conveniently be thrown in from Dunkirk or Ostend, provided that the Navy would undertake to guard their transportation.

Two further complications were then added to the situation. Firstly, German submarines were found to be operating near the Straits of Dover, threatening these lines of communication through the Narrow Seas which had suddenly assumed a much increased importance. To give them additional protection it was therefore resolved to lay minefields in the southern area of the North Sea, but the minelayers told off for this task would themselves require destroyer protection while at work. Secondly, just after the minelaying had begun, the Belgian field army, which had fallen back before the German invaders upon the fortress of Antwerp, decided to leave the defence of that place to garrison troops and retire along the coast to link up with the British. Partly to facilitate this junction, the disembarkation of the Seventh Division and the Third Cavalry Division was transferred at almost the last moment to Zeebrugge, further north-east along the Belgian coast and hence somewhat nearer Antwerp than Ostend was. A minefield already laid to protect Dunkirk blocked the approach to Zeebrugge, however, and a channel had to be swept through it – and the minesweepers protected – before the troops could pass, which they did on October 6, 7 and 8.[21]

All of this threw fresh patrolling on to the flotillas, which apart from Keyes's submarines were now the only force in the southern North Sea, and put paid for the present to a plan Keyes and Tyrwhitt had concocted for yet another attack on the German patrols in the Bight.[22] The rough weather continued into early October and patrolling off the Dutch coast to protect the British minelayers meant days of 'rolling, rolling, rolling, watchkeeping, sleeping and at intervals eating something that didn't need cooking'[23] because the weather was too bad for that.[24] On the 10th Antwerp fell, and Tyrwhitt went to sea at 4 a.m. next day with the First Flotilla to patrol close inshore with the object – or at least in the hope – of preventing the Germans from getting submarines to it and using it as a submarine base. By now the weather was much better and he set out full of hopes of a good haul. At least one of his officers, however (perhaps because he had passed through the 'Cemetery' only a couple of days before), was less optimistic and felt more like the hunted than the hunter, writing: 'I think at no time since war began have we so fully realised our danger as today...absolute fair game for any submarine that may come along and which we shall never see'[25] – words that no doubt reflected the shock many felt at the recent revelation of what a submarine could do. He was too pessimistic, however, for though two of the flotilla were attacked by U-boats they suffered no damage. On the other hand neither did the U-boats, and no others were seen. The Third Flotilla, which took over on the 13th for the usual two-day spell, had no better luck.

But now the prevailing gloom was pierced by a welcome ray of light. Two more new light cruisers of the *Arethusa* class had arrived at Harwich, the *Undaunted*, which became the leader of the Third Flotilla and so made it no longer necessary for the *Arethusa* to be that as well as flagship, and the *Aurora*. Captain Fox, who had recovered from the injuries he had sustained when the *Amphion* was mined on the first day of the war, had now returned to duty and taken command of the *Undaunted*; and since information had been coming in that German destroyers were showing activity in the Bight, he was sent out on the evening of October 16 – the very day of the *Undaunted*'s arrival – to investigate with the First Division of his flotilla (*Lance, Lennox, Legion* and *Loyal*). At 2 p.m. next day, when they were steaming up the Dutch coast about fifty miles south-west of Texel Island, they sighted four German torpedo-boats (the *S.115, 117, 118* and *119*) about eight miles ahead, steaming in line abreast at about half a mile from one another on a course slightly more easterly than their own. Seeing the British astern of them, the Germans began to spread fanwise, whereupon the *Undaunted* signalled 'General Chase'. Since it was soon evident that the British destroyers had the speed of the enemy *Lennox* and *Lance* held away to head off the easternmost boats from the Bight, while *Legion* and *Loyal* made after the others. The range fell fast, and by about 3 p.m. *Lennox* and *Lance* had reduced the easternmost boat (*S.115*) to a sinking condition while the other British pair had put the westernmost virtually out of action. Seeing that escape was impossible, the two centre boats then turned back to make a desperate torpedo attack on the *Undaunted*, but *Legion* and *Loyal* headed them off with so hot a fire that they were forced to turn away to the eastward without securing a hit on the British cruiser.

Meanwhile the other two German boats had joined, so far as they still could, in what became a close-range *mêlée* in which the Germans were hopelessly outmatched. By 4.30 p.m. the last of them had gone down, blown up by her captain's orders. Picked up mortally wounded, this very gallant officer explained before he died that he and the others had been ordered to sink themselves when they could no longer fire a shot, in order to prevent capture. One other officer and twenty-nine men were also rescued from the water. From them it was learnt that while they were scouting to see what British ships there were in these waters one of the four vessels had developed a leaky condenser, which reduced her speed to nineteen knots, and the other three had stood by her. They were a division of the Ems Patrol, but their operating so far beyond the usual limits of their area suggested that some plan was in the wind – as had been feared – to disturb the operations on the Belgian coast. The British casualties in this one-sided action, which was nevertheless calculated to secure the Straits of Dover from attack for the moment, were one officer and four men wounded. 'Just my luck!' commented Tyrwhitt. '...The very day [Fox] takes on he gets a delightful show.'[26]

He was not consoled for missing it by capturing a German vessel when he went out on the following day. She claimed to be a hospital ship searching for survivors from the torpedo-boats that had been sunk, but she had been sighted ten days before under suspicious circumstances by a British submarine and from her subsequent movements, which our submarines had continued to watch, and from the orders found in her there could be no doubt that she was breaking the rules of war by acting as a scout.[27]

The operation on which Tyrwhitt was engaged when he

made this capture was part of a successful effort to save the port of Nieuport from the German onrush along the Belgian coast that followed the fall of Antwerp. Foreseeing this onrush and seeing clearly what it would mean to the Dover area, the Admiralty on the morrow of the fall of the fortress had created a new and separate command based on Dover and under Rear-Admiral Hood, whose force ('the Dover Patrol', as it came to be called) consisted of the Sixth Destroyer Flotilla, four attached light cruisers, two submarine flotillas, and an assortment of boarding craft, trawlers and auxiliary patrol vessels. In the next few days Zeebrugge and Ostend fell and the Germans were advancing on Nieuport when on October 17 there came an anxious appeal for naval aid to be sent to the Belgians who were struggling desperately to hold out there. Hood went over at once with part of his force and three shallow-draught monitors which were operating on the coast, and opened an effective bombardment on the flank of the advancing enemy, but by the 18th there were indications that the Germans might try to interrupt his operations with armoured and light cruisers, and it was as a cover against this that Tyrwhitt had been ordered out with his full force. Two battleships from the Channel Fleet with an attached light cruiser and four destroyers were instructed to proceed through the Downs to support him, but no enemy appeared except that at daybreak on the 19th the *Arethusa* sighted a submarine on the surface and made an attempt to ram her which just failed as she dived. When later in the day it became evident that the German rush along the coast had been stopped and that Fox's smart and successful action had probably kept the enemy from attempting any intervention by sea, he sent the bulk of his force back to Harwich on the night of the 19th–20th, but remained out two days longer with a bodyguard of four destroyers. 'I shall not be sorry to get some bed,' he wrote to his wife on the evening of the 20th, 'as I have only looked at mine since Saturday night [three days earlier].'[28]

With the situation on the Belgian coast thus comparatively

stabilised it was now possible for the Admiralty to give consideration to the plan for another attack on the Bight which Keyes and Tyrwhitt had drawn up but which had had to be shelved for the time being. On the 22nd, the day after his return to harbour, Tyrwhitt was summoned to London to discuss it.

> 'I arrived at 5 p.m. [he wrote] and was at once taken to the Holy of Holy rooms, where Prince Louis, Winston and Sturdee were, and a long discussion followed. I produced my little plan (or rather, Roger Keyes's plan) and got it through right away...Well, they kept me a long time and suddenly in walked the Prince of Wales.[29] Nice little boy, very small, quite self-possessed and a gentleman...'[30]

The reason why Tyrwhitt was kept for a long time was presumably that the plan which Keyes and he had devised was now being combined with something much bigger, at any rate in its possibilities and significance. Provoked by the earliest Zeppelin raids on England, this was a scheme for an air-raid on the Zeppelin sheds at Cuxhaven, to be attempted by seaplanes of the young Naval Air Service, in whose development Churchill had shown much interest during the two years before the war. It was in fact the first feeble and primitive prototype of the enterprises carried out on an ever-increasing scale by carrier-borne aircraft during the Second World War, particularly in the Pacific. While part of Tyrwhitt's force executed the sweep off the river Ems that Keyes and he had planned, he himself with the remainder was to convey the seaplanes by night to a suitable starting-point in the Bight, where they were to be hoisted out on to the water for their take-off. The dual operation was to be supported by the battle-cruisers *Invincible* and *Inflexible,* which with a division of destroyers were ordered down from the Grand Fleet for the purpose. The Harwich Force duly left the harbour about 5 a.m. on the 24th, with Tyrwhitt, as he wrote to his wife in a letter which he began that evening, 'bursting with excitement' and hoping for great things from this novel form of attack.[31]

Both enterprises failed; the *Fearless* and the First Flotilla crept along the German coast in the dark small hours of the next morning without sighting anything, and the seaplanes were prevented from rising from the water by a heavy rainstorm, which compelled the attempt on Cuxhaven to be abandoned. Tyrwhitt, deeply disappointed, sat down to resume his letter after a spell of twenty-four hours on the bridge that perhaps goes far to explain the irritation which he now voiced and which was a good deal less than fair to the Naval Air Service:

> 'I am sick to death of everything connected with aviation...At very great risk we did our part and they utterly failed to do theirs...We did our whole business without making a signal of any sort and almost under the guns of the biggest fort in the world [i.e., Heligoland]. I am positively furious at having been made a fool of. We had two torpedoes under our keel, but thank God neither touched us. I suppose they came from a submarine but I never saw it. Freemantle, Captain of *Badger*, sank a submarine yesterday by ramming it.[32] He bent up his destroyer's nose in doing it, but no-one minds that...I am very tired and *utterly* disappointed. We had the finest show in the world at our mercy and could have done it with ease if only those idiots had known their job.'[33]

Churchill, quick to grasp the true reason for the failure, was far juster to the R.N.A.S. in a minute which he composed and sent to the Director of the Air Department of the Admiralty on the 26th, while Tyrwhitt was still beating his way back to Harwich, and which began:

> 'The failure yesterday was very disappointing. It is no

> use trying these enterprises with overloaded machines. Either aeroplanes or seaplanes with wheels instead of floats must be used,'

and went on to suggest launching them from the longest barges that could be found, each fitted with a trolley on rails actuated by an accelerating windlass. In the opinion of the eminent naval historian Captain S.W. Roskill, 'this minute could be said to mark the genesis of the concept of the aircraft-carrier.'[34] The next attempt, however, was planned to take place almost immediately, and on the same lines as before. When Tyrwhitt after his return to Harwich went up to the Admiralty on October 27, he reported to his wife that

> 'they were very sad about the failure of the business, but it was not my fault. I got considerable butter over my part in the proceedings. I had a personal interview with W.C. and told him all about it. We are going to try again and I can't help thinking we shall succeed this time.'[35]

He was too optimistic. For seaplanes to be hoisted out on to the water and take off from it a smooth sea was essential, which could hardly be counted on for long in the late autumn, still less in the winter which was now approaching. Within a few days he was writing that he was 'standing by to do another flying performance', but in his next letter he announced that 'our game was put off, and rather luckily as it is blowing very hard.' A few days later again, soon after Lord Fisher had replaced Prince Louis of Battenberg as First Sea Lord, he took him

> 'my plans for the next "game" and carried them through, and I do hope we shall pull it off this time. Third time ought to be lucky. We are going to do it by ourselves this time, no [big] ships, just my crowd and submarines. It will be exciting, but I have not the

> slightest doubt it will come off, if only we can get a fine day for it.'[36]

Nothing came of this either, however, at any rate in its restricted form. In fact, an underlying theme of Tyrwhitt's activities during the two months before Christmas, though interrupted from time to time by the alarms and excursions shortly to be narrated, was the alternation of preparations for further attempts to carry out the air-raid on Cuxhaven with disappointments, abortive efforts and frustrations.

The retirement of Prince Louis referred to above had been due to an ignorant and cruel clamour raised against him by a section of the Press on account of his German birth, and supported by a whispering campaign. These senseless slanders grew until he was driven to resign his office on October 28.[37] A few days earlier Tyrwhitt had written to his wife, who – not knowing the Prince as her husband did – had evidently been influenced a little by the campaign of smears and rumours, 'I don't think you need worry about P.L's patriotism. He's all right!'[38] That the Prince should now have been virtually forced to resign grieved him and the choice of the veteran 'Jacky' Fisher as his successor took him by surprise; but when he took Fisher his plans on the occasion just mentioned he found him 'extraordinarily nice' and had

> 'quite half-an-hour with Jacky F. all by my lone. He pumped me dry and is giving me more ships, so that I shall soon be turned out by an Admiral. I suggested this to him and he said "Never!" As a matter of fact he was really very complimentary, as he said it had come to his notice that I acted on my own initiative...He said he should always back anyone up who did things without asking first.'[39]

In fact Fisher, with his great propensity to violent likes and dislikes, had taken immediately to this new star in the naval firmament, seeing in him a fighting man after his own heart. Unfortunately he had for some time had an equally strong but totally unfair prejudice against Keyes, who in the past had dared to express to him views about submarines that differed from his own and whom he had for a long time confused with an officer named Keys who had been Naval Secretary to his *bête noir* Lord Charles Beresford. Soon after taking office he said to someone who he felt sure could be relied on to repeat the remark to Keyes 'Why can't that fellow go to sea and fight like Tyrwhitt?' Since if there was anyone in the Navy who surpassed Tyrwhitt as a fighter it was Keyes, and since the sole reason why he had not gone to sea latterly was that the Admiralty had forbidden him to do so, this was an injustice that passed all bounds. Moreover, as was soon to appear, though fortunately only briefly and then not publicly, it was a remark capable of doing harm to the relationship of the two friends.

During September and October the ordinary patrols had been hardly interfered with by the enemy. Finding this dull, the divisional commanders of the flotillas began to plan baits to be laid out off the mouth of the Ems in the hope of enticing them out. The commander of one division made a practice of towing over some floats filled with combustibles, which he would either set on fire or blow up a little before daybreak, lying off two or three miles away waiting for the Germans to come out to investigate what he hoped they would take for a mined British destroyer, while another division stood by out of sight but within easy reach. At first this produced no result, but early in November the ruse took effect; a German light cruiser and two destroyers poked their noses out of harbour, only to bolt back to the Ems the moment they sighted our forces.[40]

On November 2 Lieutenant Tennant, back in harbour after a patrol during which Tyrwhitt had kept the First Flotilla with him for its full two days in a gale that would have made it almost impossible for it to fight its guns, had confided to his diary that 'things were beginning to ease up somewhat, as well they might, since not long ago we did fourteen days out of eighteen at sea.' Even in harbour, moreover, all ships had been kept ready for sea every morning during these early days of the war, in case of enemy raids on our coasts. The first such 'tip-and-run' raid came early on the very morning after Tennant had made this entry, thus demonstrating that his belief that quieter times were beginning was premature. Shortly after 7 a.m. on the 3rd. Tyrwhitt was surprised by a signal from the *Halcyon*, a mine-sweeping gunboat stationed off Lowestoft which was then working off Smith's Knoll about twenty miles north-east of Yarmouth, that she was engaged with a superior enemy. This was in fact part of a force of German battle-cruisers and light cruisers, which at about this hour bombarded Yarmouth briefly and then made off, and it was only by good luck and continual changes of course that the *Halcyon* was able to escape with trifling damage. On receiving her signal the Commodore signalled the *Undaunted* and *Aurora*[41] (which were out on patrol with the Third Flotilla) to make at full speed for Smith's Knoll, and himself hastily prepared to get to sea with the other half of his force and make for Terschelling in the hope of cutting off the enemy's retreat. Realising, however, that it was the force already at sea that was better placed to do this, he reversed his instructions and ordered it to Terschelling, while deciding to take the Smith's Knoll position himself with the *Arethusa* and the half-dozen destroyers that had got away most quickly, sweeping along the Suffolk coast as he went. The *Aurora*, however, had not received his second order and had therefore held on for the same position, where she waited for instructions. Meanwhile the *Undaunted*, making for Terschelling with her destroyers, sighted four German cruisers which promptly gave chase to her and her flotilla.

At first the outweighted British ran off to the northward, but not content merely to escape, they presently began to turn to the westward with the design of leading the enemy south. Scenting a trap, however, the Germans gave up the chase and in their turn made off east-north-east towards the Terschelling Light. The *Undaunted* then resumed her course and followed them, doing her best to keep touch; and Tyrwhitt, who by 11.30 a.m. had reached the Corton Light Vessel off Lowestoft on his way to Smith's Knoll, set off to her aid, steaming unknowingly but unscathed through the mines which the Germans had just laid. But now came a signal from the Admiralty, which had learnt the overwhelming force of the enemy, recommending him to concentrate, and he therefore recalled the *Undaunted*. By 3 p.m. he had assembled three light cruisers and thirteen destroyers at a mid-sea rendezvous, and with this force he proceeded to sweep past Terschelling to the Bight. But nothing more was seen of the enemy, and towards midnight he swept back again and by noon next day was off the Maas Light Vessel, barring the way down the Broad Fourteens. Still there was no further trace of the raiders,[42] and normal routine was therefore resumed, a force sent out from Scapa and Cromarty under Admiral Beatty having already been recalled.[43]

With the whole of the Western Front in France and Flanders now virtually stabilised and the long deadlock beginning there, some anxiety arose in late October and November lest the Germans might switch to attempt an invasion of England, especially since it was now almost denuded of trained troops. The German submarines, too, were spreading their activities further and further afield, so that in spite of the worsening weather there continued to be plenty to keep the Harwich Force active or on the *qui vive*. Alarms of submarines, true or false, became more frequent, and some of the false ones had their comic side. Thus about 2 a.m. on November 12 an alarm signal was received that a submarine had been sighted up the Blackwater River, a shallow estuary between Harwich and the Thames. Seven destroyers headed by the *Ferret* set off in the dark through the Wallet, a deep-water channel between sandbanks off Walton-on-the-Naze. Off the Blackwater they sighted dimly a small grey object which began to flash a light, and the Captain of the *Ferret* enthusiastically went full speed ahead to ram it, but providentially a searchlight showed it to be a lifeboat with Commodore Keyes in it. He had received a rather earlier submarine warning followed by instructions from the C.-in-C. at the Nore to commandeer all suitable steamers and sink them across the entrance of the estuary, but – being very sceptical about the likelihood of enemy submarines venturing into a shallow river-mouth – had confined himself to impounding some miles of an anti-submarine net which was under construction at Brightlingsea, collecting all the available boats and beginning to lay it across the entrance. Nothing was seen of any submarine, but by the next day local inhabitants were claiming to have seen five all told, one of them chasing a destroyer at a speed which by the description must have been quite twenty knots. Eventually it transpired that all this had been sparked off by a farm-labourer who had seen a sheet of foam running through the water, caused by a flight of wild duck skimming the surface – almost literally a wild-goose chase.[44]

By now the plans for a seaplane raid on the Cuxhaven Zeppelin sheds had been carried an important stage further. The first primitive seaplane-carriers were making their appearance – not converted barges, as Churchill had suggested nearly a month earlier, but three cross-Channel passenger steamers, the *Engadine*, *Riviera* and *Empress*, which had been taken over, fitted with steel hangers capable of housing three seaplanes each, and sent to Harwich to await favourable weather conditions. In response to the increasing signs of unusual activity in the German naval ports it was now decided that the Grand Fleet should make a full-strength sweep down to the Heligoland Bight, in co-operation with the Harwich Force which was to trail its coat and act as a springboard for a raid on the Cuxhaven sheds that might serve as an additional means of goading the enemy's main fleet to action. The Force therefore sailed with the carriers on November 23, but during the night the wind and sea became too rough for seaplanes and the Germans were reported to be very much on the alert, so that the carriers were ordered back to port escorted by the destroyers, while the three light cruisers *Arethusa*, *Undaunted* and *Aurora* carried on into enemy waters accompanied by one destroyer which had become detached and joined up with them 'like a lost pup looking for companionship. Proceeding close in towards Heligoland, these four ships cruised about brazenly in full view of the island fortress, inviting the enemy to come out and fight, but without result except that the island's guns opened fire on them.[45] Tyrwhitt's version of the affair was:

> 'The whole show was not exactly a failure, but it was stopped in the middle of the night by the Admiralty. I was perfectly furious. They waited until I was well in the danger zone and then told me by wireless that a large force was patrolling in the area I was going to operate in. I had then to do a sort of disappearing trick with about half my force without making signals, etc. – a very difficult operation on a pitch-black night, and I am sorry to say it ended in a collision between two destroyers. However that did not worry me as they were going back in any case. I went on with the cruisers and we reconnoitred Heligoland who got very excited. They fired a lot of stuff (Black Marias) at us but no one of them came within miles of us... We pirouetted about for an hour admiring the view of Heligoland and as no one appeared anxious to come out after us I retired. The whole of our Fleet was hanging about within a hundred miles, but I expect they knew that just as well as we did. And I don't believe there was any reason why we should not have carried out the real thing.[46] The morning was lovely, calm and clear. It blew hard again on our return...but not much sea... Two German submarines and a seaplane came to say how-d'ye-do, but the submarines did not like the look of three *Arethusas* dodging about at 25 knots. The seaplane dropped five bombs...but they all missed. I wish she had come my way, as I was dying to try my aerial guns, but she was never in range.'[47]

During the period of this operation others of the Harwich destroyers were taking at least an auxiliary part in a bombardment of Zeebrugge. The capture of this port by the Germans had soon been followed by indications that they were establishing a submarine base there for operations against the Army's lines of communication across the Channel. On November 23, therefore, minesweeping trawlers from Lowestoft, guarded by destroyers of the First Flotilla, swept a channel through the minefield for two battleships of the Channel Fleet, which then proceeded to bombard the port for over an hour.[48] Uncomfirmed reports from Holland stated that considerable damage had been done, but what is certain is that Zeebrugge nevertheless continued to be a source of anxiety to our cross-Channel transport lines.

A period of comparative rest for the Harwich Force followed this bombardment of Zeebrugge. The Dutch coast patrol which had been its staple activity had become practically pointless, since the weather was generally so rough that destroyers could neither get their speed nor could they if required have fought their guns. The fears of invasion had not quite vanished, however, and rumours of German transports in readiness at Wilhelmshaven and elsewhere kept all ships raising steam daily at 5.30 a.m. It was during this period that the first brief rift in the friendship between Tyrwhitt and Keyes occurred. It must be remembered that Keyes had long been in Fisher's black books – which were very black indeed – and had feared with good reason that the formidable old man meant to get rid of him and replace him by someone else as Commodore (S). When on December 5 Tyrwhitt was promoted Commodore, First Class, over his head though he himself had more than four years' seniority over him as a captain, he therefore saw this – perhaps taking it in conjunction with Fisher's cruelly unjust remark quoted above – as a slight,[49] and even as a confirmation of his fears. In his understandable bitterness some expression or expressions escaped him which hurt the quick-tempered Tyrwhitt in his turn, and a short estrangement followed. On the next day Tyrwhitt told his wife:

> 'I have just written to Keyes and given him what for. I was horribly hurt at his attitude yesterday and have just given it to him in plain English...'

Four days later, however, during which interval it seems probable[50] that Keyes had unburdened himself to his deeply-loved wife Eva and received sage counsel from her, Tyrwhitt wrote again:

> 'I had reams from Roger yesterday, and it was full of excuses and apologies...but on the whole he was very sorry..., so I have forgiven him and we've made it up. I have been for a walk with him and all is peace.'[51]

One result of Tyrwhitt's promotion in which he found no pleasure was that he could no longer combine the functions of Commodore with those of Captain of the *Arethusa*, but was obliged to delegate the actual handling of her to another. As he was a perfectionist who prided himself on his seamanship, this did not make for an easy relationship with the unfortunate officer to whom this duty fell.

> 'I am no longer captain of my own ship [he wrote] and hate the whole thing. I have promoted Arbuthnot[52] to rank of Acting Commander...'

and again:

> 'I went out this morning and hated seeing someone else do it all. It is like being driven in one's own car. I take no lessons in the handling of ships from anyone, so I hate to see people making a mess of it!'[53]

Just at this juncture came the news of the annihilating victory won over Von Spee off the Falkland Islands by Sturdee, whom Fisher, who hated him of old (and also with some justice held him partly responsible for the Coronel disaster), had lost no time in thrusting out of the Admiralty. Tyrwhitt wrote:

> 'I am sick to death of sitting in harbour and nearly wept with disgust [when] we were again prevented from going out today... I am so glad for Sturdee's sake that he knocked out those German brutes. I was going to say butchers but after all they were not that. The Germans were just as much superior to poor Cradock's lot[54] as Sturdee was to the Germans, so there's no more to be said... I must write to Sturdee, as he was always very nice to me and often went out of his way to be nice.'[55]

To the enemy the news of the Battle of the Falklands had necessarily revealed that the Grand Fleet had been weakened a little by the detachment of two battle-cruisers.[56] It was therefore thought that they might seize the moment to strike a blow of some kind, and by December 14 this expectation was confirmed by reports that an attack was in preparation. Our intelligence of the enemy's movements had now been much improved by a lucky stroke of fortune. A German light cruiser had run aground in the Baltic and the Russians had salvaged from the body of a drowned signalman copies of the German Navy's cipher signal books. These they had sent to the Admiralty, where they had in due course been decoded. The result was that the British could not only intercept but to some extent interpret the German signals. It could at least be inferred that another cruiser raid on our coast was intended, though where it would try to strike was uncertain; and by the time that the German raiding forces – consisting of their battle-cruisers with the High Seas Fleet in support – were in motion early on the morning of December 15 our own dispositions were taking shape.

The Admiralty had ordered out the Second Battle Squadron from Scapa under Vice-Admiral Sir George Warrender, together with Commodore Goodenough's First

Light Cruiser Squadron and Sir David Beatty's battle-cruisers from Cromarty with some destroyers. Admiral Jellicoe gave them a well-judged rendezvous that should have enabled them at least to catch Hipper's battle-cruisers on their return from their raid, and suggested to the Admiralty that the Harwich Force should also be directed to this rendezvous. But Tyrwhitt had already been instructed to try to get into touch with the enemy off our coasts as soon as they were reported, and to shadow them; and since the Admiralty stuck to this and did not adopt Jellicoe's suggestion, when he left harbour very early on the morning of the 16th he made for Yarmouth, arriving at 6.30 a.m. and keeping his force under way in the shelter of the banks to await orders. Two hours later he received a signal that the Germans were bombarding Scarborough, and at 8.40 a.m. he started off thither with his four light cruisers and both his flotillas. His intention was to go out through the Haisborough Gat, but as soon as he was clear of the shoals he found the wind blowing strong to a gale from nearly ahead and the sea so steep and short that he felt obliged to order the destroyers back to Yarmouth and go on with his light cruisers alone. 'If', wrote Lieutenant Tennant in his diary when he was back in harbour, 'those who asked afterwards what the Navy was doing had had an hour punching into that sea they would have known!' The question was not unreasonable, however, for by a remarkable series of mischances a great opportunity of catching the raiders was missed and they managed to avoid both Warrender and Beatty. Tyrwhitt, to whom the Admiralty had meanwhile sent instructions to join Warrender with all despatch, was too far away to have any chance of making contact with them.

> 'We had a very bad time [he wrote after he had returned to harbour and gone up to the Admiralty to report], frightful weather and no fortune. *We* saw nothing, much to Their Lordships' disgust, though I think they have accepted my explanation... I never had a chance as we

started over 600 miles behind them... I dined with the Churchills last night. At least, they watched me eat a few courses and then went to the theatre. It was not very easy to talk business at the dinner table. Mrs. W. looked charming *as ever*.'[57]

The business which Tyrwhitt found difficulty in discussing over the dinner-table was almost certainly yet another plan which had been formed to bring off the raid on the Zeppelin sheds at Cuxhaven. The *Engadine*, *Riviera* and *Empress* were to be escorted by Tyrwhitt to a position about twelve miles north of Heligoland, where their seaplanes (Shorts of three different marks, with a maximum speed of 78 miles per hour) were to be hoisted out for the take-off.[58] After attacking Cuxhaven they were to reconnoitre the anchorages in the rivers, noting what ships were there, and fly westward along the coast to Norderney Gat, and thence to seaward to rejoin the carriers, which in the meantime were to move down with their escort to a position twenty miles north of Norderney. As before, it was hoped that the enterprise might provoke a fleet action, and the whole Grand Fleet was therefore to be concentrated in the middle of the North Sea in support. It was first hoped to make the attempt a few days before Christmas, but the assembling of the planes at Harwich by daylight apparently gave the enemy, whose submarines were occasionally reported off the port, some inkling of what was afoot, and the raid was consequently put off till Christmas Day – much to the chagrin and alarm of Mrs. Tyrwhitt, who had been invited with her children to spend Christmas week with the ever-hospitable Commodore and Mrs. Cayley, in a house already bursting at the seams with young people. At dusk on the evening of the 23rd, therefore, the buzz of aircraft filled the air as the nine seaplanes made their way from the air station at Felixstowe to the carriers – the first time they had flown after sunset since the war started. At daybreak on the 24th the Commodore, the three *Arethusas*, the carriers and most of the destroyers left harbour, the

Fearless and eight destroyers following at 10 a.m. to make for the rendezvous where (it was hoped) the seaplanes would be picked up again after the raid, and where a heavy attack might be expected which they were to help to repel. As they parted, two of the destroyer captains, Mackworth of the *Ferret* and Freemantle of the *Badger,* shook hands and agreed that they would be lucky if they ever saw Harwich again. A lighter note was provided by the fact that since the ships had sailed under sealed orders and 'with utmost despatch' some stewards who had been landed after breakfast to obtain 'extras' for Christmas Day could not get back on board in time and were seen on the quay frantically waving turkeys and geese and ingredients for other Christmas fare.

The weather was perfect, absolutely calm without a sign of fog. Ahead the faintest phosphorescence marked where the *Arethusa* led the way, with her two sisters following in her wake. On either hand dim shadows showed where the smaller craft were keeping station. About 4 a.m. some enemy patrol vessels were encountered. They fled, but from their intercepted wireless signals Tyrwhitt knew that they had reported his approach. This put him in a very awkward situation. He was still three hours from the position where the seaplanes were to take off, and this position was less than an hour from Heligoland and only three from where he knew that at least part of the High Seas Fleet was lying. This meant that henceforward he was advancing into the lion's mouth with a very weak force and one that on account of the comparatively slow speed of the carriers (a maximum of 22 knots) could not run away very well. On the one hand he felt that he was leading a large number of men to what might very well turn out to be disaster. On the other, he hated the idea of turning back when at last the conditions were exactly right and when such an opportunity might not occur again. At that juncture a dim light appeared above the horizon almost dead ahead and rose slowly swelling and growing brighter the while. It was in fact the planet Venus rising, much magnified by a low fog that lay over the land, and for a time all those on the *Arethusa*'s bridge took it for a fire balloon or a Zeppelin with some strange kind of searchlight. Then the navigating officer, Lieutenant Watson,[60] said to Tyrwhitt: 'Do you know that it is Christmas Day and that light bears due east?' 'It then dawned on me', said Tyrwhitt afterwards, 'that this was the Star in the East. From that moment I had no doubts or fears. I firmly believe the Almighty arranged for that star to act in this peculiar manner.'[61]

When the Force arrived at its destination lights could be seen on the horizon and as day dawned distant smoke beyond Heligoland showed where the High Seas Fleet lay, but nothing stirred on the surface of the waters to attack. Only seven of the seaplanes were able to rise from the water, however, and when the other two had been hoisted in again the Force made off for the position about thirty miles further north where the planes were to rejoin it if possible after they had done their work. Here they met the *Fearless* with her division of destroyers and sighted a Zeppelin about five miles off – 'the first that most of us had ever seen,' recorded Tennant. Then one of the raiding seaplanes appeared and was picked up, followed presently by two more which were in the act of being hoisted in when the *Arethusa* sighted a submarine. The nearest destroyers were immediately ordered to circle round the carriers, while the light cruisers, going at speed, altered course continually. Two more Zeppelins now came in sight, but all three kept their distance and after waiting for the remaining seaplanes longer than was safe Tyrwhitt began his withdrawal. The planes had in fact been hampered by a dense frost fog which they had met as soon as they crossed the coast and which made it impossible to locate the Zeppelin hangars that were their real objectives. Some did drop their bombs on other targets, apparently with effect, though the damage done was variously reported; and the appearance of the planes over the Schillig Roads so much alarmed the heavy ships lying at anchor there that they weighed in a hurry and the battle cruiser *Von der Tann* fouled another cruiser, both being severely damaged. Searching for targets in the fog had exhausted the fuel of the four remaining aircraft, however, and they were forced to come down in the sea, though the pilots of three of them were rescued by a British submarine and the fourth by a Dutch trawler which took him into Ymuiden, whence he was released a few days later as a shipwrecked mariner.

It still remained for the operation to make history in a second way. Just as it had been the first raid by carrier-borne aircraft, so now the earlier part of Tyrwhitt's return to harbour saw what was really the first air-sea engagement. In fact the operation's true significance was as the prototype of a new kind of naval warfare. Out of the sun, like their far speedier and more deadly successors in a later war, there now came three German seaplanes which dropped bombs without success. Others followed, concentrating their attack on the *Empress* which had developed condenser trouble and fallen three miles astern of the flotillas, but again without avail, thanks partly to her skilful zigzagging. The ships for their part sought to reply by directing quick-firing weapons to the sky. Then when it was evident that the German planes had made no impression one of the Zeppelins came into action, coming up from dead astern to overtake the carrier, and thus offering the smallest possible target to the guns of the light cruisers, which were trying to shell her from their position three miles ahead. When she was vertically above the carrier the airship slowed so that their speeds coincided, a compartment in her under-body opened, and through the orifice was lowered and launched a bomb much bigger than those which the seaplanes carried. A second followed and then a third, and thrice the carrier vibrated from stem to stern as the bombs burst in the water around her, while in the intervals riflemen on her decks fired back at the Zeppelin's huge gasbag. Then as the cruisers' shells burst in the air about her she drew off behind a convenient cloud and a second airship came; but when she was within range the gunners greeted her with so vigorous a salvo that she turned and made off,

CHAPTER FOUR

ALARMS AND EXCURSIONS

'Many plans and schemes are under construction,' wrote Tyrwhitt on January 4 1915. The growing activity of the German Zeppelins was causing anxiety lest they should make a raid in force on London. A memorandum which Churchill had prepared for the War Council on January 1 began:

> 'Information from a trustworthy source has been received that the Germans intend to make an attack on London by airships on a great scale at any early opportunity. The Director of the Air Department reports that there are approximately twenty German airships which can reach London now from the Rhine, each carrying a ton of high explosives. They could traverse the English part of the journey, coming and going, in the dark hours. The weather hazards are considerable, but there is no known means of preventing the airships coming, and not much chance of punishing them on their return. The unavenged destruction of non-combatant life may therefore be very considerable.'[1]

The Admiralty were in consequence hoping and planning to forestall this threat by repeating the Cuxhaven raid with more success and if possible on a larger scale. Sir John French, the commander of the British forces in France and Flanders, was meditating a drive along the Belgian coast and hoping for co-operation in the form of naval attacks on Zeebrugge and Ostend which the Admiralty were very ready to give if his offensive (which in fact was stillborn) should prove successful.[2] Plans for raiding the Heligoland Bight and attacking the German destroyer patrols had not faded from the minds of Tyrwhitt and Keyes, at least. Churchill's volatile brain had returned to a project which he had formed in the immediate pre-war days of capturing Borkum or some other island off the German North Sea coast, in order to facilitate intensive mining of the channels and river-mouths of that coast and the maintenance of submarines and destroyers in German waters, as well as to serve as a base for an invasion of Schleswig-Holstein.[3] And on January 2 a telegram from the British ambassador to Russia had brought news that the Russian high command, hard pressed in the Caucasus, were anxious for their Western allies to make a diversion against the Turks elsewhere – the germ of the ill-fated Dardanelles operation. All of these except the last would or could involve more work for the Harwich Force, despite the unfavourable season of the year.

For Tyrwhitt the early days of the new year were therefore marked by a rhythm of hasty summonses to the Admiralty (where he 'found them all very bloodthirsty'), plans and preparations, and disappointments due to bad weather. The operation dearest to his own heart was another sweep through the Bight which might repeat the success of August 28, but the Admiralty – or Churchill at any rate – was at least as much interested in another seaplane raid. Either of these ventures could be used to lure or provoke the High Seas Fleet to come out, and it is not always easy to discover which of them was under discussion – though sometimes both were – during any particular visit he made to London. Meanwhile on January 3 he went out on what he described as 'a wild-goose chase after Zeppelins and phantom cruisers' (Zeppelins had been reported approaching Chelmsford and Boston, backed by two cruisers in the North Sea) but turned back when it was established that this was a false alarm. On the 7th Captain Nicholson was despatched with the *Aurora* and the *Undaunted* and 'a large party' to 'do a deadly deed with motor launches' over which

Tyrwhitt fretted somewhat because it was the first sizeable operation that had taken place without his presence, but which proved quite successful. He himself was 'hoping to have the next go at biting the Bight' about the 10th–12th, but when he went out on January 10 he had to return frustrated next day because 'the weather and sea were too beastly for words'. He had only been back a few hours when he was awakened at 4 a.m. to receive hand-delivered letters

> 'directing me to go out to be slaughtered with practically everybody I have. It really was a weird plan and a very stupid one. I managed to choke them off and went up by the 12.19 train and told them what I thought about it. I gained my point and am now free to carry out the next performance as *I* like'

– another proof that his courage stopped short of foolhardiness. On this visit to the Admiralty, incidentally, he met an old acquaintance, Captain W.R. Hall (the afterwards famous 'Blinker' Hall), who had been obliged by ill-health to give up the command of the battle-cruiser *Queen Mary* and was now installed as Director of Naval Intelligence. Tyrwhitt found him 'very seedy' with 'some horrible inside complaint' and reported to his wife that he had 'I fear, very few months to live'.[4] Happily he was utterly wrong and the most famous and indeed legendary of all D.N.Is had in fact twenty-eight more years before him.

'The next performance', or next attempt on the Bight, which Tyrwhitt had won leave to carry out in his own way, was to have taken place on the 15th, but was called off by the Admiralty on the previous night and he was summoned instead to London for 'long interviews with Lord F. and W.C.', at which it was decided that (without prejudice to other operations less dependent on a smooth sea) a seaplane raid should be tried on the first fine day. But it was probably of the Borkum project that Tyrwhitt wrote guardedly:

> 'W.C. has a fearsome proposal which I have been working at for some time. It can't come off just yet and will take a lot of doing and arranging. It is such a secret, that I am not allowed to discuss it with anyone except Roger Keyes and even in W.C's room we always call it by the name of another place.'[5]

In the end, however, this almost certainly over-bold enterprise was ruled out. Meanwhile Tyrwhitt had hardly got back from London and resumed his gloomy contemplation of the weather which was 'preventing all our nice plans', when he was wired for on the next morning to go up again. 'I think they must have all gone off their onions...', he grumbled: 'I don't like spending my days in the train, especially without due warning' – a proviso due to the fact that if he had some warning he could sometimes make hasty arrangements by telegram to meet his wife briefly in Town; she for her part being always 'at short notice' at Ketelby to be driven hastily by Sanders to the nearest railway station. On this occasion he found that

> 'they all wanted different things at Admiralty. I was rather muddled at the end and said "Yes...Yes...Yes." Today [January 17] I have sent them what I propose to do, which is quite different to their proposals, by special motor-car and D.V. I shall be off tomorrow. It still blows like fury but the glass is steadily going up and it looks fine. I don't think there is much likelihood of anything coming of the next performance but one never knows.'

In the same letter to his naturally proud wife he wrote:

> 'Don't be too proud of me or I shall have a fall, and even I am often on the thinnest of ice at the Admiralty. I do know one thing and that is that I and Roger know Winston a great deal better than anyone else in the Navy

does [a claim that may have been justified in view of the long hours spent with him in the back seat of the car during the visit to Loch Ewe in September] ... and I like the man in spite of his bad points. He is extremely brave and I am sure longs to up and do things himself.'[6]

The reason why Tywhitt found himself a little at cross-purposes with the Admiralty on this last visit and mentally rather confused was apparently that whereas his mind was and had been for some time set mainly on a sweep into the Bight with the object of 'collecting' the German patrol reported to be still going out every night from Emden, Cuxhaven or Wilhelmshaven, the Admiralty were considering a larger context. Reports of restlessness in the German naval ports had never ceased since Christmas, and there was every reason to think that since the enemy had 'got away with' their raid on the Yorkshire coast in December they would soon try another, there or elsewhere. On January 15 more circumstantial reports began to come in of such feverish activity at Kiel and Wilhelmshaven that a sortie seemed imminent. It was because of this that Tyrwhitt had been summoned back to the Admiralty on the 16th although he had been there a few hours earlier, and it was the fitting of his scheme for 'biting the Bight' into a larger plan for anticipating any German move that was really under consideration.

On the 17th Admiral Beatty was ordered to bring his battle and light cruisers out to the west of the Bight to support Tyrwhitt's sweep, which was to serve the purpose of a reconnaissance in force; and on the morning of the 18th Tyrwhitt himself received a telegram instructing him to go ahead. He set out at once with *Arethusa*, *Undaunted*, *Aurora* (*Fearless* having gone for a much-needed refit) and thirty-two destroyers, including seven of the new M class which now had the *Aurora* as their flotilla leader. But his forecast or foreboding that not much was likely to come of the 'performance' proved to be justified. Arriving in the Bight about 6.30 a.m., he found nothing in sight, and smoke seen on the horizon at 7.50 a.m. turned out to herald only the supporting light cruisers. Afterwards the only enemies sighted were a seaplane which hastily made off and a Zeppelin which carefully kept its distance at about fifteen miles. At 11 a.m. he was ordered home, and on the way back the destroyer *Archer* was rammed by a trawler and had to be escorted to Sheerness by the *Ferret*, which herself had burst a boiler tube.[7]

What Lieutenant Watson the *Arethusa*'s navigator (who until the new year had scrupulously obeyed the regulation forbidding officers to keep diaries in wartime,[8] but had now resumed doing so) called 'the air stunt' was now fixed for January 23, and Keyes with the *Lurcher* and *Firedrake* and eight submarines had already left on that day to help to support this intended air attack when it was suddenly called off. Intelligence had come that another German sortie was imminent. According to the enemy's subsequent official statement this was provoked by the recent raid into the Bight, and its object was to clear the Dogger Bank of British fishing vessels (which the Germans had persuaded themselves were there chiefly for purposes of observation and espionage).

The force assigned to this operation consisted of three battle-cruisers, the *Seydlitz, Moltke* and *Derfflinger* (the fourth, the *Von der Tann*, not being repaired yet after the damage she had sustained by collision on Christmas Day), the heavy cruiser *Blücher*, four light cruisers and a strong destroyer flotilla. Beatty, with his battle-cruisers and Goodenough's light cruisers, and Tyrwhitt were promptly ordered to a rendezvous on the north-east part of the Dogger Bank for the following morning, while the main body of the Grand Fleet was directed to another further north. This time, unlike December 16, the whole movement went like clockwork, except that the bulk of the Harwich Force was a little delayed by fog in starting. Tyrwhitt afterwards lamented that it was a pity that the whole of it had not been late, since in that event the Germans would have passed ahead of them to the westward and could not have escaped without having to fight their way back again. As it was, he made his rendezvous with Beatty almost dead on time in the *Arethusa*, accompanied by the seven fast 'M' class destroyers led by Captain the Hon. H. Meade in the *Meteor*; while the *Aurora*, coming along with the *Undaunted* and the rest of the flotilla about thirteen miles (or half-an-hour) astern, sighted an enemy cruiser (the *Kolberg*) and four destroyers to the eastward and engaged the cruiser.

The *Kolberg*'s fire was at first fairly accurate, and the *Aurora* was hit slightly three times, but when she began to hit in her turn the enemy's fire became ragged and after a shell had exploded under her forebridge the *Kolberg* turned away to the eastward. The *Aurora* then continued on her course for the rendezvous in company with the *Undaunted*, which had not been able to get near enough to share in the action; but when further enemy forces were sighted in the distance on their starboard quarter the two light cruisers with their flotillas turned to the north-eastward to keep contact with them. This course soon brought them into touch with Goodenough's flagship the *Southampton*, through which the *Aurora* reported the presence of enemy forces to the south-east and east-south-east of her. A few minutes later the *Southampton* sighted the German main force, which had already spread for its sweep of the Dogger but hastily reconcentrated when the *Kolberg* gave the alarm and was heading for home at high speed.[9]

Meanwhile Beatty, having first seen gun-flashes to the south-south-east in the grey of the coming dawn and then received the *Aurora*'s relayed signal, had altered course to give chase, with Tyrwhitt in company. Working up to maximum speed (and in the case of the *Indefatigable* to more than the ship's supposed maximum) he could presently (by 7.50 a.m.) see the enemy's battle-cruisers on his port bow fourteen miles away. The volumes of smoke which the enemy were emitting in their efforts to escape, however, rather accompanied by her sisters. The aerial attack having now been finally driven off, Tyrwhitt made a signal.

'I wish all ships a Merry Christmas,' it ran.[62]

Though from the luck of the weather the raid's main purpose had not been attained, the experience gained was both valuable and encouraging. From 4 a.m. till noon Tyrwhitt's force had occupied the enemy's waters without a single surface ship coming out to interfere with him. The attempts to drive him off had been virtually confined to the air, and those had shown how little – in those early days – ships in the open sea had to fear from aircraft. In answer to a question asked by Balfour at the War Council on January 7, Churchill replied that they had not much to fear and added that all our more modern ships had been armed with anti-aircraft guns[63] – which the *Arethusa* certainly had, some time before. As Tyrwhitt light-heartedly put it to his sister: 'The Christmas Day business...shows that Zeppelins are not to be thought of as regards ships. Stupid great things, but very beautiful. It seemed a pity to shoot at them.'[64] After a visit to the Admiralty, where at first it does not seem to have been fully realised that the raid was really a failure, though a failure with credit, he wrote to his wife:

> 'They are awfully pleased with the Raid and most complimentary. Couldn't be nicer! I was really surprised at everybody's pleasure and delight. They want more and I expect they will get it before long.'[65]

On that note the year ended for since 1 January was the first *Arethusa*'s battle anniversary he saw the Old Year out and the New Year in by going out on December 31, in company with the *Fearless*, to look off Terschelling for Zeppelins or other means of celebrating. However he had 'no luck as the weather was too vile'.[66]

concealed their strength and movements, and he signalled to Tyrwhitt to send his 'M' class destroyers ahead to report and to follow himself in support. Tyrwhitt was then on the near or disengaged side of Beatty's line and the pace was so great that, fast as the *Arethusa* was, he found to his chagrin that he could not get to the off or engaged side without losing ground. The destroyers, however, were faster still and raced on with Meade leading until they had closed to 9000 yards. The enemy then altered course to engage them and the fire of the rear ship, the *Blücher*, forced them to turn away. But after a few rounds the Germans resumed their flight and Captain Meade carried on again till he was near enough to report definitely their strength and course. Since for the past hour the flotilla cruisers had also been sending in reports, Beatty was now sufficiently informed and therefore recalled the destroyers. After that Tyrwhitt, in order not to foul the range with his smoke, gradually dropped back with the flotillas to a position broad on the British battle-cruisers' port quarter,until at 9.20 a.m. the Admiral again ordered him to get ahead at utmost speed. But so fast were the battle-cruisers going that Tyrwhitt in spite of every effort could not claw his way to the head of the line, nor could the flotillas as a whole gain more than very slightly. In desperation Tyrwhitt ordered the 'M' class boats to go on ahead again, but this time even the *Meteor* and her fastest sisters could only creep forward by slow degrees.

The running fight that was now taking place has been described so often that, since the Harwich Force took little further part in it, it is needless to tell it again in detail. The outcome was a British success, but one that was made less conclusive – perhaps much less – than it should have been by a series of errors and mischances during the pursuit and by a hit which crippled the *Lion* and prevented Beatty from keeping control of the action. Partly through faulty distribution, most of the British fire fell on the *Blücher*, which was set ablaze, slowed down, reduced to a shambles and finally brought to a stop. The three German battle-cruisers profited by ambiguous British signalling and Rear-Admiral Moore's resultant misunderstanding of what Beatty wanted him to do after taking over the command, and were able to escape while practically the whole of the British force was concentrated on finishing off the *Blücher*. When Moore went ahead again it was, as Beatty's flag-lieutenant said, 'like trying to win the Derby after falling at Tattenham Corner'. By that time Goodenough's light cruisers were battering the *Blücher* to bits and Meade's four fastest destroyers were closing in for the kill. But the *Blücher* was fighting to the very end and as the *Meteor* was manoeuvring for position she was hit forward by a heavy shell which killed four stokers in her foremost boiler-room and virtually put her out of action. The other three destroyers took their turn and scored hits, and the *Arethusa*, coming up and holding on till the range was down to 2500 yards – 'very dashing and rather risky considering the *Blücher* was still firing', commented Tennant – gave her two torpedoes, one of which hit her under the fore-turret and one in the engine-room, at the same time as the *Blücher* fired her last torpedoes at her without effect.

Then at last, after fighting for three hours against an overwhelming concentration of fire, the German cruiser gave up the struggle. Sir Julian Corbett's often-quoted words about her can bear quotation once more – 'As an example of discipline, courage and fighting spirit her last hours have seldom been surpassed.' At 11.45 Tyrwhitt signalled that she seemed to have struck, and closed her to rescue survivors while there was time. 'She was,' he reported afterwards, 'in a pitiable condition – all her upper decks wrecked and fires could be seen raging between decks through enormous shot-holes in her sides.' She had a heavy list to port, and on her upper deck and net-shelves were clustered about 300 men, who raised a defiant cheer as the *Arethusa* drew near. When she was within a hundred yards the *Blücher* suddenly capsized and after floating bottom upwards for a few minutes disappeared.

'May humanity after victory be the predominant feature of

the British fleet' were among the last words that Nelson had penned as he went into action at Trafalgar. All the *Arethusa*'s boats were immediately lowered and 260 survivors were picked up with the help of the destroyers, in spite of the bombing of the rescuers by a German seaplane which was fortunately driven off by gunfire. When a Zeppelin seemingly bent on renewing the attack came up, however, Tyrwhitt felt compelled to call off his destroyers and boats. The *Arethusa* herself took eleven officers and 110 men on board. One German seaman being hauled up over the side by a rather stout stoker called Clark and inevitably nicknamed Nobby looked up at him and said, 'Hullo, Nobby! Fancy meeting you here!' It transpired that they had been next-door neighbours in Hull. Tyrwhitt gave up his cabin to the senior surviving German officer, the *Blücher*'s first lieutenant, 'a particularly nice man', and presented him with a box of cigarettes when he left the ship, whereupon the lieutenant broke down and 'said many things which sounded strange coming from a German'. He also 'dined and mealed' all the German officers in his fore-cabin, though he did not himself eat with them.[10]

The prisoners, however, had presently to be transferred to the *Undaunted*, as there was the wounded *Lion* to be escorted back to Rosyth, limping along at first at twelve knots but with her speed dropping lower and lower until the *Indomitable* had to take her in tow. Jellicoe, before he knew this state of affairs, had sent word that he was detaching one of the Grand Fleet flotillas to serve as a screen for her and had instructed Tyrwhitt to sweep towards Heligoland with his own force to cover her withdrawal; but after he had been fully apprised of the situation he ordered that the whole of the flotillas, with Tyrwhitt in command, should be employed to screen the two slowly-moving capital ships, which were also to be protected by a cruiser screen to the eastward. Since there was a report that twenty German submarines had left Heligoland in chase of them and they were still more than a hundred miles from their destination at daybreak on the

25th, creeping along at eight or nine knots, Tyrwhitt ordered his destroyers to fire on or ram at once any submarines that were seen without regard to any risk to their neighbours, and another anxious day and night passed before the two battle-cruisers arrived safely in the Forth about dawn on the 26th.

> 'It was not our day [was Tyrwhitt's comment on his share in the battle] and all we did was to watch the battle-cruisers slogging one another...We were very unlucky and hardly fired a shot all day, as we never got near their light cruisers and destroyers. I did eventually have a go at the *Blücher* and sank her with two torpedoes, but she was done in before I got up to her... A ghastly sight...Poor devils! I was sorry for them and even when their seaplanes were bombing us and the drowning men one could not help feeling sorry.'[11]

On his return to Harwich the second brief quarrel with Keyes blew up and fortunately cleared the air. It is a little difficult to arrive with certainty at the true inwardness of this, because of the paucity of clear statement, but a good deal may reasonably be surmised.[12] Fisher had continued to look with jaundiced eyes on Keyes, who remained on good terms with Churchill. Tyrwhitt was *persona grata* with both. Keyes's visits to the Admiralty had grown less frequent, while Tyrwhitt's had become more so and sometimes included *têtes-à-tête* with Fisher, which Keyes's never did. Keyes began to regard this with suspicion, especially as Fisher occasionally used Tyrwhitt as a medium of communication with him. He also sometimes asked Tyrwhitt questions about Keyes's submarines or about his relations with him – an example of his regrettable propensity for seeking information from one officer about another, and particularly from a junior about a senior (and Keyes was still senior to Tyrwhitt by virtue of date of captaincy). Tyrwhitt told Keyes about this and explained that he had either parried the questions or deflected them towards Keyes himself (which resulted only in his being asked to put them to him) and had emphasized to Fisher that their relations were very good.

Unfortunately there was a question at issue – indeed, it was perhaps the nub of the matter – which kept Keyes's doubts and suspicions alive. Keyes wanted a light cruiser in which to go to sea. After Fisher's cruelly unjust remark already quoted he had felt free to disregard the Admiralty's earlier veto on his going out at all, but he could still only do so in the *Lurcher* or the *Firedrake*. Now that some of the new *Arethusa* class were beginning to find their way to Harwich he had apparently asked or suggested that one might be alloted to him; though whether he had put the point directly to Tyrwhitt, as seems inherently probable, is not clear. Tyrwhitt evidently did not welcome the idea, since he wanted to build up his light cruiser strength and perhaps feared that if Keyes went to sea in a cruiser the already delicate balance of seniority and even the command of the Harwich forces might be tipped in his favour. Keyes at any rate undoubtedly felt that this was the root of the trouble and suspected that Tyrwhitt might be using his greater access to the Admiralty to sabotage his requests for a cruiser. The fact that Tyrwhitt did not mention the flare-up that followed in his letters to his wife (as he had the earlier one), taken in conjunction with some words in a later letter to Keyes about to be quoted, raises the possibility that his conscience was not absolutely clear in the matter. But two things above all have to be remembered. Both men, and perhaps especially Tyrwhitt, had been under a strain for a long time, and there are some signs about now – touchiness and irritability in his relations with some of his officers in the *Arethusa*[13] – which suggest that even his strength and nerves were beginning to feel the effects.[14] Secondly it is difficult to avoid the feeling that basically Fisher was 'the nigger in the woodpile', and that had he not been First Sea Lord or had his attitude to Keyes been what it should have been the trouble might not have developed. It is at least pleasant to record that the quarrel which took place at the end of January was followed almost immediately by a reconciliation in which Tywhitt took the initiative by asking Keyes to supper and 'having it out' with him.

Just about this time Keyes had a conversation with Churchill, who, he says, 'was well aware of what was going on' and 'had been fighting [his] battles'. (It is perhaps permissible to wonder whether a cryptic remark which Tyrwhitt had let slip in an earlier letter to his wife about a '*fracas* between W.C. and J.F. over poor little me'[15] had any relation to this business). Keyes told Churchill that it would ease the situation all round if employment could be found for him elsewhere, and was duly sent for by the First Lord on February 8 and informed that he was to leave next morning for the Mediterranean to be chief of staff to Rear-Admiral Carden, who was to command an allied squadron that was to attempt to force the Dardanelles. After his departure the direct command of the Harwich submarines devolved on his former subordinate Captain A.K. Waistell, though Fisher ordered them to work under Tyrwhitt, who wrote to his wife 'It makes my job much more simple...But don't mention this, as it is one of those things the less said about the better'[16] – the nearest he came, in any surviving letter to her, to mentioning the quarrel. Some time after Keyes had reached the Mediterranean Tyrwhitt wrote to him: 'I am so frightfully glad that we had squared yards before [you left], otherwise I should never have forgiven myself;' and again in another letter a month later: 'I can never be sufficiently thankful that we squared yards before you left.'[17] The two men remained friends for the rest of their lives.

In the first of these two letters, written some time in March, Tyrwhitt had also told Keyes that 'nothing has happened since [the battle of the Dogger Bank]. We have hardly been out.' A check-up of the *Arethusa* on her return from the battle had revealed that she ought to go to Chatham for a refit, and Tyrwhitt had intended to shift his flag to the *Penelope*, another light cruiser which had just arrived. But the *Penelope* was not yet over her teething troubles and fit for action, so that he decided to stick to the *Arethusa* for one more 'stunt' before taking her to Chatham.

The 'stunt' in question was to be another seaplane raid from carriers like that of Christmas Day, followed – after taking the carriers back to safety – by a night sweep of the Bight with the battle-cruisers once more in support. But after the force had put out at 8 a.m. on January 29 it came on to blow from the north-west and the carriers began to get knocked about with some risk to the planes they carried, so that at 1 p.m. the Commodore ordered the attempt to be abandoned.[18]

The *Arethusa* therefore went to Chatham on February 1, being recognised and lustily cheered from the batteries at Sheerness as she went up the river, and subsequently being run into the side of the dock at Chatham by Arbuthnot 'with a fearful bump', which provoked the irate Tyrwhitt to a caustic comment that in future he would prefer to take charge himself and break his own ship up. However on the following day he addressed the ship's company and praised everybody, after which he went on a few days' leave to join his wife, while Lieutenant Watson dashed up to Scotland, with Tyrwhitt's blessing, to be married.[19] When the Commodore returned to Harwich he found most of his command away on various enterprises about to be recorded, and took up his quarters for the moment on board the *Penelope*. Here he soon became bored by his unwonted inactivity, but sought diversion by going up as a passenger in a seaplane, which he 'enjoyed hugely' and by frequent visits to his friends the Cayleys, with whom indeed he presently moved over to stay for several nights. By February 17, however, since the Germans had a fortnight earlier announced that an 'unrestricted' submarine campaign would begin on the 18th, he was 'standing by for anything that might come along'. But for the next two days it blew a gale and it was only after it had abated that he could go out in a destroyer to look in vain for two U-boats which were reported to be 'nosing around'.[20] After that the *Arethusa* was ready to be collected at Chatham, from which he worked her out himself and brought her round to Harwich.

It was of course the Admiralty's foreknowledge of the unrestricted submarine campaign which had sent various elements of the Harwich force scurrying to and fro to such an extent that the Commodore's words to Keyes – 'We have hardly been out' – must clearly have referred to himself and the *Arethusa* rather than to the command as a whole. The First Flotilla had spent most of the first week of February on escort duty up and down the Channel, which Lieutenant Tennant described as 'an endless monotony of punching along in front of all and every battleship that moved in the Channel, no matter what the weather, without any hope of seeing any enemy and miles away from our proper base and our proper "Admiral".' Then it had been sent, between the 9th and the 15th, to protect minelayers which were laying a new minefield in order to block more effectively the eastern entrance to the Straits of Dover. Meanwhile the *Undaunted* had been despatched with a division of the Third Flotilla, soon followed by another, to Pembroke and the Irish Sea to give temporary help in coping with the U-boats that were becoming active there.

On the 16th, the day after the First Flotilla arrived back at Harwich, and while Tennant was lamenting that the *Ferret* had had only two undisturbed days in harbour during the past month, the *Fearless* was sent out again with eight destroyers to search in vain for several German submarines which had been reported off the North Hinder Light Vessel. On the 22nd the flotilla went out once more to give a warning of the presence of German submarines to the tramp steamers and other merchantmen that had developed the habit of anchoring for the night (when of course there were no lights showing) near the Sunk Light Vessel. Then towards the end of the month Mackworth, the captain of the *Ferret*, was instructed to take one division under his orders and proceed 460 miles to Avonmouth in the Severn estuary, from which reinforcements were about to sail to the Dardanelles, in order to escort the transports till they reached safer waters. On returning he found that the *Fearless* and the rest of her flotilla had been transferred to Rosyth, to be attached to Beatty's Battle-Cruiser Force which was now based there. Thither the division followed them, except that the *Ferret* first took her turn to refit at Chatham, 'after seven months without a breather – many thousands of miles steamed, many night watches, many gales; but nothing of that shows to the public', commented Tennant.[21]

When Tyrwhitt wrote again to Keyes towards the end of April he again reported a lack of positive achievement. 'I almost feel ashamed to tell you', he confessed, '...how much mileage we have covered without firing a gun at anything but a stray submarine or two and a Zeppelin'.[22] Included in this mileage were firing practices, sometimes aborted by the weather; a three-day 'prowl' or 'run-round' with *Arethusa*, *Penelope* and the destroyers (which had to be sent back on the first day because of rough seas) as far as Terschelling and then down the Dutch coast and up again, in which only trawlers were seen; a vain search for U-boats glimpsed briefly close off the entrance to Harwich harbour; sorties of detachments of destroyers in various directions and on various errands; and two abortive attempts to mount another seaplane raid. By now the objective had become the German wireless station at Norddeich near the Frisian coast, which Tyrwhitt had apparently badgered the Admiralty into letting him attack, but the attempts on which were to be repeatedly frustrated by bad weather. He had not been summoned to London for some time and was beginning to think that because he had not been able (or had not had the chance) to bring off anything striking since Christmas he was falling into disfavour (or, as he was modestly in the habit of putting it to his wife, had 'been found out'. He therefore drafted a plan and took it up, his own possibly highly-coloured version of the visit afterwards being that he was nearly kicked out for asking Churchill 'if we were waiting for the Germans to come and kick us', but that 'eventually they said "Well, go and blow up Norddeich and be damned to you".'

Carriers were not available, so two seaplanes were to be carried in each of the light cruisers. But first the planes were late in arriving; then on March 19 the 'jaunt' had to be postponed one day because it was snowing; and though he got away on the morning of the 20th in fine weather with *Arethusa*, *Undaunted*, *Penelope*, *Empress* (which by now was available after all) and twelve destroyers, the wind got up more and more strongly as the force approached the take-off point and the attempt had to be given up at 5 a.m. on the 21st. On the 24th the King was to visit Harwich, bringing with him the C.B. which Tyrwhitt had been awarded after the Battle of Heligoland Bight but with which he had never been free enough at a convenient time to be invested. The Commodore, who was greatly looking forward to entertaining him, had invited him to lunch aboard the *Arethusa*. But on the evening of the 23rd the weather began to look promising again for the air-raid attempt and away went Tyrwhitt, leaving George V (who had been a naval officer in his day and understood that in time of war the King's enemies took precedence of the King himself) to find precisely one destroyer left in harbour and to inspect minesweepers, trawlers, submarines and shore establishments under Cayley's escort with perfect good humour.[23]

The fine weather which had lured the Force out lasted only till between five and six next morning, when it ran into a dense fog-bank a few miles short of the taking-off position. Tyrwhitt reversed course and found the weather clearing an hour later, reversed again and again ran into a fog blanket about ten miles from the coast. Once more he turned, intending to wait and make a third attempt, but in turning in the fog the destroyer *Landrail* ran into the *Undaunted* at eighteen knots, holing her badly in the engine-room, where three men were killed and four seriously injured. The *Landrail* herself broke off thirty feet of her forecastle as cleanly as if it had been sheared off with a gigantic knife, and both ships had their wireless knocked out, so that in the fog it was an hour and a half before Tyrwhitt learnt what had happened and received a signal that the destroyer *Mentor* had taken *Landrail* in tow stern first and the *Undaunted* was on her way home with three feet of water in her engine-room and escorted by a division of destroyers. With *Aurora* and the rest he then spread and looked for *Mentor* and *Landrail*, but the fog did not lift till two o'clock next morning and he did not find them until three o'clock in the afternoon, having in the meantime had two signals from *Mentor* that successive towing hawsers had parted. 'Things [he wrote] were then very bad – horrible sea and a wreck to be handled'. He ordered Captain Nicholson with the *Aurora* to take the *Landrail* in tow, which he did very smartly, but only to repeat *Mentor*'s experience of having two towing-hawsers part in quick succession.

By now it was 6.30 p.m., still blowing hard and getting dark, and the ships were close to Terschelling and drifting fast on to a lee shore. Tyrwhitt then took on the task himself, as he had been longing to do from the beginning, and picked up *Landrail* thrice, but lost her twice because she was drifting so much faster than the *Arethusa* that the hawser could not be hauled in before the drift became too great. Shortly before 11 p.m. the third attempt succeeded and the *Arethusa* and her crippled charge set off home at four knots, after a large part of the Harwich Force had spent more than forty hours within fifty miles of the German coast. At 9 p.m. on the 26th they reached Yarmouth, and made Harwich on the following morning, where *Landrail* was handed over to two tugs for conveyance to Chatham[24] and Tyrwhitt went to bed for the first time for ninety-six hours, to snatch three and a half hours' sleep before writing to his wife:

> 'You need not repeat this, but I think more of having brought the *Landrail* back than any of the incidents we have had to do with during the war...But of course I can't say what view the Nobs will take of the matter as of course I was responsible for our getting into such an

unpleasant hole.'[25]

To his old chief in the Sixth Cruiser Squadron in the Mediterranean, Sir Douglas Gamble (now a vice-admiral recently transferred from the command of a battle squadron in the Grand Fleet to an Admiralty post) he wrote an account of the episode which evoked the following in reply:

> 'It was most kind of you to suggest that the exercises we used to carry out...were of practical value on the occasion. But, if I may say so, the success of the operation was due to the masterly manner of handling a ship which comes to you by nature. You know instinctively what she can be asked to do and you know *how* to get her to do it. That is the greatest gift a sailorman can have, and many, very many, the great majority in fact, have *not* got it.'[26]

Two days later he was standing by again 'at a moment's notice', since with the means of penetrating German signals that were now available it had been deduced that the German battle-cruisers were coming out again. At 4 p.m. on the same day (the 29th) he took his force out, but at two o'clock next morning a signal from the Admiralty cancelled all the counter operations which had been set in train and ordered him to hunt submarines instead. One was sighted off the Maas, but it dived before anything could be done. After that he spent most of the next month in a series of fruitless sorties in response to rumours or reports that the Germans were out for what, if it ever materialised, always proved to be a short run. Even when in the course of patrolling towards Borkum on April 8 the *Arethusa* called the island up by wireless in order to let the enemy know that the Harwich Force was outside waiting for them the open invitation was not accepted. Another disappointment came when after receiving information on the 11th that a German flotilla was at sea the whole Force arrived in an intercepting position off

Terschelling at dawn next day, only to be told by signal that their presence was apparently known to the enemy, who had gone back. They then carried out anti-submarine sweeps and in the afternoon sighted a Zeppelin which they chased, firing shrapnel at it, but without result. On the 17th they were suddenly ordered out, leaving at 11 p.m., to patrol off the Texel, and arrived at what they regarded as their particular hunting-ground soon after daybreak, to find the air thick with wireless messages, British and German. At 9 a.m. they were informed that the German Second Scouting Group of light cruisers had been off Terschelling five hours earlier, evidently looking for them. Having patrolled all day and seen nothing, though they heard Zeppelins about, they were ordered home at 7 p.m. On the 21st–22nd they had an almost identical experience, except that a destroyer and a British submarine had six torpedoes fired at them. On the 29th Tyrwhitt was ashore peacefully bird's-nesting – which was one of his favourite pastimes – about two miles from his ship when he heard the recall gun fired, ran most of the way back (meeting an orderly with a signal for him) and got to sea as quickly as possible with three other cruisers (the *Undaunted* having just returned from Chatham) and twenty destroyers. A wireless report had been received that Dunkirk was being bombarded from the sea, but this proved totally unfounded and the force was scarcely clear of the harbour before it ran into thick fog and was obliged to anchor off the Cork Light Vessel, returning next morning. 'I am sick to death of rushing around and seeing nothing,' grumbled Tyrwhitt to Keyes.[27]

Somewhat similar sentiments were expressed afterwards by Commander Domvile, whose activities when detached (as he frequently was) may perhaps be taken as fairly representative:

> 'I was here, there and everywhere. In the early spring, working with minelayers from Sheerness...Later escorting six-knot monitors down the Channel to Ushant with

> my 35-knot destroyer – a particularly brilliant brainwave of someone's at the Admiralty...then getting a dicky propeller-shaft put to rights in the Clyde...then fetching the *Tipperary* [a new flotilla-leader, of which he took command] from White's Yard at Cowes [and] shortly afterwards having a hole driven through her starboard side into my cabin by one of our own submarines just outside Harwich in a fog – a hole you could have driven a coach-and-four through; we nearly went down, but the bulkhead held... Later, after repairs, I was organising ocean escort work at Plymouth and chasing submarines on the west coast of Ireland... The Harwich Force was never happy so far from its home; there was always the fear of missing a good thing, but luckily there was not much doing in the North Sea at this time. Then in September I was fetching another flotilla-leader from White's, the *Lightfoot* – the first oil-burning leader – a lovely ship. [to command of which he had been transferred].'[28]

Dover, to which while still in *Miranda* he was ordered off for a time in command of seven other destroyers and to which similar detachments of temporary reinforcements were often sent from Harwich, was not popular with the Force, which considered that 'a more restless, uncomfortable harbour it would be difficult to conceive', and regarded it rather pityingly as a very inferior station. Later in the war, however, when the Dover Patrol had many gallant feats to its credit, this attitude altered.

Concentration of attention on the duties and exploits of the Harwich Striking Force should not be allowed to obscure the work of the Harwich Auxiliary Patrol. This was composed about this time of a hundred or so patrol and mine-sweeping trawlers and motor-launches, and its duties included clearing the navigational sea routes of enemy mines in the southern area of the North Sea and also attacking and destroying enemy mine-laying submarines whenever opportunity offered. Not only had the various channels used by the Harwich Force to be kept regularly swept for mines, but likewise those frequented by merchant ships, while another of the Patrol's duties was to search the approaches to the base in advance of the Force when it was returning to it. All of this was arduous and hazardous work, involving dangers not only from mines and submarines but also from Zeppelins, aeroplanes and surface craft. Of these, the greatest peril came from mines; twenty-six vessels of the Patrol were sunk during the war and many others were mined but reached harbour, and the total casualties were heavy. German minelayers were continually at work laying mines at the approaches to Harwich, and as fast as they were cleared away new minefields came into being; hence sweeping operations went on unceasingly. The vessels employed usually left harbour long before daylight in order to be in position to start sweeping at daybreak or when the state of the tide was suitable. Until they had completed their task no shipping was allowed to proceed up the channels; yet though every precaution was taken many vessels suffered disaster, sometimes through floating mines drifting down with the tide or mines being brought nearer the surface at low water. The motor-launches, handy and of low draught, were admirably suited for exploring suspected minefields and were also employed for patrol work and sometimes for light mine-sweeping operations. For the most part they were commanded by temporary R.N.V.R. officers – solicitors, stock-brokers, accountants and other professional men, some of them yachtsmen who very quickly adapted themselves to war conditions.[29]

Meanwhile in April the King had renounced spirituous and alcoholic liquors for the duration of the war and invited his subjects to follow his example, which numbers of them did. Tyrwhitt was one of these, taking a farewell glass of hot grog on the evening of April 9 and requesting his officers to join him in becoming teetotallers. This, relates Watson, made 'everybody fed up', and the effect of the gesture was partly spoilt by Churchill, who came down to Harwich two days later, lunched on board the *Arethusa*, 'drank champagne, port and brandy, and said he saw no reason why he should not!' Even Tyrwhitt found total abstinence 'a dreadful bore' and confessed to Keyes soon afterwards that he could still take no interest in his dinner and would never become a confirmed water-drinker.[30]

In the same letter of April 25 he wrote that he was

> 'now preparing to take part in a big scheme which includes an air raid on Norddeich, photographing Sylt, a bogus landing of troops somewhere else, a bombardment in the vicinity, and probably the laying of a line of nets.[31] It is quite impossible for it all to come off, as I told Oliver[32] (who is furious with the old men [Fisher and Wilson?] for proposing so many side-shows)... I made my protest but received no change...I have only been to the Admiralty twice since you left and only go when I am sent for. Winston is still very friendly or professes to be so, but I have not seen J.A.F. for a long time' –

a careful and probably unnecessary note of reassurance to Keyes. The scheme to which he referred did not materialise in its multiple form, though repeated but unsuccessful attempts to mount a seaplane raid continued during the first half of May. On the 3rd the light cruisers and twelve destroyers escorted three carriers to sea, but a wind got up and they turned back. On the 6th they tried again but ran into fog so thick that after they had twice been forced to anchor and the *Lennox* had been rammed by a carrier (though without casualties) they were recalled. On the 11th the weather conditions were perfect but on their way across the North Sea they were sighted about 4 p.m. by a Zeppelin which promptly alerted the German defences, so that it was useless to go on. Three seaplanes were launched after the Zeppelin but one plummeted into the sea from 2,000 feet and sank at once, while by the time the other two had got up the airship had disappeared. Orders were received that the Force should not return to harbour but remain at sea awaiting a more favourable opportunity; but next day the wind got up again and it was called in. After that seventh unsuccessful attempt, the 'air stunt' was given up for the time being, to the Commodore's chagrin but the relief of many.[33]

A crumb of consolation was that on the first of the month four of the destroyers when out on patrol had met and sunk two German torpedo-boats in an engagement so one-sided that they put up very little fight, most of their men jumping overboard and taking their chance of being picked up, which forty-two of them were. The commander of one of the destroyers signalled to the *Laforey*, which was taking the leading part: 'It is the custom in our fishing association to put back all fish under six inches in length.'[34]

Tyrwhitt's disappointment can have lasted little more than twenty-four hours in any case, for on May 14 he went up to be at last invested with his C.B. and to visit the Admiralty, where, he reported,

> 'I had a long day but a very satisfactory one. I have several good irons in the fire, ...all mine, and everybody including Winston and Lord Fisher rose like trout to my proposals. They have given me an absolutely free hand and I hope to do something with them. The King sent for me at 2.30 and I had a most delightful talk with him for over twenty minutes. He was perfectly charming and at the end he gave me my C.B. without any formality, which pleased me enormously.'[35]

Although he did not know it, he had been present at virtually the last moments of the Churchill-Fisher *régime* and his proposals must have been the last, or almost the last, matters over which they were in agreement, for on the next morning Fisher 'pulled down the pillars of the house', or rather, pulled down the blinds of his office in the Admiralty and walked out, refusing to return even when two days later deciphered German signals revealed that the High Seas Fleet was about to put to sea. By the 22nd not only had his resignation been accepted but Churchill, whose head the Conservative opposition were demanding as part of their price for entering a coalition government under Asquith, had been forced to tender his also.[36]

They were replaced by the Conservative ex-Premier Arthur Balfour and Admiral Sir Henry Jackson, a seaman of scientific bent who had latterly had little sea-going experience. The Balfour-Jackson *régime* could hardly have been more unlike its predecessor. Placidity replaced pyrotechnics; but if there was less friction there was also much less drive. Nevertheless when Tyrwhitt (who in the middle of the explosion in the Admiralty had expressed to his wife his hope that Fisher would not have to go, 'as he is my friend as far as I can see') had his first interview with Balfour more than a month later, he fell immediately under the spell of the old statesman-aristocrat's charm. '[He] is a delightful person to talk to,' he reported: 'He could not have been nicer and I left him prepared to die for him!'[37]

The emergence of the High Seas Fleet, referred to above, had been merely for the purpose of covering minelaying operations in the Dogger Bank area; but the news of it brought the Harwich Force to sea on the evening of May 17 in a great hurry and a rising gale. Since there was no sign of the enemy in the waters through which it patrolled, however, it returned to harbour within twenty-four hours. A similar alarm on the 29th sprang from a similar cause and had the same outcome. After that, Zeppelin-hunting became for a time the principal occupation of the cruiser part of the Force. In the first half of June three airship raids took place on various points from Northumberland to London, and Tyrwhitt's light cruisers, each carrying a seaplane, were constantly out watching for Zeppelins, though it proved very difficult to attack them from the sea either by gunfire or plane. By this time he had received two more of the new light cruisers that were being built, so that he had now six ships of this class, four of which – *Arethusa*, *Penelope* and the two newcomers, *Conquest* and *Cleopatra* – formed the Fifth Light Cruiser Squadron, while the *Undaunted* and the *Aurora* continued as leaders of the Third and Tenth Flotillas respectively. The cruisers patrolled in two relays on the look-out for Zeppelins, not without some risk, for Tyrwhitt never had enough destroyers in hand to provide an adequate screen. Most of them were called away for escort duty in the south-western approaches to the Channel, and those which remained had many similar duties to perform, such as escorting the Portsmouth floating dock to the Tyne and protecting British minesweepers and minelayers. To Tyrwhitt's representations that he sometimes had not a single destroyer to work with his cruisers, the Admiralty could only reply that the employment of his destroyers to the westward was unavoidable owing to the enemy's submarine activity in the entrance to the English Channel and the approaches to the Bristol and St. George's Channels, and the ever-increasing importance of the transport routes through these waters. The Tenth Flotilla, indeed, was at this point removed altogether to the west coast.

Not a great deal happened during this period of patrolling, however, though on June 2 the *Arethusa* and *Undaunted* sighted a Zeppelin. The *Arethusa* loosed her seaplane, but it only just managed to get off the water before being forced to turn back. She then opened fire on the airship, which made off. A few hours later a German seaplane appeared suddenly out of a cloud and dropped three bombs without hitting or being hit. During the same patrol German wireless activity on the 3rd, when the patrol was about seventy miles from Borkum, roused Tyrwhitt's hopes that the enemy might be coming out again, but this time the hopes were false and on the 4th he returned through fog to Harwich. Since this four-day patrol had followed so closely on the fruitless scouting of May 29 and 30 that the cruisers concerned had

had only one intervening night in harbour, it is small wonder that Tyrwhitt reported himself to his wife as weary and very sleepy, since 'four nights running and five out of six makes one a bit bored'.[38]

After this, however, the *Arethusa* herself did not go out on patrol for a fortnight – an unprecedentedly long period in harbour, during which Zeppelins were reported almost nightly in the neighbourhood of Harwich and often heard, though not usually seen, as they made their way inland towards the London area.[39] On June 19th the Force went to sea in the hope of intercepting some of them in daylight near the beginning or end of their flight, but in spite of patrolling to and fro for twenty-four hours across their probable route saw and heard nothing except a German seaplane which bombed the destroyer *Liberty* (while she was stopped picking up a dog that had fallen overboard) and nearly hit her.[40] It was not until July 3 that the first bombs were dropped in the Harwich area, by a seaplane, on Landguard Fort. To his slightly worried wife Tyrwhitt dismissed this as 'a very bogus affair. One airman appeared and let go a few bombs which fell into the sea and no one took any notice of him.'[41] On the night of the 7th–8th, however, Zeppelins raided Felixstowe, causing some damage. In between these two raids the Admiralty, apparently at his persuasion, had reverted momentarily to the idea of making another attempt at a seaplane raid; and on July 3, just after the German seaplane's visit, he had left harbour to carry it out. Although shadowed for much of the way by Zeppelins whose numbers increased from two to seven he reached the intended taking-off point, but the raid again proved a fiasco, since all the planes were too badly knocked about in transit or in being hoisted out to be able to fly. Nor had he any chance of bagging a Zeppelin, which he had hoped to do.

> 'I could have cried [he wrote] at my own powerlessness to do them any damage, but at the same time they dared not attempt to do any damage to us. We played about in

> the vicinity of the Germans' greatest fortress for twelve hours without seeing anything except *gasbags*. I am afraid there was no honour to be gained, but it was quite amusing... The Germans knew we were coming and had all their ships with steam up ready for sea, but for some reason or other they did not come out... I have (I hope) whetted their Lordships' appetite for something big and have put it down in black and white. It will be interesting to see if they "rise".'[42]

In expressing this hope, however, Tyrwhitt was overestimating the effect of his previous persuasiveness. When he went up again to the 'abode of love' (as the Admiralty was now called after the departure of the ill-assorted pair of Titans who had recently ruled over it) to report on the once more abortive raid and to make further proposals, he found himself gently rebuffed. 'They seem to be quite content to do nothing...', he wrote, 'and would not hear of my suggestion. Perhaps they are right, but it seems to be rather a pity.'[43] He was therefore obliged to content himself for the next fortnight with the firing and battle practices which the arrival of the *Cleopatra* and the *Conquest* had made particularly necessary, while complaining that he was 'getting bored for want of more to do' and that the command had been in harbour much too long and a good run round would do everybody a lot of good.

Something of a 'run' was provided unexpectedly on July 18 when he was ordered out to try to cut off a German submarine which had been reported about 100 miles off Peterhead, unable to dive and making for Emden. The conditions were not propitious.

> 'We...steamed straight into a gale which got worse as we went north. I had five cruisers and sixteen destroyers. They *were* a sight! Such a beastly sea and we were in a great hurry too. At noon on Sunday we were recalled, much to my annoyance, but at the same time I knew it

> was for a very good reason and between you and me it was because the High Seas Fleet was coming out after us... Nearly everybody in *Arethusa* was seasick. You would have thought they ought to be case-hardened by now. It is always the same thing after a long spell of fine weather.'[44]

Nor did better weather attend a longer run which began on the 28th, when with four light cruisers and twelve destroyers he went north to a rendezvous on the following evening with the Second Battle-Cruiser Squadron and various light forces from the Grand Fleet. The object was an operation in the Skaggerak to interrupt trade and search for enemy vessels. This produced only the very meagre 'bag' of one German trawler sunk after the removal of the crew and one suspect Danish steamer sent into a British port with a guard on board. Tyrwhitt described this visit to comparatively distant waters as 'a beastly journey...weather only suitable to mid-winter...We were all more like submarines than ships.'[45]

After a visit on August 4 from the First Sea Lord, Admiral Jackson, who was 'exceedingly nice and complimentary' though 'not possessed of much small talk', and a wild-goose chase next day to Terschelling (with a Zeppelin in invisible attendance above low cloud) Tyrwhitt was suddenly ordered to sea again on the night of the 8th on what proved a more satisfactory assignment. The German auxiliary cruiser *Meteor*, disguised as a neutral merchantman, had laid a large minefield in the mouth of the Moray Firth, then sunk a British armed boarding steamer, the *Ramsey*, north of Kinnaird Head in an unequal combat after which forty-three survivors of her crew were picked up by her enemy; and he was ordered to 'take all available light cruisers and steer for Horn Reefs to intercept her'. Tyrwhitt had come in only forty-eight hours before from a sweep into the Bight with his cruisers, but as usual he was ready, and at 10.30 p.m. he was away with the *Arethusa*, *Conquest*, *Cleopatra*, *Aurora* and *Undaunted*. Commodore Le Mesurier with the Fourth Light

Cruiser Squadron from Scapa and Commodore Goodenough with the First and Second from Rosyth were also ordered out. At 8 o'clock next morning a German seaplane passed over Tyrwhitt's squadron as it steamed northward at its utmost speed. His anti-aircraft guns failed to bring it down and it sped away to give a warning. About the same time a Zeppelin picked up the *Meteor*, warned her that British cruisers were between her and the Jade, for which she was making, and led her northward for the Skaggerak on nearly the same course as that on which Tyrwhitt was coming up, forty miles astern, but at perhaps twice the *Meteor*'s speed. Then about 9.30 a Zeppelin which may have been the same one approached his squadron and began to accompany it at a distance of about two miles, being presently joined by a second. At that point he received a message from the Admiralty that they had located the *Meteor* ninety miles west of Horns Reef at 4 a.m. This was incompatible with both Tyrwhitt's previous information and his deductions, so that after getting the message repeated he decided to ignore it and hold on for the rendezvous originally given him, after reaching which he turned westward and spread his ships at ten-mile intervals. At 12.30 he sighted the *Meteor*; but just before this her commander, Captain von Knorr, realising that escape was hopeless, had decided to scuttle her and had transferred himself with his crew and British prisoners to a neutral fishing vessel. The *Arethusa* now closed this vessel and the senior surviving officer of the *Ramsey*, Lieutenant Atkins, signalled her asking to be taken off with his men; but Tyrwhitt, who by now was being threatened not only by the two airships but by submarines, could for the time being only reply 'Steer south-west; I will return and pick you up.' The British prisoners with some difficulty prevailed on their captors to steer in this direction until another fishing vessel was sighted, to which by agreement with the Germans they were transferred and from which they were presently collected by Tyrwhitt, who reported afterwards:

> 'The Huns treated our prisoners exceptionally well.[46] They said that they knew we had been very kind to their prisoners, so they were going to do likewise. I could have captured the Huns as well, but I did not want them and besides a submarine was close to us, so I did not wait... Then I came home, followed I believe by many submarines and destroyers but they did not catch us. We had fog, dense from 4 a.m. till noon, most of the time steaming at twenty knots.'

It is hardly surprising that the Commodore was 'in transports' about Lieutenant Watson's navigation and reported that the Admiralty were very pleased with it.[47]

With the advent of the Zeppelins in the summer of 1915 Harwich became both an alternative objective for airships steering originally for London but unable to reach it and a target in itself as a fortified naval base with storehouses for all kinds of things from torpedoes and ammunition to fresh provisions. At this time only the light cruisers had anti-aircraft guns, the destroyers having only maxims on beef-block mountings. The garrison also had some anti-aircraft artillery. The usual procedure when Zeppelins were reported near was to lie low unless actually attacked, in the hope that their failure to locate Harwich by attracting its gunfire might cause them to lose their bearings and miss London. They usually flew low over the sea and when they sighted the East Coast rose to several thousand feet and followed it to the Thames Estuary, after which they headed for London. The light cruisers were therefore detailed in turn to patrol the coast from Lowestoft to Orford Ness and report instantly to the Admiralty and to Tyrwhitt any Zeppelins they sighted, taking any opportunity of intercepting and attacking them. They saw little, however, and scored no successes.[48]

Just before midnight on August 12 came the first Zeppelin raid on the Harwich area itself. Two enemy airships coming out of clouds at a height of about 10,000 feet passed over Shotley, Parkeston Quay and then the ships, dropping bombs freely. Four of these hit Parkeston village and caused casualties, including women and children; others missed the Quay and the submarines by a few feet only, and several destroyers had narrow escapes. A near-miss fell within ten feet of one, the blast knocking down everyone on deck, but nobody was seriously hurt; while in another the captain's servant forgot in his excitement that the gangway guardrails were down and fell overboard, but was fished out. The ships opened up with their guns and blazed away furiously, scoring no hits but deterring the Zeppelins from lingering.[49]

By now the *Arethusa* was due for another refit and the Commodore for another brief spell of leave; but much as he longed to see his home again for a few days he found it difficult to quit the scene of action and decided to stay for one more sortie. This was a minelaying expedition on August 17–18, which proved abortive. The minelayer *Princess Margaret*, escorted by destroyers of the Tenth Flotilla (which had now returned to Harwich) and by the Harwich cruisers lying further out to sea in support, was to lay a minefield off Amrum Bank, twenty-five miles north of Heligoland. It was a very dark night, calm but heavily overcast, and shortly before reaching the area to be mined the Force ran into a division of enemy destroyers, which at once fired torpedoes and then made off at full speed in the darkness. The torpedoes missed the *Princess Margaret*, but one hit the destroyer *Mentor*, blowing away her bows under water. It was at first decided to carry on, but a signal came from the Admiralty recalling the whole force, since directional wireless had located large elements of the enemy on the move in the vicinity. Unfortunately touch was lost with the *Mentor*, which seemed at first to be completely disabled. Her captain, Commander E.T. Inman, however, having destroyed his confidential books in case of capture and set his guns and torpedoes ready for instant action, put the rest of his men to work to shore up bulkheads, place collision mats, and do all in their power to make the ship tolerably seaworthy for the 360-mile passage home. On this the *Mentor* then set out, 'pushing the whole ocean in front of her' as Inman said afterwards, gradually working up to ten knots, and aided by the continued fineness of the weather duly arrived at Harwich.[50]

The *Arethusa* now went to Chatham for three weeks and Tyrwhitt, after returning from his brief leave, hoisted his pendant temporarily in the *Cleopatra*. Early on September 10 he went out in her, a few hours before *Arethusa* returned to Harwich, to take part in what proved to be a successful attempt to repeat the minelaying enterprise of August 17 on a much larger scale. This time three minelayers from Rosyth were escorted by a supporting force of battle-cruisers, light cruisers and destroyers from there and by Tyrwhitt's Light Cruiser Squadron, the *Nimrod* (a new flotilla leader just arrived)[51] and five of his destroyers. Three minefields were laid west and north-west of Amrum Bank and the whole operation was carried out without the enemy's knowledge, though Tyrwhitt 'had a very anxious night... and walked the bridge all night and was intensely excited'.[52]

This co-operation of the Harwich Force with a larger one from Rosyth underlines the fact that the strain on the cruisers of the Grand Fleet could scarcely have been met but for Tyrwhitt's vigorous co-operation. His force now consisted of the Fifth Light Cruiser Squadron and the Third (now re-numbered the Ninth) and Tenth Flotillas, to which were attached not only the *Undaunted* and *Aurora* respectively but also the two new flotilla leaders *Lightfoot* and *Nimrod*. Owing to the endless calls for troop-escort across the Channel his destroyers continued to be at times drastically reduced, but his activity during the last four months of the year was incessant in all weathers and some part of his force was always either at sea or in harbour at short notice. Zeppelins, some of which bombed Manningtree and Ipswich on the night of September 12–13, continued till the middle of October to be a constant source of annoyance with their bombing raids on our coast, and he spent much time in fruitless efforts to intercept them; but after that the violence of the weather that set in was more than they could face and their raids ceased altogether for the winter. He was no less occupied in searching for surface minelayers, in spite of which the enemy succeeded in laying a minefield off Harwich which made his exits and entrances more difficult and was ultimately to be the *Arethusa*'s undoing. In addition there were the patrolling of the enemy's coasts, the chasing of his submarines, the convoying of merchantmen, and a new venture which provided variety was the institution of a series of sweeps towards the Skaggerak in search of enemy vessels, particularly fishing trawlers, which were believed to be acting as scouts to give warning when our cruisers were operating.

Between September 29 and October 1 Tyrwhitt swept up to Jutland Bank, sinking five trawlers, capturing nine and allowing eight to go free as innocent. Many of the men aboard the captured vessels professed themselves glad to be taken prisoners, since this delivered them from the fear of being sent to the Western Front. In the following week he made another sweep, capturing fourteen and sinking one. On both occasions the Battle-Cruiser Fleet was kept at short notice for steam, ready to put to sea if support was needed. The prize crews which were put into the captured trawlers brought back 'mementos' (which could be less politely termed loot) in the shape of parrots, monkeys, pigeons, canaries, dogs, cats, German ensigns, binoculars, compasses and other items. The vessels themselves were taken into our service, six being sent to the Dardanelles and six to the Suez Canal. They represented a useful haul in view of the insistent demand for this class of craft for the Mediterranean. Moreover these captures had some effect in increasing the pressure of the British blockade, since all the boats were found to have been fishing on Government account and from this time on no more were seen in Tyrwhitt's subsequent sweeps. Yet his hold on the enemy's waters was never relaxed. Almost every week he was in force off the German or Danish coast, though all he met with was the Swedish *Osterland*, which he brought in as she was carrying ore on German account from Narvik to Rotterdam.[53]

At the beginning of November his difficulties with his flag-captain Arbuthnot, with whom he had never been able to get on very well, came to a head, and the latter wrote him a letter asking to be relieved. Although Tyrwhitt himself had been a successful flag-captain in the past, achieving the best of relations with his chief Sir Douglas Gamble and maintaining them in later life, he seems to have found it difficult to adjust himself to the opposite end of the relationship and to leave his own captain his proper and sufficient place in the ship. It irked him not to be in complete control of it; and moreover his own personality was so strong that only someone who himself had more force of personality than Arbuthnot apparently possessed could 'keep his end up' and make a success of a difficult position.[54] Tyrwhitt now invited his old friend Commander Domvile, who only two months earlier had been transferred from the command of the flotilla-leader *Tipperary* when she left the station to that of the even newer leader *Lightfoot*, to take Arbuthnot's place. Domvile, who had loved each of his successive ships and was extremely happy in *Lightfoot*, and moreover did not want to lose his independence, hesitated for a couple of days but then agreed, to Tyrwhitt's delight.[55]

During November the weather worsened, gales grew more frequent and patrol after patrol had to be abandoned or cut short. On one such occasion, when the destroyers had to be sent back because of the weather and Tyrwhitt carried on with the cruisers alone, the destroyer *Matchless* struck a mine on her way home which blew away her entire stern. Nobody was hurt, however, and she was brought in safely, towed by Lieutenant-Commander Taprell Dorling ('Taffrail')[56] in the *Murray*.[57] On 25 November Tyrwhitt wrote to his sister Polly:

> 'There's very little doing in my part of the world, but we still keep the North Sea fairly well churned up, although not so much as I should like to see. It is very monotonous, etc., but it is very essential for the Huns to

> know that we are always ready to pounce on them when they show up.'[58]

Meanwhile another plan for an 'air stunt' was in preparation, which he was twice summoned to the Admiralty to discuss (finding, since he had to return by late trains, London streets in the black-out 'positively dangerous... [with] taxis in every direction and it is difficult to gauge their speed in the dark').[59] This plan was for Tyrwhitt with the bulk of the Harwich Force and some submarines to take the new seaplane-carrier *Vindex* close up to the estuary of the Ems and endeavour to bomb the airship bases at Hage, north of Emden, and Hoyer, on the Schleswig coast.

At the end of November the *Vindex* arrived at Harwich. She had originally been the Isle of Man passenger steamer *Viking* (2,900 tons and 22 knots) and had been converted in September to carry four large seaplanes and one small one aft and two single-seater fighters forward, with a flying-off deck[60] and a small hangar fitted for the latter. On December 4 Tyrwhitt went out with her for what he described as a 'dress rehearsal', which was only partly successful as two of her planes were wrecked in the process, chiefly because of fog.[61] After that the bad weather continued:

> 'It blows and blows and blows and pours [he wrote to his wife on the 10th] ... I wanted to go out for a prowl round today but the weather was so poisonous that I gave up all idea of it ... I am so sick that my "air" ship [*Vindex*] is so long getting ready, but it is no use going in for air raids if the principal actors are untrained.'

On the 12th:

> 'I am, I hope, going out tomorrow for a browse round ... How tired I am of this foul weather and how I long for something to do ... I could not get off to sleep last night, a sure sign that we have been too long in harbour.'

But on the morrow the weather surpassed itself once the whole Force had got out to sea, and first the destroyers had to be sent back and then Domvile and Watson persuaded the Commodore to turn back also with the cruisers.[62] On the 20th it went out again for a sweep through the Bight to the Danish coast which was in effect a coat-trailing venture with the Battle-Cruiser Fleet once more at short notice for steam. This

> 'might have been a hair-raising expedition but we were prevented from carrying it out for two good reasons –
> (1) The trap was empty.
> (2) The weather, which was the limit and was responsible for the empty trap.
> ... I hope we shall be able to try again before long. It really will knock August 28 into a cocked hat if it comes off. I have not been so excited for a long time. We left ... in a gale and returned [on the 22nd] ... in the same gale ... Snow, hail, sleet and rain and constant gale ... I gave up all idea of carrying the job out at 11.30 a.m. yesterday and had just turned round for home when I received a wireless message from the Admiralty telling me to do the same!'[63]

He was much more disconcerted, however, by another Admiralty order which he received on the 30th, forbidding him to go out for a 'prowl' round as he wished to do and giving him a general caution not to expose his force during the stormy season unless some very favourable opportunity offered. In the course of the day a German minelayer was sighted laying mines off the Gabbard Shoal, but Tyrwhitt did not learn of this until hours after she had done her work and gone home, and he felt with justice that if he had been out on patrol he would almost certainly have intercepted her. Next day, nevertheless, he was feeling a little better, since everything was now ready for the seaplane raid to which he was looking forward, and only good weather and good luck were needed to make it a success.[64] On that note of mingled anticipation and exasperation the year ended.

CHAPTER FIVE

THE WAR JUST BEYOND THE TENNIS-COURT

'The Commodore is mad restless', confided Lieutenant Watson to his diary on January 1, perhaps not realising that '*Arethusa* Day' had come again. However an opportunity for putting to sea was provided by an Admiralty telegram instructing the light cruiser squadron to try to intercept the *Nordland*, a ship laden with ore for Germany which was believed to be about to make a dash from Norway to the Hook of Holland. The telegram contained the proviso 'weather permitting', but Tyrwhitt disregarded that and put out into an almost continuous gale, with seas so rough that some of the cruisers reported they were rolling as much as 45° each way and Lieutenant Disney of the *Arethusa* was washed overboard during the night without anyone knowing that he had been lost till he failed to appear to keep the middle watch. The squadron struggled up to the latitude of Horns Reef without sighting anything but a few trawlers – 'No one', wrote Tyrwhitt, 'has any idea how wide the sea is until they try and find something in it' – and then returned to port on the 5th. Next day it was reported that the *Nordland* had never sailed.[1] On the 10th the Force stood by to try the seaplane raid, but the weather was still too bad; on the 11th the submarines were sent out but had to be recalled for the same reason; and on the 16th the Commodore groaned: 'We shall develop into the limpet fleet if we don't get a move on soon. We have not been outside for ten days!'[2] On January 18 the attempt on Hage was made, but before the flying-off position was reached a dense fog came down which made further operations useless and obliged the Force to withdraw, although there had been no sign of enemy interference. Ten days later the attempt was repeated, after Tyrwhitt had again visited the Admiralty (where 'everybody seemed depressed') and had a successful argument with the First Sea Lord of which he reported: 'I have never seen Jackson so determined before. I thought I was going to lose the day at one time.' On this second attempt, on January 28 and 29, the weather was more favourable at first, but it worsened later. Nevertheless the Force had reached its assigned position twenty miles off the Ems estuary and had stopped to enable the *Vindex* to hoist out her seaplanes when a torpedo either grazed the *Arethusa*'s stern or actually ran under it. Captain[3] Domvile, who had recently become engaged, was looking out over the starboard side and saw the track of the torpedo comng straight towards the ship. There was no time to do anything except think that, as he put it afterwards, 'another marriage which had been arranged would not take place'; but after the miraculous miss he went ahead and turned the ship towards the danger, seeing, however, no submarines but only another torpedo which missed just ahead. The enemy were obviously on the alert; and since it was useless and indeed suicidal to carry on – the *Vindex* was not only a sitting target until she got under way but would again become one when she stopped to re-embark her machines – Tyrwhitt withdrew at full speed. As he did so the Force was enveloped in a thick fog which in any case would have frustrated the operation. 'We escaped by the skin of *Arethusa's* teeth' was Tyrwhitt's comment, but the respite was to prove very short.[4]

His problems were increased at this time by two arguments, with the Admiralty and with his wife. To the Admiralty he had written a letter on December 31 (when he was forbidden to go out for a 'prowl' and cautioned not to go out at all in very bad weather) complaining that he was not being given a free enough hand; and had received in reply what he described as 'a sort of veiled apology', approving his movements and instructing him to continue them 'as heretofore'. He cleared the air, however, by 'a heart-to-heart' talk with the First Sea Lord during his next visit to the Admiralty a few days later: 'It is quite a good thing', he commented, 'to have a row now and again, as it does clear up the atmosphere.'[5] This indeed, was often Tyrwhitt's way of tackling an obstacle, a difficulty, or a serious difference of opinion; he went at them as he would have gone at a German light cruiser squadron.

He lost his other argument, however, for his opponent was more determined than Admiral Jackson. Possibly spurred on by the news of Domvile's impending marriage, Mrs. Tyrwhitt had raised the question of letting Ketelby and moving to the Harwich area to be near him. They both wanted to be together more than his rare short leaves and her equally spaced-out visits to the Cayleys, plus an occasional snatched meeting in London, enabled them to be. But he had hitherto imposed a ban on officers' wives living at or near Harwich in case their presence distracted their husbands from their duty, and this would obviously have to go by the board if his own wife came to live there. Moreover, devoted to duty as he was, he feared lest her permanent proximity might have this same distracting effect on him. Hence at first he demurred, writing:

> 'I still look on war as the most important part of my or anyone else's business and everything must be allowed to slide which interferes with war or else it will go on for ever.'[6]

Towards the end of January, however, he capitulated – on one condition; he would not live in Dovercourt, the 'residential' quarter of Harwich; or at least if compelled to do so he would not conform to all the conventions of the code of etiquette that in those days still reigned in the Dovercourts of England:

> 'Continual rubbing wears away the hardest stone. I give in ... Let Ketelby if you can and ... I will look out for a

> house here, but do say if you want to live in Dovercourt or Shotley, and if the former do not expect me to return calls. *I won't* ... I should love to have you within reach, but there don't seem to be many resting-places out of Dovercourt and the very idea of Dovercourt fills me with horror.'[7]

He escaped it, however, for he discovered a charming and conveniently situated old farmhouse called Nether Hall at Shotley about half a mile from the pier, opposite the *Ganges* and on the way to the Cayleys' house. Into this they moved in the middle of March,[8] although they had not yet found a tenant for Ketelby, which they managed to do later, eventually selling it in 1917. The difference which it made to his life and happiness to have his family near him and to be able to have a little home life in the intervals of war was enormous, though it is the recollection of his elder daughter that he never actually spent a night at Nether Hall until after the signing of the Armistice. It was his practice, however, whenever he was in harbour and circumstances permitted, to land at 3 p.m., spend the afternoon at home and return to his ship at seven.

Although he was never interested in gardening to the same degree as his wife, he was always busy about the place, cutting down trees, mowing the lawn, making garden furniture and so forth. Quite apart from his occasional production of hencoops, garden huts and the like, the making of miniature furniture was one of his greatest hobbies and his skill in carpentry was positively professional, surprising and delighting all who saw the products of his craftsmanship. He always, even during the war, had a small carpenter's bench in his cabin, where he would while away the time when he was waiting with steam up at short notice to go to sea.[9] Fishing, the favourite pastime of his youth, was of course no longer possible until the war was over, but he was a great walker, relying mainly on long walks to maintain the physical fitness by which he set much store and sometimes combining these with his other favourite hobby of birds'-nesting. Between Keyes's departure and the arrival of his family these walks were often solitary, though when birds'-nesting was in question he was sometimes accompanied latterly by Captain Hubert Lynes of the *Penelope*, an enthusiastic ornithologist who was writing a book on birds and was afterwards a Gold Medallist of the Royal Ornithological Society.[10] Domvile also, who was likewise fond of walking, was occasionally his companion after he became flag-captain; and other officers sometimes accompanied him, notably Captains Nicholson and Lane (of the *Carysfort*) and Commander Colin Maclean, an old shipmate of his who had been gunnery lieutenant of the *Indefatigable* at the time of his engagement.[11] Later again, as Tyrwhitt's two elder children grew up, they used to walk with him.[12] Shooting, too, which had been impossible in the hectic first September of the war, became occasionally feasible again in later seasons; and when circumstances allowed he snatched the time to accept invitations to the shoots of Commodore Cayley and various local people, though he never felt quite happy when he was out of sight of his ship.[13] There was also a tennis-court at Nether Hall which was much used for tennis parties during the summers.

Rather significantly, Tyrwhitt at tennis preferred singles to doubles and was generally better when playing, as he put it, 'on his own'.[14] Warm-hearted though quick-tempered (two things very frequently compatible), he was nevertheless not at bottom a very sociable or at any rate gregarious person; in fact, even a little shy. He loved his wife and children very deeply, clove to friends like Roger Keyes and Wilmot Nicholson, and enjoyed and when he was alone frequently availed himself of the hospitable warmth of the Cayleys' beautiful home at Erwarton Hall, a Tudor mansion which was Admiralty property;[15] but parties, dinner and other (including some of those which his position obliged him to give), bored him, and he literally fled from the small change of social intercourse such as the making and returning of calls.

The sudden light of fame which beat upon him after the battle of Heligoland Bight embarrassed and in its extremer manifestations annoyed him. He steadfastly refused to allow his portrait to be painted, availing himself of the valid excuse that he could spare no time for sittings, and was appalled to discover that a profile snapshot of him had been made into a popular picture-postcard. When after the battle of the Dogger Bank the *Oxford Journal* printed a half-page picture of his birthplace with an inset of himself under the caption 'Commodore Tyrwhitt, of *Arethusa* and North Sea Fame', he wrote to his wife that it 'made him sick',[16] probably because he had not played any outstanding part in that action (from lack of opportunity) and felt that the press was seizing every opportunity of dragging him into the limelight.

The British public, of course, had expected naval heroes to emerge as soon as the war began, and the Battle of the Bight had provided two of them. The fact that both Beatty and Tyrwhitt were striking-looking men (perhaps especially Tyrwhitt, who looked so completely the keen-eyed and hawk-faced seaman the public expected) encouraged the press to continue publicizing them until some of the more sensible and responsible papers began to hint that there were other naval leaders about whom people might like to hear something. Both of the victims of what Tyrwhitt called 'this paper humbug' felt this strongly; and he even feared, not entirely without justice, that this excessive adulation might prejudice other members of the Service against him. 'I have been advertised a great deal more than I wanted', he wrote, 'and I hate it all.'[17]

In the best sense of the phrase he was a simple soul, possessing the great simple and (if one likes to call them so) old-fashioned virtues of honesty, straightforwardness, courage, patriotism, devotion to duty and inspiring leadership in the highest degree. His determination rose far above mere grim doggedness, for he had the gift (as he showed particularly in the long series of frustrated 'air stunts') of returning again and again and again to an enterprise that did not at first succeed, with an enthusiasm and ebullient optimism that carried others along with him. 'A man of indomitable courage', wrote Domville afterwards in his autobiography, 'his one object was to get at the enemy: he could not brook opposition'; apropos of which characteristic he recorded on one occasion in his diary 'We had gone back [in harbour] to our old swinging berth. The Commodore [was] slightly annoyed at our stern persisting in swinging to windward. He does not like nature to defy him!'[18] It is difficult, indeed impossible, to imagine a man more completely fitted to carry out the long, hard, dangerous, wearying and often – if only momentarily – disappointing task that had been committed to him. So his superiors evidently felt (and indeed explicitly in the cases of Jellicoe and Beatty); other commands changed hands during the war, but there was never any thought (save perhaps to promote him higher)[19] of removing the commander of the Harwich Force. More aware of his own limitations than of his qualities, he knew that he was no intellectual, writing modestly when delighted by his son's school reports that it looked as if St. John might be able to earn his living by his brains, 'which his father could never have done'. No great reader (he liked a good detective story best) or speaker ('If I live to be 3,000 years old I shall never become a speaker'), he was deficient in small talk, though usually 'very nice' in conversation, sometimes charming and very interesting when the talk fell upon war and its techniques or other Service matters.[20]

Even before he brought his family to Harwich some officers seem to have infiltrated their wives in disregard of the ban and afterwards it was of course tacitly jettisoned. The Tyrwhitt household was always at home for tea on Sundays to all who cared to drop in and were free to do so – married couples, wives, grass widowers, bachelors, miscellaneous female relatives and all alike – and Mrs. Tyrwhitt's charm and good looks won all hearts.

In addition to the many centres of private hospitality such

as this and the Cayleys' house, there was a considerable provision of public entertainment. For the lower deck there were recreation rooms and canteens fronting Parkeston Quay, and for all a cinema and a theatre to which companies of music-hall artistes were brought from London, while Saturday evening concerts were given and amateur theatricals presented in the depôt ships *Maidstone* and *Dido* or in the destroyer *Woolwich*.[21] At Dovercourt, too, the Alexandra Hotel, overlooking the water about halfway between Harwich Pier and Parkeston Quay, was a favourite port of call for officers who were on shore for a few hours, and dances were held here between two and five on Saturday afternoons – a rather grisly and cold-blooded time of day for them, some felt – as well as concerts[22] in the spacious hall of the hotel.[23] Parkeston Quay on fine mornings also became a kind of open-air club for officers to meet and chat when ashore for a short time or pausing briefly during some errand.[24]

There was provision, too, for outdoor sports and games; cricket, association and rugby football (for each of which Tyrwhitt gave a cup), hockey (Domvile playing centre-forward for the Harwich Force XI against Army teams and scoring many goals),[25] a tennis club, a nine-hole golf course on which inter-ship matches sometimes took place, regattas and sports meetings (at one of which Tyrwhitt, after conscientious training, won the veterans' race). At opposite extremes of the sporting scale there were boxing matches and croquet parties; and towards the end of the war several officers bought small yachts in which they sailed the estuaries of the Orwell and the Stour. Commander Watson, as by then he was,[26] bought a cutter; and Tennant was one of a syndicate of four who invested in a boat which was away nearly every day during the summer when its owners, or some of them, were free, generally up river when the tide suited, where they used to anchor, land in the dinghy, picnic and bask in the sun.[27]

'A comfortable way to go to war,' recorded Tennant of a

day in 1917 which began with an action with German destroyers in the small hours of the morning, followed by a return to Harwich by 9 a.m., a bath, collecting and reading the mail, a morning's duty, and then landing to play tennis.[28] But this, it must be realised, was a particularly quiet time in what was for the Force the slightly less hectic part of the war.

Nevertheless it was a novel kind of war, in a way that was not possible for the Grand Fleet far away at barren Scapa nor perhaps in quite the same degree for any other naval port, for Harwich was nearer the war than the rest, with the possible exception of Dover. In earlier centuries our ships had gone out to war and returned – if they did return – only after years, months, or at least a period of weeks. Here the war was just beyond the garden hedge, on the hither side of which there still went on what was outwardly at least a normal social life.

> 'My wife and I lived at Felixstowe [wrote Domvile in his autobiography twenty years afterwards], and I remember landing one afternoon about four o'clock to go and join her and finding a great bustle of preparation at the Felixstowe Air Station. I was informed that there were six German seaplanes sitting on the water just outside waiting for a fight, and that our Porte flying boats[29] were off to take up the challenge. When I went on board to dinner ... three hours later our machines were just back from a regular dog-fight with the Germans, in which we had had the best of it on the whole. That sort of thing made the war seem very near.'[30]

Men returned from patrol or battle and changed – metaphorically at any rate if not perhaps instantly – for tennis or dinner; or they finished their game and went out to sea, and possibly did not come back. For 'the dominant note was always the siren', as Admiral and Mrs. Watson remembered more than fifty years later; the recall signal that by day or night summoned officers and men who were on shore to hurry back to their ships. Shore leave for the various social and recreational activities which have been listed was at best limited to a few brief hours and of course subject to immediate recall. Officers sometimes ventured as far as Clacton or Felixstowe, but those who did found it expedient to ring up headquarters every half-hour or so, since they were out of hearing of the siren. No leave at all was given to the duty cruiser or duty division of destroyers (save for the postman or messman within easy recall) but once in every two or three months each cruiser had its periodical boiler-cleaning, which meant that it was out of action for two or three days and leave for longer than a few hours became permissible, enabling many to venture as far as Ipswich and other neighbouring towns.[31]

The pattern of the recall signal was that each cruiser in the harbour, taking her time from the flagship, sounded both her sirens thrice, each blast being three minutes long. To supplement the signal the Alexandra Hotel, where there were always officers' relatives and friends staying, would be telephoned and asked to ensure that all officers who might be visiting it at the time received the alarm. The hurried embarkations that followed these alarms were usually watched sympathetically by a goodly part of the population of Harwich, clustered round the landing steps. On at least one occasion the sirens sounded just as a concert was beginning in the hall of the hotel, with officers' wives and other female relatives acting as programme-sellers. There was no time for farewells; the officers left the hall at once and hurried down the unlit narrow streets of the old town to the quays, while the concert continued. This was one of the times when not all who went came back.[32] Worst of all, perhaps, was the more prolonged suspense of the wives of submarine officers, some of whom waited for weeks and weeks before giving up all hope of their husbands' return or survival as prisoners of war – 'the unacknowledged widows', as they were sometimes

Lieutenants David Beatty, Tyrwhitt and S. (afterwards Sir Stanley) Colville during their service in the Royal Yacht, 1892.

TYME
TRYETH
TRUTH
The Armorial Bearings
KCB DSO
RN

Top Left	Tyrwhitt's Coat-of-Arms.
Lower Left	Miss Angela Corbally at the time of her engagement to Tyrwhitt, 1902
Above	Tyrwhitt at the time of the Battle of the Heligoland Bight (a photograph seized on by the Press and converted into a 'patriotic postcard' which was enormously popular – much to Tyrwhitt's disgust).

THE "TYRWHITT TYR-WOO"

This wakeful bird is generally to be found on the North Sea. Always on the alert and an absolute terror to "Baby Killers"

Left A cartoon of Tyrwhitt published not long after the Battle of the Heligoland Bight.

Above H.M.S. *Arethusa*, Tyrwhitt's famous flagship, sinking after being mined, February 1916.

H.M.S. "Conquest"

Some of the severe damage suffered by H.M.S. *Conquest*, one of Tyrwhitt's later flagships, in the engagement off Lowestoft, April 1916.

The badly damaged German destroyer *V69* in the Dutch port of Ymuiden after an engagement with the Harwich Force in January 1917.

H.M.S. *Centaur*, one of Tyrwhitt's flagships in the latter part of the war.

Sir Reginald and Lady Tyrwhitt after she had joined him at Harwich.

Tyrwhitt when Commander-in-Chief on the China Station, 1927.

British, American and French warships lying off Shanghai during the 1927 crisis.

A jubilee reunion dinner of the survivors of the *Britannia* class of 1885: Tyrwhitt in the centre, with Admiral Sir Hubert Bland on his right and Admiral Sir Richard Webb next but one on his left.

Tyrwhitt as a Local Defence Volunteer at the age of seventy, 1940.

privately and sympathetically called.[33]

A number of mainly older wives and female relations, together with other local ladies, were organised (apparently by Mrs. Cayley) into a working party to provide warm garments and other comforts for the men and assist in looking after their welfare. It proved, however, rather difficult to enlist the younger women, and it was presumably someone who was more aware of this than of the positive results of Mrs. Cayley's labours who wrote to the wife of a retired admiral living at a distance, informing her that nothing in this line was being done and suggesting that she could intervene. The sequel may perhaps best be told in Tyrwhitt's own words:

> 'I had a remarkable letter from Lady ..., who I think must have been a bit off her head. She suggested that *I* should start a Ladies Working Party, etc., for Harwich and offered to send two trained women to show how to get to work. I took her letter to Milly [Mrs. Cayley], who explained what was going on at Harwich and ... about the working party which has been going on for ages. So I wrote very politely that we did not require any outside interference and that Mrs. Cayley was doing all that was necessary ... Today I received a very humble letter from Lady ... apologising for interfering, etc. Fancy me raking up all the young women in Harwich and starting a working party! ... I did not gently tell her that I had one or two other things to do!'[34]

During the twelve months after the battle of the Dogger Bank the main features of the naval operations in home waters had been the dangers from submarines and mines and the efforts to cope with them. But in the spring of 1916 both the British and German main fleets grew rather more venturesome, each seeking to take the other at a disadvantage. On the German side this quickening of the tempo was due chiefly to a change in command. Admiral von Ingenohl's unenterprising successor Von Pohl, who was dying of cancer, had now been succeeded in turn by the more active Vice-Admiral Reinhard Scheer, a strong advocate of unrestricted submarine warfare. This the Germans had been obliged by the protests of the United States to bring to a temporary halt at the end of August 1915, reverting instead to operating – theoretically at least – in accordance with international law by surfacing and stopping vessels and giving their crews time to take to their boats before sinking them. After trying unsuccessfully to obtain a resumption of unrestricted warfare, Scheer resorted instead to a series of cautious sorties by which he hoped to trap and destroy a part of the British fleet and so bring about a parity of forces which might enable him to challenge the remainder in a fleet action. On the British side mounting pressure on the Admiralty for a more offensive policy led it, as the weather improved slightly, to lend a readier ear to the strategy of seeking to lure the High Seas Fleet out by seaplane raids on the Zeppelin base at Tondern in Schleswig, which Tyrwhitt had never ceased to advocate in fair weather or foul, though mostly foul. With a German commander-in-chief who was in any case less reluctant to come out, this produced a pattern of alternative initiatives by each side which were almost bound to culminate in a major collision.

Scheer led off on February 10 with a destroyer sweep in the area east of the Dogger Bank in which a British sloop engaged in clearing one of the channels through the minefields was sunk. When the alarm was given the whole of the Grand Fleet and the Harwich Force, now eight light cruisers and twenty-three destroyers strong, rushed out, but the enemy withdrew to their base. Returning at twenty knots on the 11th through the Gledway Channel into Harwich, the *Arethusa* struck a mine near the South Cutler Buoy a few miles out – one of those which the Commodore had recently written to his wife had been laid for his special benefit. The explosion, which killed six men, occurred under the after boiler-room; the engines stopped at once and the ship began to sag and settle. In spite of the heavy sea that was running against the tide Tyrwhitt's old shipmate Commander Maclean in the *Lightfoot* got her in tow, but the hawser parted. The destroyer *Loyal* then tried, but with the same result, and the *Arethusa* drifted on to the Cutler Shoal and broke in two. Not till then did Tyrwhitt order her to be abandoned, and in abandoning her two more men were lost in a Carley raft which turned over and entangled them in the netting securing the bottom boards. The Commodore was the last man to leave her, and even after that he went back on board to search for his cat, but failed to find her. More correctly, he believed himself to be the last to leave, for after the boats had pushed off a figure appeared on deck waving and shouting – a stoker who according to one account belonged to the watch off duty and had not only been asleep when the explosion occurred but had gone on sleeping till almost too late, and according to another had been trapped below but escaped, though terribly burnt, by scrambling up the after funnel. Next day Tyrwhitt returned to find his cabin still above water and was able to salvage his books and papers; and the ship lay where she had grounded, slowly vanishing from sight, until August, after which all hope of salving her was abandoned and she was left to break up.[35]

To Tyrwhitt's chagrin, the application he made at once to be given another ship proved unsuccessful. He had already seized the chance when Admiral Jackson the First Sea Lord had visited Harwich in August to ask for and be promised the *Centaur*, which was still on the stocks, as a new flagship to take the place of the *Arethusa* when she was finished. She was one of a new class of light cruisers, mounting five six-inch guns on the centre-line and representing a further improvement on the 'improved *Arethusas*', of which the *Cleopatra* was one. The *Centaur*'s completion had already been delayed longer than he had expected, but he was now told that he must go on waiting for her and meanwhile hoist his broad pendant in one of the other ships of the squadron.

Remembering how comfortable he had been in the *Cleopatra* during the *Arethusa*'s last refit, he chose her again; but circumstances were different now and the mere prospect of having to make do till the *Centaur* was ready in May with a ship that he could not regard as his own and which had no proper accommodation for his staff and office made him grumble at her as cold and uncomfortable. However he received more than a hundred letters of commiseration over the loss of the *Arethusa*, the ship he had loved best of all that he had commanded,[36] and the Admiralty waived the formality of a court-martial for losing her (which Captain Domville would presumably have escaped in any case, since he happened to be away on his brief honeymoon at the moment).[37]

The next move in the sequence of escalating ventures was planned as what might be called a 'Keyes-Tyrwhitt Mark I' project for a sweep to the Bight on February 26 by the battle fleet from Scapa in conjunction with the Harwich Force. But once more man proposed and the weather disposed. Tyrwhitt, called on for a last-minute report on it, had to admit that it would not do, and the operation was called off. Receiving a signal to this effect in the small hours of the morning, with snow sweeping and a gale howling, even the redoubtable Com. (T) 'turned over in [his] bunk with much content'.[38]

The ball was now in Scheer's court again, and on March 5 and 6 he took the bulk of the High Seas Fleet out of the Bight to a position off the Texel which was in fact the farthest south that it ever came during the war. His object was to fall upon and destroy any British light forces that might be sent out to chase away the Zeppelins which had been despatched ahead to bomb England. This time Tyrwhitt nearly tumbled into the trap. When it was reported that a strong enemy force had been sighted off the Texel early in the morning of the 6th, steering westward, he went out at 9 a.m. full of high hopes and 'really thinking the day had come at last'. But when he sought the Admiralty's permission to intercept the returning Zeppelins at a point which he suggested, he was forbidden to do so because, as he put it, if he had gone there he would have stumbled into the arms of the High Seas Fleet. Recalled, he found 'mines everywhere' as he approached Harwich, and a small destroyer, the *Coquette*, and a torpedo-boat were blown up off the Sunk Light Vessel shortly before he entered harbour. The Grand Fleet had also swept south on the 6th, but the weather had reduced its speed so much that it had given up the attempt to make contact with the enemy.[39]

On March 9, disappointed by almost a month with only one or two abortive sallies, Tyrwhitt wrote to Keyes:

> 'The Harwich Force is not nearly so much in evidence now, as our opposite numbers the Second Scouting Group are just double our weight in guns and tons. I have very direct orders about not taking them on, but ... I have hopes of not being able to help it ... I have always grudged Nelson's remark, "Only numbers can annihilate". He should have substituted "guts" for "numbers".'[40]

It was just at this juncture that the growing dissatisfaction in the country with the Admiralty, and a campaign that was being mounted for Fisher's return to it, both came to a head when on March 7 the First Lord made a statement in the Commons on the Navy estimates. He painted what in several respects was a much too rose-coloured picture of the situation, which helped to provoke Churchill to go to the other extreme in an outburst of denunciation of the Admiralty for 'an attitude of pure passivity'. In particular he declared that he could not understand their lack of enterprise in dealing with the Zeppelin raiders and asked amid cheers why we did not go out and destroy their sheds. When Tyrwhitt, who had been trying and fighting almost week in and week out for the past year to do just that, read the account of this speech his former admiration for the speaker evaporated in an instant and he wrote to his wife:

> 'I hated Winston's reappearance and have wiped him off my list. He has done a bad piece of work and has made himself ridiculous to the world. As for old Fisher [whose recall Churchill had staggered the House by urging], if he gets back he will create Hell at the Admiralty and will do any amount of harm.'[41]

At sea it was now the British turn to move, and on March 25 and 26 Tyrwhitt's plan[42] for an air attack on the Zeppelin base supposed to exist at Hoyer on the Schleswig coast was at last carried out – an even more daring raid than that of Christmas Day 1914 on Cuxhaven because the approach was made in broad daylight. At break of day on the 24th the Harwich Force sailed to escort the *Vindex* with her five planes to a position south of Horns Reef and about forty miles north-west of Hoyer, while the Battle-Cruiser Fleet also left Rosyth on the same day, making for a point about forty-five miles west of Horns Reef in order to give close support. By 4.30 a.m. on the 25th Tyrwhitt was well inside the Vyl light-vessel south of Horns Reef and the *Vindex* was ordered to proceed further in with a destroyer escort. By 5.30 she had got her planes away and stood by awaiting their return, with her destroyers circling round her, while the Commodore patrolled east of the light-vessel.

The weather grew worse and the snowstorms heavier and more frequent, until about 7 the first two machines appeared and reported that there were no sheds or other establishments at Hoyer, but a base had been formed further inland at Tondern. Only one of the planes had located this, however, and its dropping gear had jammed, so that the pilot had been obliged to bring his bombs back. There was no sign of the others (which in fact were lost and their pilots taken prisoners); and at 7.45 Tyrwhitt ordered his two flotilla leaders, *Lightfoot* and *Nimrod*, with the remaining eight destroyers, to sweep south-east for them while he himself with the cruisers searched the Graa Deep.

So far no enemy had been seen, but towards 9 the destroyer sweep, after pushing as far as Röm island and then turning seaward, sighted two armed trawlers which they engaged and sank. While they were re-forming to carry on the search, however, the *Medusa* was rammed by the *Laverock* and so seriously damaged that she could not steam more than six knots. As the disaster had occurred right in the northern exit from the Bight and it was certain that the enemy must be aware of the British force's presence (since, even if the trawlers had not given warning before they sank, it had been located by aircraft) the situation was full of danger. The Commodore, having given up hope of finding the missing seaplanes, had just ordered the *Vindex* and her destroyer escort to return to the base, but on hearing of the *Medusa*'s plight he went off at full speed towards her. Meanwhile the *Lightfoot* had taken the *Medusa* in tow and Commander Maclean had ordered away the *Nimrod* and all but two of the destroyers that were in company, which he kept as an escort. Tyrwhitt realised that, seeing how long his presence must have been known to the enemy, to continue towing the *Medusa* during his withdrawal was very risky, but he could not yet bring himself to abandon her.He therefore ordered the *Aurora* and the destroyers he still had with him to form a screen for the *Lightfoot* and *Medusa* and began a slow retreat westward. Half-an-hour later he received a signal from the Admiralty to withdraw without delay, followed by another warning him to expect destroyer attacks during the night. But he still clung to his hope of saving the *Medusa*, merely calling back four of the destroyers that were escorting the *Vindex* to rejoin him, and holding on in a rising sea that made it more and more difficult to tow the damaged destroyer.

Fortunately Admiral Scheer, in spite of the information he had received, was at a loss to know the meaning of the British air attack with its powerful support. Since it might be a trap to catch any force he sent out, he held the main fleet back and despatched only cruisers and flotillas. Meanwhile the gale grew in violence every hour, and it became evident that the *Medusa* could not be saved. The towing hawser had parted, and the Commodore gave orders for her to be abandoned and sunk.[43] He then sent the bulk of his destroyers ahead and with his light cruisers steered a course to pass to the north of the enemy's North Sea minefield. About 10 p.m. Captain Loder Symonds in the *Cleopatra* was aware in the intense darkness of the flaming funnels of two German destroyers steaming across his bows. Putting his helm over he made for the second one and rammed her very neatly amidships, practically cutting her in two. The crash of the impact was followed by what seemed to be two explosions, one possibly a boiler explosion in the enemy destroyer and the second, which caused some damage to the *Cleopatra*'s stern, due to either a mine or a depth-charge. Moreover her sudden alteration of course had brought her across the bows of the *Undaunted*, which, as the squadron was steaming in close order and without lights, could not avoid crashing into her. The result was that the Commodore's movements were even more dangerously hampered than before he abandoned the *Medusa*. The *Cleopatra* was only slightly damaged, but the *Undaunted*'s bows were stove in and her collision bulkhead could not stand the strain of a speed of more than six knots. In the confusion, too, the squadron and the flotillas had become scattered and were ignorant of each others' movements. Fortunately Scheer had recalled everything for the night in view of the obscure situation and the heavy weather, but as he might be expected to come out in the morning the Harwich Force was still in grave danger. Tyrwhitt therefore remained in company with the *Undaunted* during the night and on the morning of the 26th ordered three of the other light cruisers to cover her passage to the Tyne for repairs, while with the rest he closed the Battle-Cruiser Fleet, after which the whole force swept back towards the German coast. In the meantime the remainder of the Grand Fleet had come out from Scapa and Cromarty on the evening before, in spite of snowstorms and a heavy gale, in order to be prepared for eventualities. It seemed, to the Admiralty at least, that an action was inevitable and that it must begin long before the British battle-fleet could appear on the scene, since the south-westerly gale was still raging with undiminished violence. Scheer had in fact come out in force, but at 6.30 a.m. his cruisers reported that the sea was so rough that an engagement was impossible, and he gave up the attempt as hopeless, having perhaps missed his chance. Whether an engagement could indeed have taken place at all is doubtful, but if it had it would have been under conditions favourable to the enemy. For some hours Beatty and Tyrwhitt continued to cruise in German waters near Horns Reef, but about noon they gave up all hope of an encounter and turned for home.[44]

From about 6.30 on the following morning, as they struggled back, Mrs. Tyrwhitt was spending most of her time in the drawing-room at Nether Hall, constantly scanning the horizon through glasses for the return of the *Cleopatra*, which did not arrive at Harwich until 5 p.m. It was, she wrote to her sister-in-law Polly, 'a terrible time' – her first experience of 'the drawback of being on the spot' and knowing just when the ships were out and when they were long in coming back.[45]

For a little time afterwards, while Scheer was quietly maturing his plans for his next move, German offensive action was confined to air-raids, and when the raids ceased again temporarily he was held back by the German Government, which believed that a British attack was imminent. This impression probably arose from the extensive preparations which were being made for an attempt on the Zeppelin base now located at Tondern and also for a large mining operation off the Belgian coast. This was a project which Admiral Bacon had cherished for some time, of a mine and net barrage against the German minelaying submarines of the Flanders Flotilla. The idea was to close the passage between the Thornton Ridge shoal and the Belgian coast by a double line of mines extending across the entrance to Zeebrugge, supplemented by mine nets on the same line. The considerable force detailed to cover the minelayers included twelve of the Harwich destroyers, eight of the 'L' class and four 'Ms'. In the early hours of April 24 a double line of mines fifteen miles long and a barrage of over thirteen miles of mined nets were laid and the minelayers and their escort returned to port, leaving some drifters to finish their work with the nets, supported by the 'M' class destroyers and two monitors. While engaged in this they were attacked by seaplanes, though innocuously, and three enemy destroyers also appeared. The *Milne* had been detached to search for a submarine, but the other three 'M' boats immediately broke away after the destroyers and chased them. This brought them under a heavy bombardment from shore batteries during which the *Melpomene* was hit by a shell which did not burst but penetrated her engine-room and stopped her with it flooded. The *Milne*, which had hastened to rejoin, went alongside *Melpomene* to prepare to tow her, but entangled her own port propeller in the towing-cable during the process and put it out of action. The *Medea* then came up on the *Melpomene*'s other side, and the three ships withdrew in sandwich formation. The German destroyers, seeing their opportunity, reappeared from under the shelter of the batteries, but the *Murray* engaged them single-handed until the *Medea* slipped her tow and joined her. The monitors also opened fire, and the enemy went back to cover and stayed there, while the *Melpomene* was towed and escorted out of range of the batteries by her sisters, which by zigzagging and laying a smoke-screen escaped with some casualties in the *Medea*.[46]

While this was taking place Scheer's next sortie was already beginning – a tip-and-run raid on Lowestoft and Yarmouth. The High Seas Fleet left harbour at noon on the 24th, with Rear-Admiral Boedicker commanding the striking force in the absence of Hipper, who was ill. This force consisted of four battle-cruisers (originally five, but the *Seydlitz* struck a mine and had to be sent back), four light cruisers of the Second Scouting Group, and two fast destroyer flotillas with their cruiser leaders. The Admiralty were soon aware that the enemy had put to sea, but at first did not know their objective. After alerting the Grand Fleet in the afternoon, at 7.05 p.m. they ordered it and the Battle-Cruiser Fleet to sea. An intercepted German signal at 8.14 then revealed that a bombardment of Yarmouth was intended, but it was not till towards midnight that the Harwich Force was called out. On this occasion it was somewhat depleted for various reasons (including the absence of the twelve destroyers engaged in the operations off the Belgian coast) and comprised only the *Conquest* (in which Tyrwhitt was now flying his pendant), *Cleopatra*, *Penelope* and *Lightfoot* with the only seven destroyers that were immediately ready, the *Nimrod* following with eight others.

Tyrwhitt's original instructions had been that when ordered out he was to make for a mid-sea position between Southwold and the Hook of Holland on the enemy's presumed track and try to lead them towards our main forces. Just before he left harbour, however, information which the Admiralty had just received was relayed to him that the German battle-cruisers would be past this position within two hours, steering westward towards Yarmouth. This made it evident to him that his instructions had been based on a false appreciation and at best would enable him only to intercept the enemy on their return. He therefore decided to act on his own responsibility and make straight up the coast for the point of the German attack. The odds against him would be overwhelming, the moon would soon be up, and with dawn at hand when he arrived it would be too light to attempt a torpedo attack. He might however entice the enemy to chase him and draw their fire away from our coasts and upon himself. About 3.50 a.m. with the first glimmer of dawn beginning to brighten the sky to seaward, he sighted Boedicker's force about ten miles away to the northward, and after sending an urgent signal to Jellicoe and Beatty and standing to the westward towards Lowestoft for a few minutes to give the enemy a good sight of him, he turned south again at full speed as though seeking to escape. But Boedicker was not to be drawn and held on for Lowestoft, which he proceeded to bombard, merely detaching his light forces to chase Tyrwhitt. Even these soon turned away again, and seeing that he was not followed the Commodore stopped his retirement. The lessening thunder of the bombardment now told him that the enemy were moving away from him, and at 4.20 it ceased altogether. Clearly they must be heading for Yarmouth, and in an effort to save it he turned north again to regain contact. Ten minutes later he sighted Boedicker's light forces and began to engage them at extreme range. Hearing the sound of this engagement to the southward, the German admiral broke off the bombardment of Yarmouth, steamed to the support of his light cruisers and destroyers, and opened fire on Tyrwhitt from a range of 16–18,000 yards which made any reply impossible.

The Commodore immediately turned his ships back sixteen points together, but for thirteen minutes he was under a heavy fire that considerably damaged the *Conquest*, now the rear ship, which was struck by five twelve-inch shells and lost twenty-three killed (including Tyrwhitt's servant) and thirteen wounded. She could still steam twenty knots, however, and the only other damage inflicted on the Force had been by one hit on the *Laertes* which wounded five men and put a boiler out of action. Fortunately, too, Boedicker was rather lacking in enterprise and presently put about in his turn and withdrew, perhaps because he feared that Tyrwhitt's force might be only a screen for something much stronger.

To some extent Tyrwhitt's spirited action had achieved its object. Even though he had not been able to lure the enemy away in the first place, he had ultimately done so; and though Lowestoft had suffered severely[47] Yarmouth had hardly been touched and the enemy were now withdrawing rapidly eastward towards their battle-fleet with their work only half done. But the indomitable 'Com (T)' had no intention of resting content with that. As soon as he found that Boedicker was no longer pursuing him he reversed the rôles, turned once more himself, set off at his utmost speed in pursuit of the enemy, and by 8.30 had once more sighted their smoke, when the Admiralty ordered him to return to his base. Meanwhile Beatty, and far astern of him Jellicoe, had both been struggling through heavy seas in the hope of cutting off Boedicker or Scheer (who had also turned for home) but before midday it became evident that the pursuit was hopeless.[48]

Beatty, who held his one-time shipmate Tyrwhitt in very high esteem, lost little time in arranging a meeting with him on May 17–18 at which they relieved their feelings by holding a furious post-mortem on the Lowestoft raid. The outcome of this mutual letting-off of steam was a letter from Beatty to Jellicoe on May 18 that was really intended mainly for Admiralty consumption. Among the several passages of very strong condemnation of the War Staff for persistent failure to co-ordinate the movements of the various units operating in the North Sea were these:

> '...The 24 April was an object lesson which makes me weep when I think of it. There was absolutely no reason why every unit should not have been on the move three and a half hours before it was!! Commodore T. and Harwich Force did not actually leave Harwich until eleven o'clock p.m. He received many contradictory orders and when eventually pushed out was told to do his best!! He had no idea where I was, or when I might be expected or where I was going to. I had no idea of anything appertaining to the Harwich Force – neither their position, composition or disposition... It amounts to this, that we were without general principles and had no plan, no combination and no decision. The opportunities of inflicting damage were priceless; they were thrown away ... Commodore T. could have brought off a torpedo attack; our submarines could have been in the

> right place at daylight; the battle cruisers and indeed the whole of the Grand Fleet could have been three and a half hours further south. The possibilities arising out of these *facts* are incalculable...'[49]

Beatty's main point was that the system of working from different bases 'in watertight compartments' prevented proper use being made of opportunities; but Jellicoe thought that as far as the Harwich Force was concerned it was best for the Admiralty to give it its orders, since any reversion to the original idea that he should do so must cause delay. Less than a fortnight later, on the day of Jutland, came the supreme failure of the Admiralty to give 'Commodore (T)' his head, and the biggest opportunity, perhaps, was missed.

Before Beatty wrote this letter, however, the British in their turn had moved again, but with no more success than in the Hoyer raid. In this venture the Harwich Force took no part. It was light cruisers and destroyers from Rosyth which on May 3 and 4 escorted the *Vindex* and the *Engadine* to a position off the island of Sylt from which a bombing raid on the Zeppelin sheds at Tondern was intended. The battle-cruisers and (more remotely) the battle-fleet also took up positions which it was hoped would enable them to cut off the High Seas Fleet if it came out. But the raid failed like all its predecessors and the High Seas Fleet, deterred by bad weather and uncertainty as to the situation, came out only belatedly, when the Grand Fleet had given up and retired.

The revelation of how open the east coast of England lay to a raid had now given a further fillip to a reconsideration of the fleet's distribution which was already going on. It had also had the effect of making the Admiralty more nervous about the southern part of the North Sea (an important point to be borne in mind in view of what befell the Harwich Force on the day of Jutland). 'The enemy', they wrote to the Commander-in-Chief, 'have practically tested our weakness in southern waters and will probably act on the offensive in those waters shortly'. Pointing out that Tyrwhitt had at the moment only one light cruiser available,[50] they asked Jellicoe to take steps to safeguard the threatened area at least until the Commodore's damaged ships were repaired. At his suggestion the Third Battle Squadron (of pre-dreadnoughts) and Third Cruiser Squadron were detached from the Grand Fleet, placed under the orders of Vice-Admiral Sir Edward Bradford (who commanded the battle squadron) and ordered to proceed to Sheerness and to regard the Swin – the northern passage of the Thames estuary – as their war anchorage. On the other hand, since the Commander-in-Chief felt that the Grand Fleet had not enough destroyers to provide a sufficient screen for the heavy ships, two divisions (eight boats) of the Ninth and Tenth Flotillas were sent north from Harwich to Rosyth on the eve of Jutland, in which they were the only units of the Harwich Force to take part.[51]

At the time of the Admiralty's message to Jellicoe, however, the Force had just acquired an additional light cruiser and Tyrwhitt a new flagship. The idea that he should wait for the *Centaur* had eventually been given up, and instead it had been at first proposed that he should have the *Canterbury*, the last of the 'improved *Arethusas*', which was to be ready in April. Early in that month a further change was made and the *Carysfort*, of the same class as the *Centaur* but now much nearer completion, was substituted for the *Canterbury*, which went instead to the Grand Fleet in time for Jutland. Captain Domvile, who since the loss of the *Arethusa* had been employed in organising the coastal motor-boat base at Queenborough near Sheerness and in building the boats themselves, duly went to the Clyde to take over the *Carysfort*, conduct her trials and bring her round to Harwich, where she arrived on April 30.[52] The idea of these coastal motor-boats, it may be mentioned, had originated with officers of the Harwich Force. They were designed to be sufficiently light to be hoisted at a cruiser's davits, and the intention was that each cruiser of the Force should carry two and that they should then be transported over to the German coast to make a torpedo attack on the ships lying in the

Schillig Roads.[53] This operation, however, after repeated postponements, was eventually given up altogether.[54]

In the latter part of May both Jellicoe and Scheer were preparing to move again. The latter, however, moved first. By interception and decoding of German signals the Admiralty gathered on May 30 that he was probably coming out next day and duly alerted Jellicoe and Beatty (who were actually at sea well before the enemy), as well as warning Tyrwhitt to stand by for possible action at daylight with all available light cruisers and destroyers. Had he been unleashed then to join the Grand Fleet (as the Admiralty had given Jellicoe to understand early in the war that he would be in the event of a fleet action)[55] he would presumably have reached the Commander-in-Chief by dark; and if his force had taken part in the subsequent night operations the moves that enabled Scheer to escape might not have gone uncomprehended and unreported. As Lieutenant Louis Hamilton of the *Moorsom* (one of the Tenth Flotilla destroyers sent up to Rosyth just before the battle) confided to his diary 'The destroyer business in the night at Jutland was an awful mess-up. If only they had allowed Com. T. to be there ... things might have been very different.'[56] Jellicoe himself told Domvile some weeks later that the absence of the Harwich cruisers and flotillas had constricted his actions during the fatal night.[57] But the Admiralty felt that the first consideration must be to guard against the possibility that Scheer's sortie might be only a blind to cover some design in the southern area – that under cover of it, for instance, a detached squadron might come through the southern part of the North Sea and combine with the strong German destroyer forces in the Belgian ports to overwhelm the Dover Patrol and then fall on shipping in the Downs or the eastern part of the Channel. They therefore held Tyrwhitt back; and all during the afternoon he strained at the leash while the intercepted, half-read battle signals told him clearly enough what was happening at sea. Eventually he asked for instructions, but still none came, and at 5.15 p.m. he could bear it no longer and gave orders to put out, at the same time informing the Admiralty that he was putting to sea. Crossing his signal came a reply to his former request for instructions: 'Complete with fuel. You may have to relieve light cruisers and destroyers in Battle-Cruiser Fleet later.' Disregarding this, he held on hopefully until the effect of his last telegram should be known, but before he had reached the Cork Light Vessel there came another signal that could not be disregarded: 'Return at once and await orders.' His only immediate comment, made to Domvile, is said to have been: 'I might as well have gone on mowing the lawn!'

Eventually at 3.30 in the morning of June 1 he received orders for steam and went out half-an-hour later with five light cruisers, two flotilla-leaders and sixteen destroyers; but all he met was the damaged battleship *Marlborough* which was still in danger from the attacks of enemy submarines, and all he was able to do was to provide her with a welcome escort of destroyers and enable her to proceed in safety to the Humber. A little later he was informed that he was not needed for anything else and instructed to return to harbour.[58] Had he been allowed to proceed when he went out on his own responsibility on the previous afternoon he would still, of course, have arrived too late to affect the situation; but it is difficult to avoid toying with the thought that if there had been a 'Jacky' Fisher – with all his faults – at the Admiralty to send him straight out at dawn on the 31st Scheer might twenty-four hours later have found the Grand Fleet still between him and his base, with all the long day before it, and the sun might have gone down that evening on a yet more Glorious First of June.

CHAPTER SIX

'THE CONTINUING OF THE SAME UNTO THE END'[1]

In view of the failure to make use of the Harwich Force at Jutland, the question of co-ordinating its movements better in future with those of the Grand Fleet was among the matters discussed at a conference held at the Admiralty on June 25 which was in effect a post-mortem on the battle. It proved difficult, however, to reach a clear-cut solution of the problem. The Admiralty appreciated that the Force ought to co-operate with the battle-fleet if possible, but unfortunately though they had means of knowing when the German fleet was putting to sea they did not usually know immediately what its plans were, and until they could be sure that these did not involve any southward move Tyrwhitt could not be definitely ordered to join Jellicoe. Indeed, the enemy's plan might be such that to order him north at once might mean exposing him to being cut off and crushed. Moreover there was the fact that the German flotilla on the Flanders coast was steadily growing and was now too strong for the Dover destroyers to face it unaided, so that the Harwich Force might be needed to help it hold the Straits in a sudden crisis. The question was therefore left in abeyance for the time being, though after the affair of August 19 (shortly to be recorded) it was laid down that if the enemy seemed to have no intention of operating south of the latitude of Yarmouth the Force would be ordered to join the Grand Fleet – a decision which still left possibilities of doubt and hesitation.[2]

The Admiralty's case for refusing to lay down a hard-and-fast rule was strengthened, however, by the fact that after Jutland Scheer seemed to have decided to use Zeebrugge as a destroyer training base and to detach flotillas from the High

Seas Fleet to carry on a kind of guerilla warfare from it. Early in June it was learnt that the German Second Flotilla had been sent there, and the correct conclusion was drawn that it was meant to threaten, and if possible raid, our communications with Holland and our shipping in the Downs. In the small hours of June 8 twelve of these German destroyers appeared to the east of Dunkirk, where they were engaged by some vessels of the Dover Patrol. Six light cruisers and many destroyers were therefore ordered out from Harwich in support, but the enemy decamped before they could arrive.[3]

At this time the British forces in Flanders Bight, which was about to become an increasingly important theatre of operations and a scene of fierce raiding and counter-raiding, were distributed between Dover, Dunkirk and Harwich. At Harwich there were – when the Force was at full strength – the Fifth Light Cruiser Squadron, consisting at the moment of five ships; the Ninth Flotilla (*Undaunted*, *Lightfoot* and 21 'L' class destroyers) and the Tenth (*Aurora*, *Nimrod* and fifteen of the 'M' class). The eight boats of the First Flotilla, though based on Harwich, were permanently attached to the Third Battle Squadron at Sheerness. The Dover Force consisted of the light cruiser *Attentive*, a flotilla-leader, 24 destroyers, 14 monitors and eight 'P' or patrol boats. The Dunkirk Force had to be made up by detached elements from the other two and usually comprised from four to eight destroyers. But owing to the frequent refits which the destroyers in particular needed and the constant calls for reinforcements in the Channel whenever U-boats were reported to be operating vigorously there, the total striking force that could be mustered in the area rarely exceeded four light cruisers and thirty destroyers. The repeated demands from others for aid burdened and handicapped Tyrwhitt considerably, on top of which the Admiralty ordered him to detach two of his cruisers and eight destroyers to reinforce the Dover Patrol. One of the cruisers detached was the *Cleopatra*, which struck a mine a few weeks later while engaged in this service but managed to get into dock for repairs. Tyrwhitt took advantage of this to persuade the First Sea Lord to let him have the cruisers and four destroyers back again at Harwich in August. The destroyers were particularly useful, since he had only three with him at that moment, all the rest being away on what he described as 'odd jobs' – two divisions hunting submarines from Portsmouth and on the Dogger Bank respectively, another looking after minesweepers and two more occupied in a new and arduous duty which had recently been imposed on him.[4]

This last was the Dutch convoy, colloquially called at Harwich the 'Beef Trip'. The traffic route between the Thames and Holland was the easiest of all the routes to attack, since not only could it be raided by a quick dash from Heligoland Bight but on its flank lay Zeebrugge with its flotillas of submarines and destroyers. In June 1916 the British Government concluded a trading agreement with the Dutch by which a large amount of food that had hitherto been sent to Germany was allocated to Britain. The transport of this considerably increased the number of passages of ships on this route, and moreover it was anticipated that since they were carrying food which had been diverted from Germany they would be a special target, probably for destroyer attack. Towards the end of the month the Admiralty therefore ordered the Harwich Force to keep under permanent patrol a route running roughly from the Sunk to the Schouwen Bank and thence to the Maas. A force of two light cruisers and from five to ten destroyers, frequently under Tyrwhitt's personal command, was generally allocated to this; and events were not long in justifying the wisdom of the step.

After a few patrols had taken place without any incident of note, Tyrwhitt put to sea on the evening of July 22 with the *Carysfort*, *Canterbury* and eight 'M' class destroyers, ordering the *Canterbury* with one division to watch the route near the North Hinder while he himself took the Maas section of the patrol with the other. At about the same time a German flotilla left Zeebrugge, setting a course for the North

Hinder in the hope of capturing some of the merchantmen; and at 12.15 a.m., with the Hinder nearly abeam about two miles off, the *Carysfort* and her division sighted three of them dead ahead. Outweighted, the enemy at once turned to the eastward and made off, pursued by the *Carysfort*, which had just succeeded in bringing them under fire when a squall of rain practically blotted them from sight. Seizing the chance, the Germans put up a heavy smoke-screen, turned sharply to starboard, and when the horizon cleared again had disappeared from view. Tyrwhitt then ordered the *Canterbury* and her division to turn south-east and try to catch them near the Schouwen Bank, while he took his own division on to the Maas to cut off their retreat if on meeting the *Canterbury* they should turn north again and try to slip in to Emden along the coast. At 1.45 when the *Canterbury* was about ten miles north-west of the Schouwen Bank the German destroyers, now six in number, were sighted ahead, steaming at high speed for Zeebrugge. Captain Royds altered course to port to close them, and an exchange of fire at about 5,000 yards began at 2.10; but the *Matchless*, just returned from the dockyard, could not keep up, and the captain of the *Milne* felt that he must stand by his sub-divisional leader. This left two destroyers chasing six Germans and overhauling them, with the *Canterbury* dropping astern though still well within range; and since the boats were fast approaching the minefield off Zeebrugge Captain Royds called off the chase.[5]

This brief engagement showed that our dispositions were well adapted for protecting the Dutch route; but on the other hand it was equally clear that the Zeebrugge flotilla, though too far outnumbered and outclassed to dispute our command of the Flanders Bight, had nevertheless considerable capacity for mischief. Before the end of July, therefore, the arrangements for the protection of the route grew into a definite convoy routine. The convoys were spaced at intervals of two or three days, each consisting of four to nine ships with a direct escort of a light cruiser and four destroyers, while a similar force patrolled at the Schouwen to cope with any German destroyers that might come out from Zeebrugge. Eastbound and westbound convoys were synchronised, the westbound leaving Holland at the same time as the eastbound passed the North Hinder Light Vessel; and the escort of these convoys became a principal – and often blasphemously execrated – activity of the Harwich Force. The crossings were at first made at night in order to add to the difficulties of an attacking force, but it was presently realised that this had the disadvantage that ships in the convoys were inclined to straggle owing to their differences of speed; indeed, when the head of a convoy reached safety the remainder were sometimes spread out over fifty or more miles of sea. After a straggler had been picked up by the enemy on September 21 Tyrwhitt therefore made a radical change of routine, abandoning the principle of direct escort for the time being. Under the new orders which he issued on October 15 the passage was made entirely in daylight and the route was divided into eight sections, each occupied during the passage by a destroyer zigzagging at fifteen knots. The convoy method, that is, was replaced again by the patrolling system. In November, however, there was a further reversion to an improved form of convoy (with the slower ships eliminated altogether), by which the eastbound trade always sailed first and was met off Orford Ness by a strong escort which saw them safely in to the Hook of Holland before the westbound trade came out to be escorted back. Until the German resumption of unrestricted submarine warfare in February 1917 the only escorted vessel lost since the 'Beef Trip' began was the unlucky straggler of September 21.[6]

On August 13, however, the destroyer *Lassoo* was lost while escorting a Dutch convoy. On the previous day she and the rest of her division had left Harwich for this duty, but since the merchantmen had not formed up in close order at the rendezvous the convoy had become considerably scattered by dawn on the 13th. While the *Lassoo* was zigzagging to and fro in front of it as a protection against submarines she struck a mine which broke her back, a stoker and three officers being killed by the explosion. Her three sisters came up to the rescue, getting out their explosive sweeps since it was at first thought that she had been torpedoed; but when it became increasingly evident that she had been mined two went on to continue protecting the convoy while the *Lance* remained standing by. Both her boats and the *Lassoo*'s were lowered and the ship's company of the latter were ferried across with such of their belongings as they could collect, except for the captain, Lieutenant-Commander Butler, and about a dozen men who remained behind since there seemed to be a slight chance that she could be towed home, as the weather was calm. Although she was gradually sinking deeper into the water amidships as one bulkhead after another collapsed under the pressure of water, Butler and an engine-room artificer went down into the foremost boiler-room in the pitch darkness to see if it was possible to shore up the after bulkhead, but found it too close to the back of the boiler for anything to be done. Preparations for taking the remains of the ship in tow had just been completed when this bulkhead collapsed and she fell over on her beam ends to starboard. On Butler's orders the men still on board dived from the forecastle into the sea and were picked up by the boats, except the unlucky E.R.A., who had got oil on his boots while in the boiler-room and so slipped backwards in trying to climb over the side of the ship, became entangled in the berthing-rails and went down with her as she broke in two. Butler himself walked out along a now horizontal funnel and managed after being sucked under once to get hold of a coir fender which kept him afloat until he was picked up.[7]

On August 18 Admiral Scheer now decided to try again to whittle down the Grand Fleet, either by catching part of it at a disadvantage or by luring it into a submarine trap, or both. His plan was to attempt a battle-cruiser raid on Sunderland with his main fleet in support and with Zeppelins operating in advance and to the northward of his route to prevent his being taken by surprise by the whole Grand Fleet as he had been at Jutland; while submarines were disposed off the British coast and on both flanks of his fleet. Once again interception and decoding of German signals warned the Admiralty that a sortie was imminent and enabled the Grand Fleet to put to sea before the enemy. Tyrwhitt was ordered to be on the look-out for the German force at Brown Ridge by early dawn on the 19th, and left harbour at 10.30 p.m. on the 18th in the *Carysfort* with the Fifth Light Cruiser Squadron, the *Lightfoot* and eighteen 'L' and 'M' destroyers in company. He had not even been told that Jellicoe would be at sea (though he felt sure that he must be), much less given any information of his position, course or intentions.

Arriving on the Brown Ridge at 3 a.m. on the 19th, he began patrolling it at twenty knots and continued doing so until shortly before 10 he received a signal from a British submarine which revealed to him that the High Seas Fleet was to the northward. Having relayed this to the Commander-in-Chief in case he had not yet received it, he began steaming north, still at the same moderate speed of twenty knots in the hope of slipping in on the Germans' line of retreat.

Meanwhile a German submarine had torpedoed and sunk one of Jellicoe's light cruisers, and since she had not been seen and it was therefore not known whether the cruiser had been mined or torpedoed, Jellicoe feared that he might be leading his fleet into a minefield and turned back northward until the matter was cleared up, thus losing four hours.

Scheer for his part had received a report from Zeppelin *L 13,* which had sighted the Harwich Force but had not identified its components correctly, that about sixteen destroyers with some cruisers and battleships were coming up from the southward. Believing that his chance had come of destroying a smaller and weaker detachment that was nevertheless big enough to make its destruction an important victory, he gave up the intention of bombarding Sunderland, turning south towards the approaching force and away from the Grand Fleet, which by then had resumed its course towards him. At 12.45 Tyrwhitt, who had neither seen anything of the enemy nor as yet received any signal modifying his original orders, decided that he ought to return to the station they had assigned to him and also turned southwards. Next Scheer learnt by a signal from one of his submarines that Jellicoe was coming down on him, though still sixty-five miles away, and at 2.35 gave up the chase of the Harwich Force and turned for home. Jellicoe, who at first remained unaware of what had happened and only gradually gathered in the course of the afternoon that the enemy were well on their way back and all chance of intercepting them had gone, then sent Tyrwhitt a succession of orders the later of which cancelled the earlier and all of which were delayed in getting through. Nevertheless the Commodore succeeded in grasping the situation, turned to the course which seemed to him to give the best chance of establishing contact with the enemy, and achieved that contact. About 5.30 the *Lightfoot* reported that she had sighted a considerable number of vessels steering east, and he first of all turned south to get enough room to avoid being cut off and then turned again and began to dog the High Seas Fleet.

Scheer, seeing that Tyrwhitt was following him, made preparations to receive a severe night attack by stationing a powerful group of destroyers astern of his line. Jellicoe, however, now sent a signal stating that he was too far away to give any support; and Tyrwhitt, realising that even if he attacked he could not delay the High Seas Fleet sufficiently to provoke a fleet action, turned away and presently received further orders to return to his base.[8] To the Commander-in-Chief he wrote privately two days later, more apologetically than was necessary:

> 'I am afraid we failed you on Saturday and I am kicking myself for not standing on for another hour instead of turning at 12.45 p.m. I imagine I should have sighted the enemy if I had. It will probably seem inexplicable to

> you, but I had not the slightest idea where you were ... I hope I was right in not making a night attack. I could have made one but I don't think I should have succeeded in doing any harm and should most certainly have been badly cut up as the night was not very dark. There was not time to make a detour to get ahead of them, especially with their Zeppelins in close attendance ... I was groping in the dark all day!"[9]

Jellicoe was convinced that the object of Scheer's operations had been to draw our fleet over submarines, and the loss of two light cruisers (a second had been torpedoed during his return to Scapa Flow) had strengthened his view that we should give up trying to bring the enemy to action every time he left harbour, in disregard of submarine and mine risks. He therefore proposed that in future the Grand Fleet should not go south of latitude 55°30′ (corresponding roughly to a line drawn from the Farne Islands to Horns Reef), unless there was a really good opportunity of bringing the High Seas Fleet to action in daylight, and that even if there was it should not operate to the east of longitude 4°E. or south of the Dogger Bank. This change of fleet policy was accepted by the Admiralty in September, and meant that the duty of defending the North Sea and the British coast south of the Tyne henceforth devolved more completely upon the local defence flotillas, the Humber and Harwich Forces, and the Third Battle Squadron (now commanded by Vice-Admiral de Robeck).

On the other side of the North Sea, however, a more or less corresponding change of plan had also taken place, for the pendulum of German policy had swung back again towards reliance on submarine warfare. The last sortie of the High Seas Fleet in force (apart from a final abortive one attempted in April 1918) took place on October 18, when in accordance with the new strategy the Grand Fleet was merely put at short notice for steam, though Tyrwhitt was ordered to take his force to sea and assemble to the west of the North

Hinder, where it waited expectantly until news was received that Scheer had returned to harbour.[10]

It must not be imagined, however, that the Harwich Force – or at any rate its commander – had any intention of allowing the initiative to rest with the enemy. For some time past Tyrwhitt had been pressing the plan, already referred to,[11] of a raid on the Schillig Roads by coastal motor-boats conveyed across the North Sea by the Force. The Admiralty nevertheless do not seem to have regarded this with favour. Some objection or another was always forthcoming, and eventually they stipulated that it was not to be attempted without a previous air reconnaissance, since there were rumours of a boom across the anchorage in the Roads. To carry out this reconnaissance it was proposed to use what were colloquially called 'Porte flying-boats' after Squadron-Commander J.C. Porte who commanded the Felixstowe Air Station.

An early pioneer of naval aviation, Porte had been invalided out of the Navy as a lieutenant in 1911 and had then devoted himself to the development of commercial aviation in both Britain and the United States. Returning to this country on the outbreak of war, he had rejoined the Royal Naval Air Service and had worked tirelessly to develop large flying-boats, disregarding the tuberculosis which led to his sudden death in 1919 at the age of 36. In his dedicated way, it has been justly said, he was as much one of the pathfinders of naval aviation as the better-known Samson or Longmore.[12]

Another specialist, but of a different kind, who was also engaged in preparing for this reconnaissance was Erskine Childers, an R.N.V.R. lieutenant who had taken part in the Cuxhaven raid of Christmas Day 1914. 'A quiet little man with the courage of a lion,'[13] as Domville has described him, Childers was the son of a Victorian First Lord of the Admiralty. He was also an ex-trooper of the Boer War, Clerk to the House of Commons, gun-runner and a yachtsman with a considerable knowledge of the German North Sea coast and the Frisian Islands. In 1903 he had published *The Riddle of the Sands*, one of the earliest, best written and most successful of the pre-war alarmist novels which had depicted a German attempt to invade Britain.[14]

After repeated postponement owing to bad weather the reconnaissance was carried out on October 29, two machines (with Childers in one of them) being got away from the carrier *Vindex*. Both returned safely, though they were chased back by German aircraft and the escort was shepherded on its return journey across the North Sea by two Zeppelins. The crews' report was disappointing, however, for they had met thick fog inshore and had not succeeded in locating any boom. Childers and his pilot had actually landed on the water inside the harbour and discussed the position, but had decided that there was nothing else they could do. No other chance of carrying out this reconnaissance occurred, and as the Bight was being gradually mined up, mostly by the Germans but also by the British in an attempt to seal in the U-boats, the attack on Schillig Roads never came off. Instead the C.M.B's, though unsuited for operating on the high seas, were presently employed on reconnaissance work inside the minefields, over which they could safely pass while other craft could not.[15]

It was at this time, too, that Tyrwhitt, who was one of the few naval commanders completely convinced of the value of aircraft accompanying the fleet, carried out some experiments in towing an R.N.A.S. Coastal airship behind a light cruiser, with the object of increasing its range. This was done successfully at 26 knots, and he went on to experiment with methods of refuelling and relieving aircrews. These also succeeded, the former by passing up petrol cans on the end of a line in the first place and later by means of pressurised fuel-hose, the latter by a bosun's chair from a height of 100 feet – and in rough weather at that. In view of these promising developments a special streamlined type of naval airship called the Zero was designed for work with the fleet, but the idea was eventually abandoned since it was felt that towed airships would make a fleet's whereabouts known to the enemy at too great a distance and would be too vulnerable to gunfire once the enemy were within range.[16]

By now the long-awaited *Centaur* had arrived at Harwich on September 11, having been collected from Swan and Hunter's yard on Tyneside by Domvile, who viewed with displeasure the novel arrangement by which all her guns were mounted on the centre line, since it gave him 'only one gun at the front or business end'. She arrived at Harwich with a 15% list which at first refused to right itself, but Tyrwhitt nevertheless insisted on turning over to her from the *Carysfort* next day. Soon afterwards her steering gear broke down when he went to sea in her and he transferred his pendant to the *Conquest*; but the defect was soon repaired and he returned on board, after which her teething troubles seem to have been over.[17] The dispersion of his ships and especially his destroyers to Dover and elsewhere continued, however; and his recovery of some of them from Admiral Bacon in August proved brief, for in October the Admiralty ordered him to reinforce the Dover Command with the *Carysfort* and four destroyers in addition to the four that were still there; and a few days later they instructed him to send the *Lightfoot* and another four as well. For some time after that the Harwich contingent detached to Dover stayed constant at one light cruiser, one or two flotilla leaders and twelve destroyers, though the actual vessels were continually being changed. These vessels were very hard-worked, in view of the Admiralty's and Bacon's well-founded anxiety lest German light forces might attempt to raid the several targets open to them in the Narrow Seas;[18] and Tyrwhitt grumbled in letters to both De Robeck (for whom he had an admiration that he did not feel for Bacon) and Keyes that the Vice-Admiral at Dover was driving them so hard that they were being knocked to pieces.[19] He was also ordered, late in December, to send the *Nimrod* and eight destroyers of the Tenth Flotilla to Dunkirk 'for service during the dark nights in the event of a raid'. These, however, were replaced by the

Grenville and eight other destroyers which were sent south from Scapa to assist in a large minesweeping operation on the Swarte Bank, after which Tyrwhitt was told by the Admiralty to keep them under his command for the time being. This left him with eight light cruisers, two leaders and ten or a dozen destroyers (whose number varied from day to day, since there were always some temporarily out of service because of defects).[20]

The mixed character of the Force that resulted from this reinforcement presently proved to have a disadvantage which showed itself during an operation in the new year, and was partly responsible for its lack of success. The senior officers who had come from the Grand Fleet had been trained under a more centralised *régime* and were inclined to a stricter obedience of orders and less given to the exercise of initiative than those who had been longer with Tyrwhitt. Like Beatty, 'Com. (T)' believed in imbuing his officers with his spirit and with an understanding of his general principles and then leaving them – or rather, expecting them – to act on their own interpretation of these principles in moments of uncertainty or crisis. Thus when a situation arose in which each of the newly-arrived captains had to decide for himself what to do, their judgments tended to differ.

On 22 January 1917 the Admiralty became aware through the usual media that an enemy destroyer flotilla would be leaving the German rivers for Zeebrugge that afternoon as a reinforcement almost certainly intended for operations against the Straits. The task of intercepting this reinforcement naturally fell to the Harwich Force. With five hours' steaming Tyrwhitt could get his cruisers and destroyers between the Schouwen Bank and the Maas, which the Germans would probably not pass until about midnight. At 11.40 a.m. therefore, he was ordered to 'intercept the enemy with destroyers' and to take his light cruisers to sea 'in support, to assist after daybreak'. At the same time Bacon was instructed to send six destroyers to Harwich without delay, as a result of which Tyrwhitt was able to put to sea at

5.30 with six light cruisers, two leaders and sixteen destroyers. As the enemy had the choice of either passing down the coast by the Maas and Schouwen Bank light vessels or making for Zeebrugge down the central part of the Flanders Bight past the North Hinder, Tyrwhitt's dispositions had to cover both possibilities. He therefore ordered his destroyers to take up patrolling stations in two detachments: the first, under the commanding officer of the *Grenville*, of the Maas; the second, under the commanding officer of the *Nimrod*, off the Schouwen Bank. The light cruisers were also divided into two detachments. The first, consisting of the *Centaur*, *Aurora* and *Conquest*, was to proceed to a patrol line about twenty-five miles east of the North Hinder; while the second, consisting of the *Penelope*, *Cleopatra* and *Undaunted*, was ordered to a line about ten miles to the westward of the first. Both lines, which were parallel to each other, ran roughly north-east and south-west. The weather was fine and clear but bitterly cold; in fact Tyrwhitt, Domvile and Tennant all recorded it independently as the coldest night they had ever known at sea. All the ships arrived on their patrol lines well before midnight, and for the next three hours they saw nothing, by which time their decks were coated with ice.

The German flotilla had chosen a route passing about midway between the North Hinder and the Maas, and at 2.45 a.m. it ran into the *Centaur*'s division. There was a brief exchange of fire, in which the *Centaur* was handicapped by the icy conditions, being unable to reload at first because the rammers were frozen into the tubs, so that she could only get off six rounds in ten minutes. Tyrwhitt, after swerving to avoid a torpedo which just missed his flagship, then tried to head off the Germans to the north-eastward, but the flotilla managed to escape under a heavy smoke-screen and resumed its course for Zeebrugge. It was not unscathed, however, for the *V69*, struck by a shell, was rammed by the *G41* and both were so badly damaged that they could only limp slowly away, though Tyrwhitt remained unaware of this. Meanwhile it was evident to the other patrols from the flashes of the guns that the Commodore was engaged; and shortly after three they received a signal from him giving the enemy's position and course, followed by another informing them that the enemy had scattered. Neither signal, however, was accompanied by any order, either to close the scene of action or to remain on their patrolling stations. Commander Dundas in the *Grenville* had no doubts that on the news received his duty was to stay on the patrol line, and made a signal to his destroyers to close him, which two of them obeyed; while the other two, not having taken in this signal, made off to the northward to cut the enemy off from the Bight. The captain of the *Nimrod*, whose destroyers were patrolling on two lines, made off to the north-eastward with one line for the same purpose while the other line kept its station to the west of the Schouwen Bank. Captain Lynes of the *Penelope* promptly took his detachment eastward towards the sound of the guns.

The result was that practically all the British forces lost their cohesion and their original dispositions were broken up. Although when the Commodore realised this he ordered the destroyers back to their assigned positions, the bulk of the German flotilla was able to pass through them without further mishap, steering a course that took them between the *Nimrod*'s and the *Centaur*'s patrol lines and passing the Schouwen Bank Light Vessel about 3.53 unobserved by the four destroyers which were still patrolling near it. The damaged *V69* encountered the *Penelope*'s division, however, and the three cruisers switched on their searchlights and plastered her with shell at close range. Convinced that they had sunk her, they then switched them off again too quickly for this to be checked, and by some miracle she survived and struggled into Ymuiden, where she was ultimately not even interned, since the British could not prove that she had put in to escape pursuit by their ships. The other damaged straggler, *G41*, managed to reach the Dutch coast and steam along it to Zeebrugge. 'A little later [than the *V69*'s miraculous escape]', recorded Domvile, 'a most terrific explosion reddened the lovely starlit sky far away to the southward.' Another German destroyer, which though undamaged had lost touch with her flotilla, had stumbled across the *Simoom*, one of the *Nimrod*'s detachment, and got a torpedo home on her which blew up her magazine, after which the German turned sharply eastward and escaped back into the Bight. The *Morris* took off the *Simoom*'s survivors, though she remained afloat till morning, when Tyrwhitt ordered the *Nimrod* to sink her. Her Commander, Inman, who was killed by the explosion ('a splendid man and a great friend of mine', wrote Tyrwhitt), had already been torpedoed almost at the same spot in the *Meteor* in October 1915, though on that occasion he had managed to make port. The Commodore now wound up the operation as quickly as he could, though the mishaps were not yet over, for on the way back to harbour the *Undaunted* burst a gun on discharge, through the bore being iced up, and lost two men killed and several wounded.[21]

The results of the night's work were most disappointing. In spite of advance warning of the enemy's movements and great superiority in strength the Harwich Force had failed to prevent the enemy from not only getting past but inflicting in passing more damage than they received. Basically the failure was due to the hazards then inseparable from a night action. 'The results were not very fruitful,' wrote Tyrwhitt to his sister Polly, 'but they never will be from night fighting.' But he himself had been at fault in leaving his senior officers without guidance on what proved to be the main problem of the night's work – whether to act independently or to remain on their stations and wait for further orders – and in his report he explicitly justified Commander Dundas for doing the latter. Nevertheless things might have gone better if the Force had possessed its usual homogeneity and uniformity of principles. According to the same letter from Tyrwhitt to his sister, he was strongly criticized for this failure by Lord Curzon in the small War Cabinet recently formed by the new Prime Minister Lloyd George, but was immediately championed in the same body by Balfour with equal force; and on the following day Jellicoe, now First Sea Lord (who told Tyrwhitt of this himself when he visited the Admiralty on January 26), seized the opportunity of one of his now frequent attendances at the War Cabinet to take up the cudgels on Tyrwhitt's behalf and silence criticism.[22]

When Jellicoe had been transferred at the end of November 1916 from the command of the Grand Fleet to the Admiralty, Beatty had succeeded him as Commander-in-Chief. Other changes had included the transfer of Vice-Admiral de Robeck (to Tyrwhitt's regret) from the Third Battle Squadron at Sheerness to the command of a battle squadron at Scapa. In the political field, Balfour had been replaced as First Lord by Sir Edward Carson, with whom Tyrwhitt had a long interview during the visit just referred to, and of whom he reported:[23]

> 'He has a brogue that you can *see*. I always thought Elias and Co.[24] were not deficient, but theirs is a lisp compared to Sir E.C's. He was very pleasant and told me that he knew nothing about his job and wanted to know more.'[25]

To Beatty he paid two visits at Rosyth at his request, soon after the new Commander-in-Chief's appointment. The first of these however, in mid-January, was spoilt by Beatty being suddenly required to put to sea on what proved an abortive mission before he had had an opportunity to talk to his visitor.

> 'There were many things of the greatest importance [he wrote apologetically afterwards] I was anxious to discuss with you. Indeed, I could talk to you for a week on some of them. But I'll ... ask you to consider the feasibility when the weather is suitable of an operation or series of operations on the enemy's coast ... When we have stirred them up in the past we have always fetched something out, but have invariably gone away *too*

> *soon*. Stir them up one day and be there the next, when they have really woken up, is my theory, and stir them up in more places than one *at the same time* is my idea. What do you think?
>
> Your Zeebrugge scheme I return. I am not very well qualified to give an opinion, but I am all for doing something and we must use our imagination, and for that reason I like it ... We must keep them busy ...
>
> The time of the year is against us just now, but we must be prepared for a generally more active development when the spring comes... But if anything is to be gained I am ready *now*. Let me know what you think. Any ideas are very welcome, the wilder the better. One can always tame them down. What we lack is imagination.'[26]

On his second and more satisfactory visit in mid-February Tyrwhitt found that Beatty had heard poor reports of the morale of the crews of the Harwich submarines, which was said to be low owing to their heavy losses. These reports he vigorously rebutted, though he admitted that the losses had been severe, 'because the Harwich submarines have done all the work in the Bight'. To Keyes he wrote apropos of this:

> 'The Harwich submarine losses nearly all occurred in the Bight. That was the fault of the Admiralty, who kept up that patrol long after it became a great danger [i.e., as a result of German mine-laying]. Now they only wander up and down outside the mined area;'

adding admiringly of Beatty:

> 'D.B. was splendid... he impresses me more every time I meet him. He has a wonderful grasp of the situation and absolutely fills me with confidence and hope of the future.'[27]

After a third visit early in June he wrote:

> 'It fills me with admiration the way he has captivated everybody and the absolute faith that everybody has in him. There's no doubt that he is the right man in the right place.'

On this occasion Carson also came up to Rosyth and during his stay had 'a long-heart to-heart talk' with Tyrwhitt, in which 'he was awfully nice and said all sorts of things which were quite undeserved', though it was presumably the less personal part of their conversation which made Tyrwhitt feel 'thankful that we have such a good man at the head of affairs'.[28, 29]

Beatty's allusion, in his letter quoted above, to Tyrwhitt's 'Zeebrugge scheme' referred to a matter that was now much in the minds of the British higher command – the vexed question of whether, and if so how, the Belgian coast ports and Zeebrugge in particular could be attacked in such a way as to destroy their usefulness, and also that of Bruges, as advanced bases for submarines and destroyers. Bruges, about eight miles from the sea, was in fact the real base, Zeebrugge and Ostend being only exits from it, though if they could be effectively blocked this would seal Bruges up. To all appearances they were almost invulnerable, but there was one relatively weak spot – the lock at Zeebrugge, whose destruction would practically put an end to communication by water between it and Bruges. Even to block it would cause a useful though temporary interruption, and Admiral Bayly had suggested a blocking operation in the autumn of 1914 and again two years later without any notice being taken of his suggestion. The idea had only been discussed for the first time when Tyrwhitt renewed it on 25 November 1916 with a proposal to put the lock out of action by sinking a ship in it under cover of a smoke-screen, a gas attack and gunfire.

When he found, at a conference with Admirals Jellicoe, Bacon and Oliver in the autumn of 1916, that this was not favourably received,[30] Tyrwhitt submitted another and somewhat more comprehensive plan for capturing the mole and the town beyond, which he suggested should then be made the starting-point for a military expedition against Antwerp. Bacon, however, criticised this strongly as impracticable. He did not believe that parties landed on the mole and elsewhere could penetrate as far as the locks, much less carry the town. As for a military expedition against Antwerp, the military authorities, so far as he knew, would neither approve of it nor undertake it. He himself preferred, and was authorised, to plan a bombardment of Zeebrugge, even though this would have to be carried out at long range and for a limited time only, in view of the powerful coastal artillery by which the place was protected. The operation also needed conditions of wind and weather which prevailed only at rare and irregular intervals, so that it was postponed several times before eventually being carried out on May 12. The Harwich contingent lent to the Dover Patrol took part in it, the *Lightfoot* with a group of destroyers cruising near the Thornton Banks ready to act as a covering force if the enemy's destroyers tried to interfere, while the *Nimrod* with four others zigzagged round the bombarding squadron as a submarine screen. But although nearly twenty shells almost hit the locks, none actually did so; and though it was at first thought that the bombardment had had a measure of success, it was really a failure.[31]

Before this had been realised, Bacon followed it up by a bombardment of Ostend dockyard for which Tyrwhitt's whole command turned out to provide the covering force. At 9 p.m. on June 4 he left Harwich and headed for Thornton Bank with four light cruisers (*Centaur*, *Concord* – a new arrival which was his reserve flagship and to which he shifted his pendant when *Centaur* went to refit – *Canterbury* and *Conquest*), together with *Lightfoot* and eight destroyers. Half an hour later he was followed by *Undaunted*, *Cleopatra*, *Aurora*, *Penelope* and eight more destroyers, whose orders were to guard against enemy interference from the neighbourhood of the Schouwen Bank. After reaching his station at 2.15 a.m. he began his patrol on a south-westerly course. Just after half-past two, when he was about half-way between the Bligh and Thornton Banks, he sighted two destroyers ahead which he at first took to be part of Admiral Bacon's forces; but almost immediately they opened fire, which he returned after turning away about four points to starboard to get his whole broadside to bear. After sustaining the concentrated fire of the whole squadron for a few minutes the Germans fled for Zeebrugge; but one, *S20*, was already badly damaged and lagging behind. Ordering Commander Hodgson to pursue them with his division, Tyrwhitt then resumed his patrol with the light cruisers and the remaining division. The Germans made a smoke-screen which concealed them for a few minutes, but the crippled *S20* was soon overhauled and sunk by the *Satyr*, which picked up nine survivors. The *Taurus*, the leading British destroyer, chased the other fugitive until she had brought the range down to 5,000 yards, scoring a number of hits; but by that time the shore batteries had opened up on Hodgson's division and Tyrwhitt recalled it to rejoin him in his covering duties. The British had suffered no damage or casualties in this engagement, and the bombardment of Ostend did sufficient damage to make it likely that if it could have been repeated often the enemy's sorties from the Flanders bases would have been very much hampered. Unfortunately the great difficulties of the operation made this impossible.[32]

'1917 was a busy year,' wrote Domvile afterwards. The Harwich command continued to have more frequent contact with the enemy than any other British force except the Dover Patrol. It was still hoped that it would be able to join forces with the Grand Fleet if events pointed to a meeting with the High Seas Fleet. It carried out most of the reconnaissance work in the southern part of the North Sea and into the Bight, in whose outer waters to the seaward of the minefields laid by both sides it was constantly operating, though it could no longer come so close to the German coast as in the early days of the war. Its objects here, besides providing as before the covering force for any aerial operations carried out from seaplane-carriers, were: to intercept any German light forces which might be intending to operate off our coasts or might be on passage between German ports; to surprise and attack enemy minesweepers and support our minelayers – which involved leaving Harwich in the evening, steaming northward all night until to westward of the minefield being laid, and patrolling until the minelayers were sighted leaving in the morning; to attempt to destroy Zeppelins which might be engaged on reconnaissance or raiding work; and to capture enemy merchant ships trading between Dutch and German ports, or neutrals trading in contraband with Germany. At Harwich it was also well placed to attack Zeppelins at sea on their return from raids over England; and it continued to cover the passage of the Dutch Convoy and to be constantly called on to provide reinforcements for the Dover Patrol or to assist in its operations.[33]

The duty of protecting the Dutch Convoy imposed a heavy strain. Since the route was only eighty miles long and the water was shallow all the way it was very easy for the Germans to lay mines in it or to attack with submarines, and it was practically impossible to keep the times of sailing from the Hook secret from them, though they were now varied as much as possible. In March the new destroyer *Skate*, to which Hamilton had just been appointed, was torpedoed off the Maas barely three weeks after her arrival at Harwich. The explosion left nothing of her abaft the after gun, but her crew were taken off and she was taken in tow by the *Nimrod* for a time, after which the crew returned to her and she managed to make port under her own steam. 'The chief engineer', Hamilton recorded, 'the most delightfully vague person I know, was reading a book on his bunk [when she was hit] and didn't even get up as he thought it was someone blowing up a mine.'[34] In December a disaster occurred. The Germans had laid lines of floating mines twenty yards apart secured together by wires near the Maas Buoy off the Hook, with the result that three out of four in a division of brand new destroyers – the *Surprise*, *Tornado* and *Torrent* – were sunk with a loss of twelve officers and about 240 men. The catastrophe had some features in common with the *Cressy-Hogue-Aboukir* disaster more than three years before, in that when the first vessel struck a mine a second went to her aid, only to be blown up herself, after which the third met a similar fate while she was trying to rescue the crews of the other two. The captain of the surviving ship, the *Radiant*, Commander G.F.S. Nash, undeterred by the terrible danger, thereupon steamed to the spot where the survivors were struggling in the icy water, lowered his boats and was able to save many lives. Several of his officers and men jumped overboard to save those who were drowning. Even so, hardly a quarter of the crews of the three ships survived; but none at all would have been saved but for the coolness and gallantry of the *Radiant*'s captain and ship's company. That their ship ever got clear without also coming to grief was a miracle, since when the chart of the German minefields was handed over after the Armistice it was discovered that more than 400 mines had been laid in this locality. The *Valkyrie*, a new large flotilla leader, was also mined on this occasion, but was towed safely to harbour with a broken back.[35]

After this Tyrwhitt made a point of invariably going himself to escort the traffic; and the convoys, which latterly had reverted to night crossings, were again taken across during the day. The Germans then laid a minefield in the way and the route had to be swept regularly in front of the convoys, which slowed them down. In all, during the year 1917 520 eastbound and 511 westbound vessels were convoyed with the loss of only four ships by submarine attack, one by destroyer attack, and one by a mine. The price paid for this success was the loss of four destroyers by mines and one by collision, and the damage of three destroyers and a flotilla leader by mine or torpedo and of five destroyers and a light cruiser by collision; the frequent collisions being due to the conditions under which the traffic was carried out at night without lights for part of the time and to the prevalence of fogs. At the end of the year, indeed, five light cruisers were undergoing dockyard repairs owing to collisions or engine trouble, leaving only three operational.[36]

In April the Admiralty had received news that German merchant shipping was showing signs of life after three years of complete inactivity. A small coasting trade had begun between the Bight and Rotterdam, and Tyrwhitt was directed to prepare plans for stopping it. Thinking that it would be unwise to keep a large intercepting force off the Dutch coast, he first tried to stop the traffic by means of submarines. Four 'E' class boats were stationed along the coast of Holland and a destroyer force held in support out of sight of land; but the first attempt on these lines made in June was unsuccessful. One Dutch steamer was stopped by *E47* and then released, and nothing else was sighted. Shortly after the force had returned to harbour the Admiralty learnt from Holland that four German steamers had left Rotterdam on the 23rd, escorted by a torpedo-boat, and that others would follow. Tyrwhitt therefore again ordered out four submarines and two divisions of destroyers, but this time nothing was seen at all. He then decided to alter his plans. Assuming that the enemy must know that he was attempting to stop the traffic and were therefore being very cautious, he concluded that their most natural plan would be to have their ships sail from Rotterdam on the nights when the Dutch trade was being escorted across to England, since they would probably expect that the bulk of the available Harwich Force would be engaged in this. As the Force was at full strength at the moment, however, he arranged that a large part of it should be assembled and ready to act on those very nights.

The new plan worked. On July 15 he received information that German ships would leave Rotterdam during the night, and accordingly sailed that evening with all eight of his light cruisers, two flotilla leaders and fifteen destroyers. About 4.30 next morning six enemy merchantmen were sighted off the Camperdowns steaming in formation, and were chased by the *Undaunted* and some destroyers in disregard of neutral Dutch waters. Two beached themselves and were destroyed by gunfire, and the rest were taken, though some of the shots fired to heave them to fell in an internment camp for Germans on land. This violation of Dutch neutrality worried Tyrwhitt a little. 'We certainly were a bit Hunnish,' he wrote to both Keyes and his sister Polly, but made clear to both that he would be prepared to do it again. The success of the stroke, however, was only temporary. Impressed, as Tyrwhitt had calculated that they would be, by the size of the force employed, the Germans suspended the traffic for a time; but in August news came through that they had resumed it, after which a light cruiser and four destroyers were sent out each day to intercept it, and numbers of their merchantmen were brought in.[37]

It was shortly after this that Tyrwhitt's new flagship became a casualty. On October 24 he was informed that some enemy destroyers were about to make a dash from Zeebrugge to Germany, and went out with 'the four Cs', as they were called (*Centaur*, *Concord*, *Carysfort* and *Canterbury*), a flotilla leader and four destroyers, in what proved a vain attempt to stop them. The odds were against him, since at that time of year the enemy could make nearly the whole journey in the dark, when the range of vision was approximately one mile. After his force had 'toiled all night and caught nothing' (as Tennant put it) it turned homewards in the teeth of a south-west gale which presently rose to hurricane force. The *Centaur* had been reduced to about three knots when her depth-charges were washed overboard and exploded with a force that at first created the impression that she had struck a mine. To quote Domvile's account:

> 'About noon there was a terrific explosion and the ship quivered and shook as if in her death-agony, and the fore-topmast came down with a crash. I must admit that for a brief moment I thought we were for it, as there

> would have been no chance of saving anyone in the weather prevailing ... When I reached the scene I found many compartments flooded, but fortunately the rudder still worked and two of our four propellers were functioning ... We had an anxious twelve hours [but] ... eventually we made harbour about midnight and I never reached the familiar old spot more thankfully.'

The *Concord* then became the flagship for a time.[38]

The gradually increasing size of the Force, which by the end of 1917 comprised nine light cruisers, four flotilla leaders and twenty-four destroyers, meant that in at least the newly-commissioned ships which arrived from time to time, and indeed in all, there was an adulteration of personnel. The experienced and trained men had to be spread more thinly; and the intervals between the various operations just described were seized on, as Tennant – who had returned to Harwich in the *Concord* after two years with the Grand Fleet – put it, 'for instilling a little seamanship and gunnery into our Crystal Palace sailors and boys who began to form an alarmingly large proportion of the ship's companies – the older hands being continually withdrawn for new construction'.[39]

These exercises, and indeed what may be called the home life of the Force, were occasionally disturbed by Zeppelin or in one or two cases aeroplane raids. 'Air raids were frequent', grumbled Domvile, 'and my poor wife had many bombs round our house. Every German with a bomb left seemed to drop it on Felixstowe on his way home.'[40] In June orders were given that the anti-aircraft guns were to be manned daily in harbour from an hour before sunrise to 6 a.m., but it was a little after seven o'clock in the morning when on July 4 twelve German aeroplanes attacked the air station and the ships, scoring some hits and causing some Service casualties. Bombs also fell in Harwich, Dovercourt and Felixstowe – though apparently without injuring any civilians – and must have put Mrs. Tyrwhitt and Mrs. Domvile (as well, no doubt, as many others) in a position to exchange bomb stories.

> 'The Huns rained bombs here yesterday [wrote Tyrwhitt to Polly] and did remarkably little damage, although there were some casualties ... Angey and Co. had a very narrow escape. Two bombs fell in Packard's yard next door, which blew off the roof of the cowshed just after sixty-odd cows had been milked [some of them possibly by the thirteen-year-old Bobby, who was learning to milk as her contribution to the war effort], ruined a small orchard and damaged everything within a radius of fifty yards. Nearly all our windows are broken, but not our spirits. The kids are frightfully pleased with the whole show and want more.[41] The maids are rather upset.'[42]

Honours and decorations had now begun to crowd upon Tyrwhitt. On 3 June, 1916, he had been awarded the D.S.O. in the birthday honours (as Watson was in the following year). In April 1917 he was appointed a naval aide-de-camp to the King; and on July 15 the honour of knighthood was bestowed on him. This was only the second time in history that it had been given to a post-captain, which was still Tyrwhitt's substantive rank; the previous occasion being 78 years earlier. Allied decorations followed in September, when he was made a Commander of the French Legion of Honour and awarded the Italian Military Order of the House of Savoy.[43]

From time to time visitors from the world outside the Navy made their appearance at Harwich. One such was the Hon. and Rev. Leonard Tyrwhitt of the Staffordshire branch of the family, whom he had not previously met and who was a younger brother of the Commodore's kinsman Sir Raymond and of the Hon. Hugh (now dead) who had been his captain in the *Surprise* in 1896–8. Besides (or despite) being a canon of Windsor and Vicar of Rolleston the Rev. Leonard was an army chaplain who had spent a long time on the Western Front, where he had been wounded and to which after his recovery he was about to return. He came down to Nether Hall for a night in November 1916, accompanied by his sister Hester whom the Commodore described as 'very Tyrwhitty and possessed of all the Tyrwhitt traits'. He and his wife took to both of them immediately and all four were spending a hilarious evening roaring with laughter over the family failings and characteristics when in the middle of dinner he received orders to put to sea. Since his cousin declared that the one wish of his heart was to see a naval engagement he took him with him, and to Leonard's great delight when they were off the Schouwen Bank with six light cruisers they sighted five German destroyers approaching from Zeebrugge. These turned and fled, throwing out a heavy smoke-screen, but not before the *Centaur* had opened fire and straddled them at 9000 yards. 'He thoroughly enjoyed his outing', wrote Tyrwhitt: 'I liked him very much. He's very much a man of the world and a very good parson into the bargain. I should imagine he is also a very fine character.'[44] In July 1917 Domvile also produced an ecclesiastical cousin, none other than the Bishop of London, Dr. Winnington Ingram, who came to stay a few days with him and his wife at Felixstowe and won all hearts. 'I have never met such a charming man,' wrote Tyrwhitt.[45]

A visitor who came in the course of his professional work, in the following September, was Colonel à Court Repington, the famous war correspondent of the Times.[46] In his diary he wrote:

> 'Tyrwhitt met me at the station. A very attractive figure ... We went aboard the *Centaur* ... and had lunch. I went all round the ship with the flag-lieutenant. She lies at the head of the line of light cruisers nearest to the open sea. A long talk with the Commodore alone after lunch over the charts of the North Sea. Then we went on to the Porte flying-boat yards, and saw these new aircraft

put out and come home. Tyrwhitt took me back to the station ... T. is under the orders of the Admiralty directly, but he has a working agreement to act under Beatty if they are out together, and he and Bacon of the Dover Patrol help each other ... There is a flotilla of submarines in Harwich Harbour not under T., but they again work together ... Roughly Tyrwhitt's domain extends from latitude 54°30'N. to about 51°30', right across the North Sea to the Dutch, German and Danish coasts. He has nine light cruisers and twenty-four destroyers ... Usually one light cruiser and a couple of destroyers ... are under repair ... In Tyrwhitt's cabin there hangs a small board on which is shown, by little brass labels which ... hang on hooks, the position of each vessel under him ... It is 'form at a glance', as T. says, and the exact situation of the whole command can be seen in a moment ... Tyrwhitt showed me the North Sea charts on which are marked the positions of the German and British minefields, so far as they are known. There are two large German minefields off Harwich, in the region of the Galloper light and to north of it, and various channels through or round these are kept open by our minesweepers. There is also the long main channel, N. and S., suitable for all craft, which is kept open all up the E. coast.[47] All these are swept every day, but three times a week the Germans mine them with their submarines and shortly after I came on board the *Centaur* one of the mine-sweepers returned with the survivors of another that had been blown up. These German minefields are not, however, the main obstacle to the activity of our light cruisers and destroyers in the North Sea. The real obstacles are our own minefields, which extend in a semi-circle across the German North Sea shores, from about Blaavand Point in N. latitude 55°30' off the coast of Jutland to the Dutch territorial waters off the coast near the Texel ... Thus Tyrwhitt can no longer get into the Bight of Heligoland, and moreover our ships escorting or towing the new Porte flying-boats cannot escort them or take them within 120 miles of the German ports and towns overdue to be bombed. These minefields no doubt obstruct the German Navy too ... but the Germans can sweep channels if they like and the main object, the barring of the road to the submarines, has wholly failed in its purpose.

I said that these minefields seemed to me antagonistic to the principles of Nelson, who always gave every opportunity to the enemy to put to sea, because it was there he 'expected to realise the hopes and expectations of his country' ... T. said that that was the position, and he could not be off the German coasts with his light craft because he could not now get there. In fact his instructions to his officers were that he did not expect them to cross the line of the mined area, leaving it thus open to them to take the risk if the occasion warranted it, but covering them if they did not. He knew that the public thought he was always off the German coasts, but he was not, for the reasons stated, and he could not range beyond Terschelling ... The *Centaur* was as spick and span as the *Queen Elizabeth* and the same light-grey colour. So smart does she look that when some American sailors came on board the other day they said 'I suppose you never go out of harbour!' ...

I asked Tyrwhitt about his formations when cruising. Line ahead, he said, gave the submarines too good a target by day, so he usually moved in certain formations which he explained to me ...

For Tyrwhitt the Zepp is finished. He prefers the Porte flying-ships, which have a range of 600 miles, to take five men, and can drop 1000 lbs. of explosives. This is for the large Porte with, I think, 230 feet spread tip to tip and weighing five tons. The smaller sort is only eighty feet[48] ... Harwich and its surroundings have been constantly bombed, but no real damage has been done

> and the great sheds are untouched. It is probable that the Archies [anti-aircraft guns] ashore and on the cruisers make the Huns wary ... One of his officers told me that T. never leaves the bridge while at sea and spoke with enthusiasm of him, adding that he was a bit of a tartar. The demeanour of all who came to him to report showed that they knew who was the master of the Harwich Forces.'[49]

Repington moved constantly in high society and had talked to many or most of the great figures of the western world, but this part of his diary leaves a distinct impression that he had not only had a breath of sea air but knew that he had met someone out of the common run.

CHAPTER SEVEN

THE END CROWNS THE WORK

During the latter part of 1917 Tyrwhitt suffered some embarrassment through the indiscretions of Commander Carlyon Bellairs, M.P., who several times voiced publicly the idea that because of his outstanding services he ought to be specially promoted to flag rank over the heads of all those senior to him on the captains' list. In an article in *Truth* in July, applauding his being made a K.C.B., Bellairs attacked the anomaly that whereas a junior officer could be promoted for meritorious service a captain, however distinguished, could only move slowly on in his proper place in the procession. 'At the normal rate of progress', he wrote, 'Commodore T. will become a Rear-Admiral in October 1919, and nothing on earth save a cataclysm or a change in the regulations can accelerate his advance.' In another article in October, castigating the defensive spirit which he claimed ruled at the Admiralty, he became more demanding, declaring that 'Sir Reginald Tyrwhitt must not wait until over fifty captains senior to him have been promoted to rear-admiral;' and in the House of Commons at about the same time, while announcing that he would not mention any names, he complained that the captain who, as far as he could find out, was the greatest strategic genius in the Navy would not get his promotion until 1920. Tyrwhitt, personally embarrassed and also offended by Bellairs's transgression of the unwritten law that the internal concerns of the Service should not be discussed in Parliament by serving officers, sent him the following curt note –

'I should be grateful if in future you will refrain from

> taking a personal interest in my professional career. I am perfectly content to leave my advancement, etc., in the hands of my superior officers, who have risen by merit to the positions they hold in the Admiralty.'

This 'stinging rebuke to a too intrusive advocate' (to quote a leader on the subject in the *Morning Post*) Commander Bellairs at Tyrwhitt's request read in the House in the course of making a full and ample apology.[1]

Nevertheless, whether or not it owed anything to Bellairs's advocacy, the unprecedented step was taken less than three months later, and on 14 January 1918 Tyrwhitt was promoted Acting Rear-Admiral over forty-eight captains. For a moment he was inclined to regard this signal honour with mixed feelings, for in three and a half years of war his previous rank had become, especially in its shortened form of 'Com. T.,' an affectionate and admiring nickname, famous throughout the Navy. There were many rear-admirals, but there was only one 'Com. T.'; he was unique. Another consideration, though perhaps a secondary one, was that as an admiral he would, according to precedent, have to give up his post of aide-de-camp to the King, of which he was very proud. However he took advantage of a visit by His Majesty to Harwich soon afterwards to broach the subject, whereupon the King insisted that he must retain the post, saying with royal tact that he would be proud to have an admiral among his A.D.Cs.[2]

Meanwhile the waiting policy to which the main fleets of both sides were committed continued to have no effect on the activities of the forces in southern waters, where the alternation of attack and *riposte* went on without interruption. On the very day of Tyrwhitt's promotion a force of German destroyers made a flying raid on Yarmouth. Tyrwhitt put to sea to intercept them within an hour and a half of their first shells falling on the town; but they had already retired and his forces saw nothing of them, returning to harbour at noon next day.

The next fortnight proved a very energetic time. The flagship first had two 'beef trips' in three days, followed by a minelaying excursion to the Bight, the return from which through fog was very difficult. Four days after that the Admiralty, convinced that the Germans were at sea, bundled the Force out, but the fog came down again so thick that it had to anchor in the channel abreast of Felixstowe in a long line stretching right back into the harbour. This check mattered little, since the Germans had not in fact come out. But the Admiralty continued, as Tennant grumbled, to lead the Force 'the dickens of a life, frequently sending them to look for or intercept German destroyers which never materialised'. Concern was caused also by a proposal to remove the North Hinder Light Vessel on the ground that it was too helpful to U-boats laying mines off Harwich or making for the Channel. This was met by a protest that it was also very useful to British vessels returning at night or in thick weather, which used to check their position by the North Hinder and then shape a course in through the minefields to Orford Ness.[3]

On February 20 the Admiral's final flagship arrived from Pembroke dockyard – the *Curaçoa*, 'a fine little ship' according to Domvile, who may have been inclined to look with some retrospective favour on her since she was to be his own first flagship fourteen years later. Tyrwhitt, however, also considered her 'a great improvement even on *Centaur*', and hoisted his flag in her on the 21st, just in time for the King's visit.[4]

At this time his health was beginning to trouble him a little again. Despite his robust physique the unsparing demands which he made upon it were not without their effect, and the indigestion and internal pains from which he had suffered early in the war do not seem to have completely cleared away. In May 1917, suspecting that he might be suffering from incipient appendicitis, he had consulted an eminent specialist, Sir Alfred Fripp, who gave him a very thorough examination followed by a reassuring report.[5] Fripp had afterwards become a great friend of his and had developed the habit of occasionally running down to Harwich, staying overnight for a brief rest and change, and sometimes giving him a check-up. In the early part of 1918 he felt somewhat unwell again, and his face took on what his anxious wife described as 'that horrid strained look that used to worry me so'.[6] On March 4 he was sent for by the First Lord and ordered to take three weeks' leave, during which he was to forget the war and keep as far away as possible from any ship. On the 13th he handed over temporary command to Captain St. John and left with Lady Tyrwhitt to stay with some friends near Kelso. Here he fished the Tweed all day and every day and returned to take over again on April 3, declaring himself as fit as a fiddle, though Lieutenant-Commander Watson thought he still did not seem completely recovered.[7]

He was, however, anxious to get back, all the more so since the great German spring offensive of 1918 had begun on March 21. This had been anticipated for some time beforehand (though its magnitude and where it would fall had not been foreseen); and though it was doubtful whether it would be accompanied by any naval moves in the North Sea the flag officers in the southern area had felt it advisable to take special precautions against renewed raids on the Channel. Before his departure, therefore, Tyrwhitt had ordered a striking force of two light cruisers and five destroyers to be maintained on patrol by relays in the centre of the Flanders Bight. But apart from a short and fruitless coastal raid by destroyers on March 20–21, which did not involve any elements of the Harwich Force, the Germans made no particular attempt to second their land offensive by operations at sea.[8]

On the British side, however, further aerial reconnaissances were made in the neighbourhood of Heligoland Bight. By now the Bight itself was so thoroughly mined that it was only at considerable risk that any British vessel could approach within a hundred miles of it, so that emphasis had shifted back again to the air as the only feasible medium of attack and of preliminary reconnaissance. For these purposes large barges cut away aft and capable of being sunk till they were half awash were built, to carry large seaplanes when towed by destroyers. The first operation in which these were used was carried out in Tyrwhitt's absence by the Harwich Force on March 19, when a strong force of light cruisers with destroyers towing six of these barges arrived off Terschelling at daybreak. It proved difficult to get the seaplanes' engines warmed up and running after a cold and wet night's journey across the North Sea, but this was eventually achieved and the planes made a reconnaissance. A second similar expedition followed soon afterwards.[9]

By now Keyes had returned from the Mediterranean, received his promotion to flag rank, and after a short period of service in the Grand Fleet and another at the Admiralty in charge of the Plans Division had replaced Admiral Bacon in command at Dover. Months earlier Tyrwhitt had written to him: 'How I wish they would put you at Dover! Then we could get going at Zeebrugge in earnest. I have a lovely scheme which I submitted but it has been received with stony silence.'[10] Keyes, however, had not even seen Tyrwhitt's plan when he worked out in conjunction with Captain Dudley Pound the Director of the Operations Division the more elaborate one for simultaneous attacks on Zeebrugge and Ostend which he put into operation on April 23. Nevertheless the fact that the main features of this so far as Zeebrugge was concerned were a blocking operation and an assault on the mole such as Tyrwhitt had proposed led shortly after the war to statements, embarrassing to both men, which found their way into print that his plan had been based on Tyrwhitt's or even merely taken over from him. The relationship of the two schemes, however, is placed beyond doubt by a letter of February 1919 from the latter to Keyes:

> 'I must confess that I feel very small when I compare my effort with yours, as it is so very incomplete; but as

> I said before it was only an outline and would probably have been improved on if it had met with Their Lordships' favour and sanction. It pleases me all the more ... that our ideas were so much in common, and I think I can truly add they always have been.'[11]

In the actual enterprise, which after two postponements was carried out on April 23rd (St. George's Day), the Harwich Force played only the limited role of an outer guard; for which purpose Tyrwhitt patrolled the approaches to the Flanders Bight with seven light cruisers, two flotilla leaders and fourteen destroyers.[12]

Seaplane operations now came into fashion again, as Watson (who was promoted Commander in June) put it, but the weather frustrated three attempts that were made within as many weeks in May. During that month the *Concord* established her record since her commissioning in 1916 by steaming 5000 miles, merely in the course of the normal variety of tasks – patrolling at night off Ymuiden in the hope of catching German destroyers, supporting minelayers, escorting seaplanes and dashing suddenly to sea after reported enemy vessels. On the 31st, the second anniversary of Jutland, a great effort was made to lure the High Seas Fleet out to its destruction. The Grand Fleet cruised off the minefields of the Bight while the Harwich Force, acting as the bait in the trap, went right in through them, after which the light cruisers patrolled inside them while the destroyers went on further to positions off Borkum and Heligoland. But nothing was sighted, while on the other hand one destroyer, the *Shakespeare*, was mined; though the *Centaur* took her in tow and got her home. After that the Harwich Force retired on the Grand Fleet and waited for some hours more to see what it might have put up, but still nothing appeared.[13]

Nevertheless this penetration of the Bight seems to have encouraged the idea at the Admiralty that the Force might be called on to repeat it for a different purpose. The Germans had made one of their several changes of signal-code and for the time being their signals could no longer be decoded. A scheme was therefore evolved and put into operation from June 10 by which the Harwich Striking Force was to make nightly sweeps through the minefields into the Bight and try to intercept a German patrol from which a signal-book might be captured. As Domvile put it, somewhat differently:

> 'We had one or two rather mad expeditions into the Heligoland Bight in which we were very thankful for our paravanes,[14] as we were constantly cutting mines, mostly our own. I cursed the genius at the Admiralty who first mined the Bight and then sent us into our own minefields.'[15]

It was, however, just off the Sunk, outside Harwich, that the *Conquest* was mined on June 13. Fortunately the *Curaçoa* was exercising not far away and was able to tow the damaged vessel round to Sheerness. But next day the *Centaur* was mined in the Bight 'on one of the fool expeditions', to quote the exasperated Domville again. The *Canterbury* took her in tow but later cast off and escorted her while she steamed stern-first 250 miles across the North Sea and after twenty-four hours got safely into the Humber. During the latter part of her painful passage she was also guarded by Tyrwhitt himself, who had not originally gone on this sortie but came dashing out from Harwich with reinforcements to the rescue.[16]

After this the ventures through the minefields by cruisers and destroyers were discontinued; but instead Tyrwhitt began sending coastal motor-boats (each carrying a torpedo and capable of thirty-five knots) across them towards the mouth of the Ems with orders to attack all the enemy minesweepers that they could find. On these occasions the light cruisers left their cutters ashore and carried the C.M.Bs at their davits till the edge of the minefields was reached. Of the second such enterprise Hamilton (now commanding the *Taurus* and the youngest destroyer-captain at Harwich by three years) grumbled; 'One always has the feeling that the little snipes will get lost and one will mess about for hours looking for them;' and indeed one did fail to return on this occasion but was picked up two days later when the *Taurus* and three other destroyers went out again for the purpose. On the third venture one boat did not return and had to be given up. The fifth attempt, which was combined with a seaplane venture, was disastrous for the C.M.Bs. On the evening of August 10 four light cruisers and thirteen destroyers sailed from Harwich for a point about twenty-five miles north-west of Vlieland, which they reached just after six o'clock next morning. Five of the destroyers were towing barges with aircraft, while the rest acted as an anti-submarine screen for the cruisers, each of which was carrying two motor-launches. Had the C.M.Bs and the seaplanes been able to get away together all would probably have been well, but the seaplanes could not take off from the water after being hoisted out because the weather was *too* fine and there was not a breath of wind stirring. The six motor-boats which managed to get away therefore made their start to the eastward without air escort, and Tyrwhitt did not recall them since arrangements had been made for a flight of planes from Yarmouth to meet the Force. These did arrive soon after 7 a.m., but Tyrwhitt's signals to them did not get through and they acted independently for the rest of the morning.

Unfortunately the launching of the C.M.Bs had been watched by four German seaplanes which waited till they neared the Dutch coast and then, with reinforcements, swooped down on them and opened fire with their machine-guns. From time to time they also dropped bombs, but none made a hit. The boats put up a gallant fight with their Lewis guns as long as their ammunition lasted, and even brought down one German plane into the sea; but about 8.15 it gave out and they were helpless henceforward. One boat reached the shore, and since they had been driven into Dutch waters a Dutch torpedo-boat came out later and took two others in tow. The remaining three were sunk. Unaware of their fate, the Harwich Force patrolled all day waiting and searching for them in the intervals of engaging German seaplanes which came out in considerable numbers. Very few of these, however, ventured to come near enough to drop bombs in the face of the ships' high-angle anti-aircraft guns.[17]

The operation, however, had a dual purpose; its other object being to bait a trap for a Zeppelin. Several abortive attempts had already been made to do this, the plan for which had been devised by Colonel C.R. Samson, commanding No. 4 Group of the Royal Air Force (which had recently been formed by the amalgamation of the Royal Flying Corps and the Royal Naval Air Service). One of the destroyers was towing a lighter fitted with a flying deck and carrying, not a seaplane, but a Sopwith Camel aeroplane, the most efficient type of single-seater fighter which the R.A.F. then possessed. The latest Zeppelins in commission at this time had a ceiling of from 20,000 to 22,000 feet, and the relatively heavy seaplanes could not climb high enough to tackle them. Even the Camel's service ceiling was reckoned to be only about 18,000 feet; but Samson had calculated that if it kept out of sight from the Zeppelin (whose visual range he estimated at seven miles or more) until it had climbed to 15,000 feet before attacking it should have a very good chance of success. Indeed, he had endorsed the copy of a memorandum on attacking Zeppelins with which the pilot of this machine, Lieut. Culley, had been provided: 'If you follow the rules you are certain to bring her down'. About two hours after the motor-boats had been got away, Zeppelin *L53* hove in sight and Culley was hastily helped into his machine while the towing destroyer worked up to full speed, thus giving just enough air speed to enable him to get into the air. He rose rapidly and after about forty minutes disappeared from sight in the clouds. The Zeppelin remained in the sunshine till about 9.30, when she was observed to have altered course for home and to have begun to climb quickly. Clearly her crew had become aware of their danger. Presently she also passed out of view. Ten minutes later the watchers in the ships heard a faint rattle of machine-gun fire which lasted for a few seconds; then they saw a sheet of flame spread across the white cloud-bank and the blazing Zeppelin falling.

At the suggestion of his flag-lieutenant, Anthony Floyer, and after hastily consulting a hymn-book, Tyrwhitt ordered a signal to be made to all ships: 'See Hymns Ancient and Modern, Number 224, verse seven' – which is

> 'O happy band of pilgrims,
> Look upward to the skies,
> Where such a light affliction
> Shall win so great a prize.'

This apt signal was long remembered among the many stories told of him, though the circumstances were usually garbled in the telling. Another two hours passed, however, before anything more was seen of Culley; and hope had nearly been abandoned, since it was realised that his petrol must soon be exhausted, when he came circling down out of the heavens amid a roar of cheering and landed close to a destroyer, which promptly picked him up and also salved his machine. He had had to climb to 19,000 feet to get his prey. His hands were frozen, one of his two guns jammed, and he was unable to follow Samson's advice that the best attacking position was to dive from above, but he had run along underneath the Zeppelin, pumping incendiary bullets into her from his remaining gun. Tyrwhitt gave him a cigarette case with 'Hymn 224, v.7' engraved on it and recommended him for the Victoria Cross. Possibly because it was felt that Samson had spelt out his task for him, however, he was only given the D.S.O., though the officers and men of the Harwich Force felt that the courage and skill with which this eighteen-year-old youth had carried out his instructions deserved the higher award.[18]

By now the end of the war was beginning to come into sight. Two destroyers, the *Scott* and the *Ullswater*, were sunk on August 15 by a mine and a torpedo respectively while escorting the Dutch convoy, though the casualties were comparatively light.[19] After that came an unprecedentedly long period of six weeks' quiet during which the Force did not go to sea at all as a whole.[20] Then at the end of September, with the Allied armies advancing, the Germans began the evacuation of Flanders. Tyrwhitt had had his forces standing by for some days in readiness to intercept the German destroyers which might be expected to make a break for home from Zeebrugge, and on the 30th he received orders to put to sea for this purpose. The weather was so rough, however, that the Admiralty presently recalled him. Back in harbour by 7 p.m., he set off again at midnight, but without result. Writing to Keyes next day, he blamed the Admiralty rather than the elements, declaring that

> 'they were caught napping and did not expect them to break out so soon... When they got the news it was too late; we started five hours after the Huns and were of course too late. Their Lordships also made the stupid mistake of not letting the cruisers go alone. We were hampered by the destroyers (it was blowing a full gale) and they could not keep up. I left them behind, but in any case I doubt if we should have been within two hours of the Huns.'[21]

For the next week or so repeated efforts were made to catch the German destroyers which were now making a bolt for it; but still without success, for the odds were very much in favour of the enemy. The nights were moonless; there were many channels among the banks near the mouth of the Scheldt by which they could slip out near high water, while to keep up a patrol in these narrow channels with a strong cross-tide would have meant the danger of many ships grounding – 'half the flotilla ashore the first night' was the way Hamilton put it. Nevertheless, as he added, it was refreshing to have a war again after being at peace for so long, and on October 4 part of the command did have a last 'scrap of a kind'. Information was received that German submarines returning from sea were going to be met by minesweepers at a certain position in the Bight, and destroyers were ordered out to intercept them, while the light cruisers patrolled ten miles away in support if required. But nothing was sighted except two armed trawlers which were easily mopped up. 'Home for tea' was the laconic ending of Commander Watson's entry in his diary for that day.[22] The 'beef trip' continued, but two destroyers were now considered sufficient escort. On October 23, four days after the Germans had completed the evacuation of Zeebrugge, there was one final expedition into the Bight; a motor-boat operation had been contemplated but Tyrwhitt decided to leave the C.M.Bs behind as too unreliable and sailed with seaplanes and Camels only. Once more the weather proved frustrating; the seaplanes could not get off the water and three Camels out of four broke up on their lighters. Some German aircraft appeared, however, and were driven off without casualties on either side by the last shots which the Harwich Force was to fire in anger.[23]

Nevertheless the general expectation was that the German Navy would end the war, not with a whimper, but with a bang; that it would come out at last and fight a fleet action to a finish – as indeed most of its officers would have done if they could. In readiness for this the Force stood by day after day, and all refits and even boiler-cleaning were put off for the present.[24] But then rumours of the mutiny in the High Seas Fleet began to trickle through. In the afternoon of November 7 there was a premature report that the armistice had been signed; a signal to that effect was made, but cancelled in the evening. Shortly afterwards a signal was made to *Concord* (half of whose ship's company were ashore at a canteen concert), *Curlew* (a recent addition), and eight destroyers to raise steam with all despatch and prepare to slip at 11 p.m., at which hour they went out for a day and a half's final patrolling in an effort to catch some German steamers which were expected to make a dash out of

Antwerp and attempt to intern themselves in Holland – in which they succeeded by creeping along the Dutch coast within territorial waters.[25] Even this was not quite the last kick of the war for the Force, for on November 9 when a considerable number of officers and men were ashore enjoying their teas the syrens sounded the recall for the last time. For this alarm a report of a brief tentative sortie by two German cruisers was responsible, but after getting as far as Terschelling they turned back, and the Force did not go out.[26]

Two days later, at eleven o'clock in the morning, the war ended and the syrens sounded once again, but this time in celebration, not in summons, and as part of a scene of tremendous enthusiasm, with bands playing and cheers pealing out again and again from every ship. From *Curaçoa* Tyrwhitt made the signal:

> 'On this day of rejoicing I wish to thank the captains, officers and ships' companies of the Harwich Force for the unbounded gallantry, zeal and endurance they have invariably displayed during the war.
> The Harwich Force has made its name and will not be forgotten during the future annals of history.
> I particularly wish to call attention to the uniformly good conduct and cheerfulness of the Harwich Force during this long period of war, and trust that in the general rejoicings of to-day the Harwich Force will remember the good name of the Force.
> It is well to remember that though peace is assured a period of hard and possibly unpleasant work is at hand. I know that I can trust the Harwich Force to carry out any work ordered in the same cheerful spirit that they have shown throughout the war.'[27]

In the evening he and Lady Tyrwhitt entertained the captains and commanders to dinner at the Alexandra Hotel. Domvile prepared the menu – one of the wines being described as

'Kaiser, 1918 (bottled in Holland)'[28] – and the evening was gay and festive, but what the little flag-captain enjoyed most

> 'was the cheerful light flooding out through the open portholes in the ships' sides over the dark waters of the harbour – portholes that had been closed for four and a half years... It was going back on board that night and seeing those glorious scuttles that really brought it home to me that the war had ended'.[29]

On the same note Tennant recorded that 'the Armistice seemed very strange – the ships at eight hours' notice, the harbour a blaze of lights, late and night leave to officers and men.'[30]

The losses of the Harwich Force during the war had been two light cruisers – the *Amphion* and the *Arethusa* – and fourteen destroyers – the *Louis* (sunk 31 October 1915), *Medusa*, *Lassoo*, *Simoom*, *Laforey*, *Setter* (lost in collision 17 May 1917), *Mentor* (torpedoed 7 August 1917), *Recruit* (mined and sunk 9 August 1917), *Surprise*, *Torrent*, *Tornado*, *North Star* (lost at Zeebrugge 23 April 1918), *Ullswater* and *Scott*. In addition the *Tipperary* and *Turbulent* were lost at Jutland after being transferred to the Grand Fleet.[31]

On November 14 Tyrwhitt left in the *Curaçoa* for Rosyth to take part in the meeting with Admiral Meurer, the representative of the German Navy who was coming to receive instructions for its surrender according to the terms of the Armistice. This meeting – there were in fact four meetings in all, at which Tyrwhitt was present only for some parts of the time – took place on the two following days, and it was arranged that all the German submarines should be surrendered to him at Harwich and a specified number of surface ships to Beatty in the Firth of Forth. When this arrangement became known at Harwich there was much disappointment and even discontent among officers of the Force that the German destroyers were not also to be made to surrender there, since they felt that it had had more dealings with them during the war than any other section of the Navy. A story, possibly *ben trovato*, also became current that during the discussions with Meurer the following exchange had taken place:

M: 'Will you guarantee the safety and honour of our submarine crews?'

Beatty: 'Admiral Tyrwhitt, can you guarantee the safety of the German submarine crews?'

T: 'Yes, sir.'

B: 'Admiral Tyrwhitt will guarantee their safety, but their honour is entirely in their own hands.'[32]

The surrender of the first batch of German submarines took place on November 20. Domvile, to his great chagrin, was unable to watch it, having on the return from Rosyth fallen a victim to the influenza epidemic that was sweeping through the Force in common with the whole country, and being still in his bunk. At 4.30 a.m. the Force weighed anchor and steamed out to meet the U-boats at a rendezvous off Lowestoft. Tyrwhitt had given strict orders that there were to be no demonstrations, but few or none wanted to demonstrate. Indeed, there was still doubt in everyone's mind about what might happen even at the last moment, and at 7 a.m. all hands were closed up at action stations to be ready for any eventuality. Fifteen minutes later a German transport (which was to take the submarine crews back to Germany) hove in sight, followed closely in single line by twenty of the latest type of U-boat, disposed in four divisions of five boats each. As the Force steamed past them on an opposite course the destroyers were detached and took up positions such that each division of the enemy was in charge of three of them, one leading and one on each beam. The cruisers (*Curaçoa*, *Centaur*, *Coventry*, *Danae* and *Dragon*, the last two being comparative newcomers)[33] then made a sixteen-point turn and, steaming ten knots, slowly overhauled the procession in front of them, which was more than five miles long.

About 10 a.m. a second rendezvous was reached, where the destroyers *Melampus* and *Lurcher* and several motor launches were waiting with prize crews from the submarine depot-ship *Maidstone* aboard, which were now put on board the U-boats. The German captains were required to sign assurances that their boats were in good running order and ready for sea in all respects, and that no 'booby-traps' or other unpleasant devices had been arranged aboard. Each boat then ran up the White Ensign and proceeded into Harwich harbour with the prize crew in charge and the Germans fallen in on the forecastle. The German crews, already more or less mutinous, had apparently not been told by their officers that they would be taken into a British port under the British flag, and the majority immediately concluded that they were about to be paraded through the streets. Once assured that this was not so, most of them became very communicative and obliging and spared no pains to explain all the intricacies of their boats to the victors. As soon as the submarines were safely berthed their crews were transferred to the transport, which then steamed back to Germany. Further surrenders by batches followed until more than 170 boats had been handed over.[34]

The dispersal of the Harwich Force now began, though before they began to leave for new assignments the commanding officers of the destroyers gave a dinner to Tyrwhitt on November 30.[35] The *Concord* had already sailed to carry Paderewski, the great Polish pianist and patriot, back to his native country, of which he became the first President. Of the ship's departure from Harwich Tennant reflected: 'How different to some others – dashes out in the middle of the night to catch enemy destroyers, feeling your way out in fog to be at a rendezvous at a certain time, slipping and going to sea at 4 a.m. on a wintry morning to bring back your butter and eggs by the beef trip.' On the voyage Paderewski, as a token of his gratitude to the Navy and admiration for it, entertained the officers by playing on the wardroom's battered and never very grand piano without allowing a flicker of the agony this must have caused him to cross his features.[36] On December 3 the *Centaur* and the *Coventry* left for the Baltic, to which a naval force was now being sent. On the 6th the Admiral slept ashore for the first time and on the 11th he took five days' leave, followed by a longer spell of twelve days in the middle of January, which he spent shooting in Wales.[37] 'I am wondering what to do next,' he wrote to Keyes: 'I have no fixed idea, except that I should like to go abroad, but I gather all the light cruiser squadrons are already filled up.'[38] This was correct, but already the rumour was beginning to run, presently to be proved true, that he was to be offered the Gibraltar command.[39] The *Curaçoa* was now detailed to convey the Queen of Norway and Crown Prince Olaf, who had seized an early opportunity of visiting their British relatives once the war was over, back to their own country. Tyrwhitt, however, remained behind in order that Her Majesty might have his cabin,[40] and received instead an invitation to spend a few days with our own royal family at Sandringham, travelling up from Harwich to London on January 28 in the same special train that had brought Queen Maud down, after he had received her and escorted her on board his flagship. To his wife he wrote:

> 'The Queen of Norway arrived before her time and I only just arrived on the platform after the train had stopped! Fancy me being late! Luckily they take some time to move, so I was at the door before she got out of the carriage ...
>
> I ... arrived here [York Cottage, Sandringham] at nine o'clock and was shown straight into the dining-room. The King was alone except for Godfrey.[41] We had coffee and talked for about half-an-hour and then I was taken to the drawing-room and presented to the Queen and Princess Mary ... It was not so bad as I expected. I remained with them until about eleven o'clock all by

> my lone and kept up a conversation of sorts. The Queen is really charming, but shy, like me! Then to bed, where I had not enough bedclothes. I was frozen.
> 5.45 p.m. Just returned from shooting. I enjoyed it immensely and did not do so very badly ...
> I found brekker rather a trying meal, as the King's parrot took a violent fancy to me and insisted on sitting on my shoulder and making violent love.
> I being the only guest always have to sit next to the Queen. She is not very talkative, but I managed to blurt out a remark now and then ...
> Dinner is the next ordeal, but I expect if I get quickly on to the second glass of bubbly my tongue will become looser and things may hum a bit ...
> It really is very wonderful and I sometimes wonder if I am dreaming ...'[42]

From Sandringham he had to hurry to Oxford to receive the freedom of his native city, which he had been asked in the previous December to accept – an honour which had provoked the comment to his sister Polly: 'I am horrified at the idea ..., but I suppose I shall have to go through with it ... I don't hanker after these sort of things!'[43] The ceremony took place on a typical English winter's day, with a stern grey sky and a temperature about freezing-point, but this did not prevent a great crowd from lining the route along which the Mayor and Corporation walked in procession escorting the new freeman. On the following day the Convocation of the University bestowed the honorary degree of Doctor of Civil Law upon him. He also visited his old school as a guest of honour and gave a simple but forthright address to the boys on the theme 'Start with ideals and stick to them and cultivate a mind of your own. Don't be talked over by others from doing what you consider to be the right thing.'[44]

On April 9 he was formally offered, and accepted, the appointment of Senior Naval Officer at Gibraltar from July 5 following, when it would fall vacant.[45] Later in the month the Navy, or a representative section of it, were the guests of the French nation for a hectic week. The ports visited were Cherbourg and Brest, Beatty taking four of the newest and most powerful battleships and a destroyer flotilla to the former and Tyrwhitt four of his light cruisers and a flotilla to the latter. He also took with him his son St. John, who had just passed into Osborne with considerable ease and was bursting with pride and excitement to be accompanying his now famous father.[46] From each of the two ports the flag officers and about 450 other officers and men went on to Paris on April 23, which was now the anniversary of the Zeebrugge Raid as well as St. George's Day. During the journey of Tyrwhitt's party from Brest an episode occurred which was characteristic of the man. The train pulled up at a wayside station where a British breakfast had been specially provided at a large café just across the road. A young English journalist, the only member of his profession accompanying the party, spotted as he climbed down from the train a figure in shirt and trousers having a good sluice under a water-tap and recognised the heavy eyebrows, the prominent nose and the jutting chin. Hurrying over in a rush of youthful enthusiasm, as Tyrwhitt wrestled with a collar-stud, he began: 'Excuse me, sir, I represent the *Daily* ——...,' and then stopped, paralysed by a glance that would have halted most men. There was a brief pause, and then the journalist received what he described as 'a couple of verbal salvoes that rocked the stationary train'. As he walked crestfallen across to the café with a companion, the latter chuckled: 'I ought to have warned you! He doesn't like newspaper men, and he's inclined to firework displays before breakfast!' They sat down and had begun breakfast when a figure loomed up at their table, seized a chair and settled in it. 'Now', said Tyrwhitt with a twinkle in his eye, 'let me get outside some bacon and eggs and we'll have a chat. I don't like being interviewed with my head under a tap, you know!' The story the young man subsequently sent off brought him a congratulatory letter from his editor and a pleasant line of thanks from Tyrwhitt.[47]

When the two British naval contingents arrived in Paris they were plunged into a bewildering succession of receptions, lunches, dinners, visits to the Opera (the first of which Tyrwhitt found 'very fine' but the second 'very long and rather dull') and speeches (which were all made by Beatty with much aplomb despite his one *faux pas* of declaring that 'he always knew when he went out with the Grand Fleet that he had the French Navy behind him!'). After that came visits to Versailles (where Tyrwhitt inspected the furniture with the eye of a craftsman if not perhaps exactly that of a connoisseur), Rheims and Verdun, the last two of which gave the visitors some idea of what their allies had been through. At Rheims Tyrwhitt found 'not a single house intact' and saw only one window with any glass in it. The party were shown round the shattered cathedral by Cardinal Luçon, 'such a splendid old man', who had remained in the city throughout the war and to whom they gave three rousing cheers when they left, in recognition of an old man's fortitude. Afterwards they lunched in the Caves Pommery, with the Marquis de Polignac ('who owns the champagne business', as Tyrwhitt put it) as their host, where they 'swam in champagne'; and then motored to Verdun over roads so appalling that Tyrwhitt was twice bumped up against the roof of the car he was in, cutting his head the second time. At Verdun they were conducted over forts and trenches by three very pleasant young French officers, one of whom Domvile declared was the best guide he had ever heard, knowing every inch of the ground from bitter personal experience.[48]

On his return to Harwich Tyrwhitt hauled down his flag and said good-bye to the force he had led so tirelessly and successfully through four and a half years of war. To the accompaniment of tremendous and unceasing cheering he was rowed ashore at Shotley from *Curaçoa* by six captains – Cayley, Lynes, St. John, Domvile, Maclean and Engineer-Commander Griffith – through an avenue of gaily-dressed minesweepers and drifters. A further farewell ceremony and demonstration followed at Shotley R.N. Barracks, where he took particular care, since he had never before had a public opportunity of doing so, to thank the officers and men of the Harwich minesweeping service for their magnificent work. Then, with the cheers still pealing out, 'Com. (T)' and Lady Tyrwhitt got into their car and drove home.[49] For, as Watson wrote long afterwards,

> ' "Com. (T)" was his title when first he led the Harwich Force to war and by that title he was always remembered by those he led so well... His love was for the sea and for the direct and personal leadership of the Force he was proud to command. The plans for the many operations, the training and supervision of his squadron and the consummate skill with which it was handled, were his and his alone; and nothing delighted him more than to exercise the seaman's gifts of eyesight, hearing and judgement as his squadron swept outwards or homewards through the narrow channels of the North Sea... His captains were his staff and their confidence in him was unbounded. He never spared himself and when at sea kept watch for hours at a time, ever searching the darkness or the far horizon for the first signs of the enemy – a lonely figure in his corner of the bridge, as strong as a rock and as silent. That he held the command of the Harwich Force for four long years of war was certainly unique but it was far more than that. It was in truth one of the greatest examples of courage, endurance and devotion to duty in the annals of our Navy. To every other leader in that war... came periods of rest or at any rate of change of duty which refreshed the spirit and gave new strength; but for Com. (T) there were only incessant anxiety and continuous strain borne to the end without faltering... His responsibility may not have been as heavy as that of other leaders, but none can have experienced for so long the constant strain and anxiety of operations in enemy waters, the

frequent loss and damage of his ships, and of the rush to sea at all hours of the day and night to meet the risks and dangers which it was impossible to foresee but easy to imagine.'[50]

CHAPTER EIGHT

GIBRALTAR AND THE MEDITERRANEAN

After six weeks' leave which he enjoyed immensely, first visiting his mother's family home at Bewerley and then having some good fishing in Ireland, the Admiral sailed for Gibraltar in a P. and O. liner which he not unnaturally found slow and dull, his wife and family following a fortnight later in another. Arriving on July 9, he took over immediately from his predecessor Vice-Admiral Sir Heathcoat Grant, who sailed for England on the following day. The Governor of the 'Rock' at this time was General Sir Horace Smith-Dorrien, and Tyrwhitt found both him and his wife charming and congenial, so that they got on very well. Lady Smith-Dorrien, who was very active, introduced him to squash rackets, a game which he had never played before but at which in spite of his age he afterwards became proficient.[1] A few weeks after his arrival he was notified that a baronetcy had been conferred on him in recognition of his great services during the war, and since this involved the choice of a territorial title he decided upon 'Tyrwhitt of Terschelling', in memory of the countless times when that island had been a landmark or a turning-point in his patrols. A parliamentary grant of £10,000 was also bestowed on him. On the other hand it was not until December that his acting rank of rear-admiral was made substantive – not, in fact, until he would have reached that rank by the normal course of progress up the captains' list – which made him feel 'somewhat sore'.[2]

Despite the social, residential and sporting amenities that his new post offered, the amount of dockyard administration it involved was both new and uncongenial to him and made it an unwelcome contrast to the excitements and stresses of the wartime years. By November he was writing to Keyes:

> 'I am not in love with Gibraltar and I hate the sight of the Dockyard and everybody in it. We are constantly having strike troubles and they bore me to tears. Hunting has just begun. It is not very grand but it passes the time. I have five animals of sorts, just enough to mount the family and one spare. The Mount [his official house] is a charming residence. We are very lucky in the Governor and Lady Smith-Dorrien...'[3]

To another fire-eating old friend, Rear-Admiral Sir Walter Cowan, who was commanding the British naval forces in the Baltic and conducting the naval side of the 1918–20 war of intervention against Soviet Russia, he confided that the hunting at Gibraltar was

> 'a poor sort of game but better than nothing and gives one an excuse for a day off the Rock. Angey and the family... all ride hard and thoroughly enjoy it all... I scooped two cups out of three for the Hunt Cup... It is rather late in life to start riding races, but I did enjoy it. I have not ridden a race since the old *Alexandra* days... I find this place d...d expensive and the Mount is an expensive place to run.'[4]

Besides uncongenial dockyard administration, the amount and cost of the entertaining which his new post involved (being a shore appointment) were more than he liked. Lady Tyrwhitt, on the other hand, took to this entertaining with *éclat* and it was now that her talents as a hostess blossomed and became much admired. It was presumably she who prevailed on her husband to engage a French chef, over whom he had a passage at arms with the Admiralty which he described to Keyes:

> 'I have been having rows with Their Lordships. They

> first refused to let me have a French cook and then docked me of thirty shillings a week table money, all in one act. As I had the cook and intend keeping him,[5] it was a blow, as wages are pretty stiff, but what did raise my ire was a paragraph at the end of the letter which said I was to deduct the surplus table money from the time of my appointment – a matter of £135. I... quoted their own order which refers to overpayments for which the officer concerned is not responsible... They have not seen fit to answer my letter for six weeks... The family love the place. I wish I liked it as much as they do. I am afraid I am not cut out for this sort of job.'[6]

It was therefore with much relief and pleasure that he learnt, after a tenure of just over a year, that he was to relieve Rear-Admiral Sir George Hope in the command of the Third Light Cruiser Squadron in the Mediterranean Fleet.[7] Removing his family to Malta, he hoisted his flag in the *Cardiff*, another of the improved 'C' class cruisers which he had come to know so well at Harwich, and to his delight was able to secure as flag-captain his very old friend Colin Maclean who had been his shipmate in the *Indefatigable* and one of his ablest and most trusted officers in the Harwich Force. Maclean wrote to Cowan:

> 'I am just starting off to join *Cardiff* as flag-captain to Tyrwhitt and I don't mind telling you that I wouldn't dream of going as flag-captain to the ordinary common or garden admiral as [like Tyrwhitt himself] I'm not a society bird, but somehow this job is quite different.'[8]

Tyrwhitt also again took with him his equally trusty secretary Paymaster-Lieutenant-Commander Kenneth Badcock, a most devoted officer who had served him in this capacity throughout the war and continued to serve him until his retirement in 1933. Badcock, in spite of his devotion and a tendency to stammer, was never afraid of speaking his mind to his formidable chief when he deemed it necessary – a trait which Tyrwhitt, who had little use for those who could not stand up to him, much appreciated.[9] At the beginning of February Tyrwhitt was sent up to Constantinople by the Commander-in-Chief in the Mediterranean, Vice-Admiral Sir John de Robeck, in order to relieve temporarily Rear-Admiral Richard Webb (who had been in the same term with him in the *Britannia*) as Senior Naval Officer there, the arrangement being that they were to have alternate spells of three months each in this capacity.[10] The situation in the Near East at the time was both complex and potentially explosive; in fact the war in that part of the world had not really been wound up. A peace treaty had been signed at Sèvres in the previous August with the nominal government of Germany's late ally Turkey, but by this time that government had lost all authority over the country. Constantinople had been occupied by Allied forces, while Anatolia, the heartland of the Turkish Empire, was virtually independent under the control of Mustapha Kemal, a very able general who had greatly distinguished himself in the Gallipoli campaign. His hold over the nationalist movement of which he was the leader had been strengthened – as also had the movement itself – by the landing of a Greek force at Smyrna with the sanction of Lloyd George, the British prime minister, who had been persuaded by M. Venizelos the prime minister of Greece to give his approval to Greek territorial ambitions in Asia Minor. These ambitions, however, were anathema to France and Italy, both of whom had interests in this area and were alarmed by Greek aspirations there. The humiliating terms of the Treaty of Sèvres had then given a further fillip to the nationalist movement and to Mustapha Kemal's power; and when in January 1921 the Greek forces advanced inland from Smyrna, only to meet defeat at the Kemalists' hands at Inönü, the situation was worsened and Allied disunity increased since the French and Italians adopted an increasingly pro-Kemalist policy. A second but separate problem was provided by the imminent collapse of the White Russian campaign in South Russia against the new Bolshevik *régime*. This campaign had previously received encouragement from both Britain and France, and both countries were now faced by the obligations of extricating the remnants of General Wrangel's White Russian army and doing something if possible for the crowds of refugees who were fleeing before the advancing Bolshevik forces.

Tyrwhitt found Constantinople far from congenial, though this was probably partly because his position involved him in a great deal of what he described as 'toshy paper work which bores me to tears' and which he always detested though he applied himself to it with a dogged conscientiousness. He was also worried by finding himself in the midst of a complicated political situation to which, even though the major responsibility of coping with it did not lie on his shoulders, he was required to adapt himself, carefully keeping in step with the other British authorities involved.
To his brother Beauchamp he confided in March:

> 'The general situation is very difficult to explain and as I have only a very vague idea of it myself I won't attempt it, especially as it alters daily. This is the land of intrigues. No one trusts anyone and everyone lies like a toothdrawer if any advantage is to be gained.'[11]

To his wife he was even more candid, writing a few days later:

> 'I have come to the conclusion that I am not cut out for a diplomatist. I don't seem to get the hang of matters here and have not the brains to compete with so many people who all think and act differently. I don't think the C.-in-C. [de Robeck] thinks much of my efforts either.'[12]

He was perhaps a little too modest, for he certainly achieved one thing of some importance by establishing and maintaining excellent relations with the two other principal British representatives on the spot, Sir Horace Rumbold the High Commissioner in Constantinople and General 'Tim' Harington the commander of the troops, as well as with the French Admiral, De Bon, 'an old dear with a snow-white beard and a nice red face'.[13] He had met and liked De Bon during his visit to France in 1919, and also his charming niece the Countess de Marondière, who with her husband was now keeping house for him in the commandeered former residence of the Grand Vizier. They became very friendly, with frequent exchanges of hospitality facilitated by the Countess's perfect command of English – though before his short tour of duty was finished Tyrwhitt was launching out more and more boldly into conversational efforts in French. When the time came for him to depart De Bon declared that the relations between England and France in Constantinople had never been so satisfactory or amicable as during the last three months.[14] General Harington, who had been General Plumer's chief of staff in the Second Army during the war, but whose hour in history still lay ahead of him, was a man after Tyrwhitt's own heart. That the converse was also the case was shown by a remark of Harington's, also made shortly before the Admiral's departure, which carried the clear implication that after meeting one or two admirals who had fancied themselves in the political sphere it had come as a welcome relief to have as his *vis-à-vis* a plain straightforward fighting-man of his own stamp.[15] To Sir Horace and Lady Rumbold, too, Tyrwhitt took immediately, and they to him; he played golf and squash with Sir Horace, and was soon writing appreciatively to his wife that they were nice homely people when they were by themselves.[16]

Buried within this comment, however, lies another reason, though a less weighty one, why he disliked this tour of duty. As time went on, he came to feel that there were too many functions which he could not escape, too much hospitality (even though he enjoyed some of it), too many dinner parties to attend or give.

> 'I shall grouse like the devil [he wrote] if I find a long list of night engagements when I come back [to Malta]. I shall require rest. Here I never or hardly ever get a quiet dinner on board and I am bored to tears with them all. I positively look forward to going to sea for exercises.'[17]

Occasionally the dinner parties could be unwelcome for another reason, as when he wrote of an invitation to one at the Italian Embassy:

> 'I don't look forward to it one little bit and intend to take a revolver with me as I have to go through awful slums to get there. People are often held up here by ruffians of all sorts and no-one goes about alone if they can help it. Riding yesterday we had two Indian troopers with us, which I thought rather silly. One soldier invited me to go for a walk and incidentally mentioned that I had better take a few marines with their arms. I told him that there were none on board who would enjoy walking behind me.'[18]

He did in fact take frequent walks on shore with Captain Maclean as once he had walked with Keyes and then Domvile at Harwich; he played tennis and squash rackets, though handicapped or prevented for part of the time by trouble in his right arm which sounds like a bad case of 'tennis elbow' but which did not prevent him from 'knocking the heads off ... two young soldiers who rather fancy themselves' at squash;[19] and at least once he had some hunting of a sort. On this occasion the meet consisted of about thirty army officers, half-a-dozen naval officers and the same number of ladies, only one of whom still rode side-saddle, while the pack was 'a motley crew' of elderly fox-hounds of doubtful origin, beagles and one couple of 'sooners', the last possibly being distantly related to foxhounds. 'We had quite a good run', he reported '... for about half-an-hour and lost, ... but I don't know what we were hunting – wolf, fox or jackal!'[20] He also spotted an island which seemed to him likely to provide good birds'-nesting and looked forward to finding time for it, though when he did so it proved 'rather a frost', for the island housed only thousands of common gulls and a few cormorants.[21] He was more successful, however, with his hobby of miniature furniture-making, producing in particular a model of a bow-fronted knee-hole table for his house in Malta and something else unspecified which he gave to Princess Bariatinsky, 'a dear old lady [who] talks English perfectly'.[22] He found diversion too, in several times visiting the great bazaar of Constantinople with Captain Maclean, where they bargained for and bought rugs, carpets and silks.[23]

Soon after his arrival at Constantinople he made a brief excursion into the Black Sea in the *Cardiff*, calling first at the port of Constanza and from there paying a visit to the Rumanian court and capital which was vaguely described as on business connected with the defence of the country against the Bolsheviks. During the war a large part of Rumania, which had joined the Allies in 1916, had been overrun by the German army, and the devastation that had resulted made Tyrwhitt's journey to Bucharest slow and rather uncomfortable. All the carriages of the train in which he travelled, even his reserved coach, had been stripped of their cushions, leaving only bare canvas seats; most of the windows lacked glass and were boarded up; and there was no heating. When the Danube was reached the passengers had to get out (since the bridge had been blown up and not yet repaired) and walk a quarter of a mile through ankle-deep mud to a bridge of boats and then another quarter of a mile on the far side to another waiting train. This was in the same state as the first – except that it did include a restaurant car which managed to serve quite a good lunch – and doddered along at about ten miles an hour, stopping at every one of the wrecked stations. On the morning after his arrival at Bucharest he and his flag-lieutenant called on the British minister, Sir Herbert Dering, and afterwards lunched with King Ferdinand and Queen Marie, who was a daughter of the Duke of Edinburgh under whom he had served in his now far-off midshipman days.

> 'They were all very affable and had no frills [wrote Tyrwhitt]. The Queen was particularly nice and talked about old times. I sat next to Princess Elizabeth, who is pretty but rather dull. I found it difficult to keep up a flow of chatter.'

The King offered the use of the royal train for the return journey, since it happened to be going to Constanza in any case to meet a visiting prince. The party were thus able to travel back in greater comfort and to remain in their carriage while it was ferried across the Danube on lighters.[24] The *Cardiff* then sailed for Batoum, where Tyrwhitt at first thought he might have to remain long enough to evacuate the British mission and all British subjects, since fighting was going on between the Bolsheviks and the Georgians about eighty miles inland. As the Georgians seemed to be holding their own and he was due back at Constantinople, however, he decided that he was not justified in staying more than two days, though he wrote to Beauchamp that he would 'love to have been let loose' on the Bolsheviks. Within a week after his departure the Georgians were defeated, and the *Calypso* and *Caradoc* had to be sent hurriedly to carry out the evacuation and bring numbers of other refugees away to Constantinople to join the many thousands who were already there. White Russians of good birth and former wealth were in some cases driving cabs or even sweeping crossings to keep themselves alive, though there were sufficient who still had some means to maintain a very expensive Russian café, where Tyrwhitt and Maclean had an excellent dinner. 'All the waitresses are Russian ladies and some are very pretty,' wrote the former. 'All the Russians who can afford to dine there do so, and it is rather nice to see them kiss the hands of the waitresses.' The remnants of General Wrangel's army, camped in the neighbourhood of Constantinople and on the island of Mudros, were to all intents and purposes refugees also, having traded their arms and equipment to the French in exchange for food.[25]

As his three months' tour of duty at Constantinople drew towards its end Tyrwhitt's expressions of dislike for the Turkish capital became more emphatic. At the beginning of March he 'wished he was out of this beastly place'. By the 13th he was 'hating Constantinople more than ever' and expressing a wish that he might 'never see this beastly place again'. 'I never hated a job before', he ended this long letter.[26] A month later, however, with release only a week away, he was regarding the prospect of having to return to 'this hole' in August for another three months after Webb's next spell with wry resignation. 'Three solid months – oh Lord!' he groaned. 'Never mind, I am off this day week.'[27] Nevertheless there is perhaps some risk of a false impression, or at least of over-simplification, if these outbursts of exasperation and the expressions of distaste for Gibraltar already quoted are taken too much at their face value or isolated from their setting. It seems probable that, like many others in many walks of life at that time, Tyrwhitt did not find it easy to settle down again after the prolonged excitements of war to the peacetime exercise of his profession. Quite apart from this, he had in any case little taste for either dockyard administration or diplomacy and not much gift for the latter at least. But it has also to be borne in mind that he was given to forcible statement, and with reference to his service at Constantinople that he loved his wife and family very deeply indeed – though he would never hestitate to put duty before even them – and hence separation from them tended to darken his view of any place.

Meanwhile in March the Greeks had renewed their advance in Anatolia and been repulsed again. In August and September they tried once more and were even more decisively defeated. By this time the French had made a secret and separate treaty with the Kemalist or nationalist government which had been set up at Ankara, and both they and the Italians were supplying large quantities of arms to its forces, so that Allied unity of purpose had completely broken down. Lloyd George, for his part, had shifted his attitude and that of the British government to one of neutrality in the war between Greeks and Turks. In this a long lull followed, mainly because both sides were 'about fought out', as Tyrwhitt put it at the end of his next spell of service at Constantinople. This had begun in the middle of August, after he had taken the Light Cruiser Squadron for its summer cruise, and lasted till the middle of November. Again he found himself involved in much entertaining but managed to get plenty of riding and this time some excellent hunting. His arm was still troublesome though improving and he thought it prudent not to attempt tennis, but played a good deal of squash, boasting privately to his sister Polly that he knew of only one man in Constantinople who could beat him. The darker side of life was well in evidence, however, for the Russian refugees, of whom there were about 27,000 in the city, were in sad case, supported by British charity in spite of which some of them were literally dying of starvation. Many Turks were starving too, 'and yet', wrote Tyrwhitt,

> 'to see Constantinople you would think it a most thriving city. All the shops are full to overflowing. No dearth of anything to people who have money to buy with. The Bazaar people are making fortunes as even the well-to-do people are selling their things every day.'[28]

He himself bought little except two 'old-fashioned Turkish dresses' to serve as fancy dresses for his wife and elder daughter (who had just put her hair up, enabling her proud father to declare that he felt 'quite elderly with a grown-up daughter'). Towards the close of his term of service he was required to provide safe transport into exile for Crown Prince

Carol of Rumania, who had renounced his rights to the throne (though, after his father's death he returned to become King Carol II). Since the Prince's destination was Madeira and Tyrwhitt's flagship the *Cardiff* was due to go to Gibraltar for a refit he assigned her for this duty and turned over temporarily to the *Centaur*. The Prince and his Princess, he reported, had had to leave Rumania in such a hurry that they arrived in Constantinople with nothing but the clothes they stood up in.[29]

In the summer of 1922 the Turkish nationalists took the offensive against the Greeks in Anatolia, routing them on August 26 and driving them in headlong retreat towards Smyrna, where they arrived a few days later as a disorderly rabble. Admiral Sir Osmond de B. Brock, who was now Commander-in-Chief in the Mediterranean with Domvile as his flag-captain, received news of this on September 2 when he was on his way from Malta to the Adriatic and at once abandoned his cruise and made for Smyrna, where he arrived next morning and began to make arrangements for the evacuation of British subjects. A few days later, with the Turks approaching the town, the Greek troops an utterly demoralised mob incapable of any resistance, and the population (a large proportion of which was Greek) panic-striken and searching frantically for the means of escape, the Greek High Commissioner begged the Allied admirals (there were also French and Italian warships in the port) to take the town over and arrange its orderly surrender to the Turks.

It was eventually arranged that the Allies – as they were still called – should land detachments to protect their own national interests as far as possible, send a delegation to meet the Turks and use their good offices in turning the town over peacefully. On September 9, however, the Turkish advance guard arrived just as the delegation was getting ready and the terrified population fled to the water's edge, where as many as could cram themselves into them took refuge on the numerous lighters that were in the port. The Turks, however, behaved with restraint, being just as anxious to be rid of the

250,000 Greeks and Armenians as the latter were to leave. Brock arranged to visit the Turkish commander next day in order to confer about an orderly surrender of the town, and Tyrwhitt arrived in the *Cardiff* just in time to accompany him and Domvile. He had been cruising off Sardinia prior to going up to Constantinople for another three months as Senior Naval Officer there, when he received Brock's orders to join him at Smyrna. Of the interview with the Turkish general he wrote:

> 'We had a very friendly reception. O. de B. had to ask some very pertinent questions, one of which was – are we at war with the Kemalists ...? The Turkish general would not answer until we had said that we were not at war and were strictly neutral to Turks and Greeks. He then said that he was not at war and became quite pleasant. The real object of the visit was to arrange for all British subjects (of which there are several thousand) to embark if they desired to do so. That has since been allowed ...'[30]

He went on to describe the situation in general:

> 'The Turks are behaving wonderfully well and there has not been much bloodshed except in the Armenian quarter [where some of the inhabitants had 'asked for it' by throwing bombs]. I heard that that was thoroughly combed out last night by the Turks and I need hardly add the result ... [They] have practically swept the Greek troops into the sea. About 30,000 of the latter embarked before the Turks arrived, and the rest are mostly captured or being hunted by the Turks.
>
> The Greeks behaved disgracefully, committing every possible atrocity during their retreat. They were not content with burning the villages, murdering, etc., etc., the inhabitants, but they cut down all the fruit trees and destroyed every bridge and culvert in over a hundred

miles of railway. I can't put on paper what they did to their horses when they had no further use for them ... It is impossible to believe that human beings could be so vile. The only reason was to prevent them falling into the hands of the Turks. They could easily have shot them.

The town is fairly quiet, though a good deal of shooting goes on at night, but I saw little sign of bloodshed on shore.'[31]

Unfortunately on the 13th a fire broke out in the Armenian quarter. Its origin was never established with certainty, but it was thought likely that it was caused by an attempt of the Turks to remove all traces of the massacre which they had been methodically carrying out in that quarter. Driven by the high wind, it increased rapidly and within twenty-four hours the city was blazing from end to end. The flames burnt their way down to the two-mile-long quay, to which the panic-stricken population had flocked with all of their goods and chattels that they could carry and where they were now rushing madly about, shrieking with terror. Admiral Brock ordered all boats from the British ships to be sent inshore and to bring refugees aboard them regardless of nationality, since all British subjects had already been embarked. The French and Italians concentrated on their own nationals, of whom there were a great number in Smyrna, and took off 15,000 and 9,000 respectively. 'I am afraid', wrote Tyrwhitt, 'that many were drowned trying to swim off; we could see them jumping into the sea, but none actually swam off.' The rescued refugees were transferred as rapidly as possible to merchant vessels, which took them to Malta, Athens or Mitylene. Next day Brock departed in his flagship the *Iron Duke*, leaving Tyrwhitt to carry on the British share of the operation.

There was still much to be done, presenting many and great difficulties. The city was still burning and the waterfront crowded with people hoping to be embarked, but for the moment there was no more space in any of the steamers left in the harbour, all of which were sailing or else about to sail, loaded to the brim with human cargo. Fortunately the newly-appointed Turkish governor of Smyrna, Kiazim Pasha, had been persuaded by Domvile before he left to promise that there should be no further molestation of the civil population, and he kept his word; but there were many thousands of people who did not know this or did not trust him and still clamoured to be taken away. On the 16th the battleship *King George V* left with British refugees for Malta, and Tyrwhitt was left with the *Cardiff* and a destroyer. Not until the 20th did two colliers 'clean and empty, but that is all you can say', become available and enable the work of embarkation to be resumed. Between 8 a.m. and 7.30 p.m. on that day the British performed the feat of taking off and somehow packing into these two ships 1200 men ('nearly all very old') 2950 women, 1900 children, 230 babies 'and one goat, which was carried on board by a splendid little old woman of at least 65 on her back'. Although they were all good-humoured and grateful they were sometimes very difficult, constantly rushing the barriers which had been put up. Moreover all the women and children and many of the men had to be lowered in cradles into the holds of the colliers, since they could not climb down the iron rung-ladders at least thirty-five feet high. Tyrwhitt complained afterwards that his strained arm, which had still not completely recovered, had been put back three months again by the unaccustomed exercise of handling women and children. He found it embarrassing, too, that in spite of his bushy eyebrows and sometimes forbidding expression women always chose him to take care of their babies while they looked for the rest of their families.

On the 22nd another 3500 refugees were crammed into one of the colliers which had already returned from Mitylene empty (but no longer clean). This time the barriers were rushed at the start by a number of able-bodied men who had then to be ejected, so that time was lost and the work was even more tiring. On the 23rd another 'cargo' was loaded, making a total of over 15,000 refugees for whose embarkation Tyrwhitt and his officers and men had been responsible; after which he was relieved by his old friend Wilmot Nicholson in the *Curaçoa*, who continued the evacuation and by the beginning of October was reported to have got something like 100,000 refugees away. Tyrwhitt himself then proceeded with the *Cardiff* to the small town of Chanak on the Asiatic side of the Dardanelles.[32]

It was on Chanak that the attention of the world was now focussed, for the victorious Turks had advanced upon it and towards the Asiatic coast of the Bosphorus with the object of crossing into Europe and chastising the Greeks further. In both these areas small neutral zones had been created by the Armistice of 1918 and occupied by Allied troops, but France and Italy now withdrew their contingents, leaving the British alone to confront greatly superior numbers of Turks.[33] The British Cabinet, on the other hand, decided that Turkish reoccupation of the Straits and re-entry into Europe must be resisted by force if necessary, and instructions to that effect had been sent to Admiral Brock and General Harington, hastily followed by reinforcements in the shape of three battleships and various other vessels from the Atlantic Fleet and a division of troops. At the same time the otherwise disunited Allies had agreed to invite the nationalist government at Ankara to send representatives to negotiate a final treaty of peace with Greece and also with themselves, which would be substituted for the discarded Treaty of Sèvres. For a time, however, the situation remained very precarious and a new war between Britain and Turkey seemed likely as the Turks invaded the neutral zones. A single incident would have sufficed to precipitate an explosion, but with superb nerve and brinkmanship Harington held his position without provoking or being provoked to hostilities and with equal patience and tact conducted preliminary negotiations with Kemal which led to a more formal conference at Mudania, which Sir Horace Rumbold, Brock and he then attended on

Britain's behalf. This conference was in session when Tyrwhitt arrived in the Straits from Smyrna and was placed in charge of the Bosphorus itself with a flotilla of destroyers, another of motor-launches, a seaplane-carrier and some submarines in addition to the *Cardiff*.[34] By now there were also the three Atlantic Fleet battleships *Malaya*, *Revenge* and *Ramillies*, at Constantinople, and the Mediterranean Fleet lay in support of the Chanak position. This, in fact, was probably in less danger than the single line of trenches across the Ismid peninsula on the Asiatic side of the Bosphorus, which Tyrwhitt visited and did not think very formidable. By October 6 the Mudania negotiations were making so little progress that Harington had been authorised, if this deadlock continued, to give the Turks a 36-hour ultimatum to clear out of the neutral zones. War seemed very near again; the fleet prepared for action, and it was Brock's intention if hostilities began to open them by bombarding the Turkish troop concentration opposite the Ismid line, placing Tyrwhitt in the van of the operation. 'My picnic begins at 08.00 a.m. tomorrow if it is war,' he wrote to his wife on the 10th. 'Personally I am very fond of the Turks, but much as I like them, I don't feel inclined to be dictated to by them.'[35] Meanwhile, however, a better atmosphere had prevailed at Mudania and in the early hours of the 11th a convention was signed by which the Turks agreed to withdraw from the neutral zones pending the outcome of the peace negotiations which were to be opened at Lausanne.

Tension now eased again for a time, but the danger of war was by no means over yet. In November the newly-appointed Kemalist governor of Thrace, Rifet Pasha, whom Tyrwhitt described as 'a most unpleasant little beast', arrived in Constantinople and immediately became very aggressive, virtually ordering the Allies out of the city. The fleet had relaxed its readiness somewhat since the Mudania Convention had been signed (giving Tyrwhitt the opportunity of one or two games of squash rackets with Domvile, who was a good match for him);[36] but it now prepared again for possible war. This time, however, France and Italy made common cause with Britain, and presently things quietened down again as the Lausanne conference met and began its deliberations, which – with one temporary breakdown – dragged along until July 1923.

As the likelihood of war became less and less Tyrwhitt's dissatisfaction grew. 'I hate all this standing by to fight', he wrote to his friend Walter Cowan in December, 'especially when one knows there is nothing to fight about and also that there is not going to be one. At the same time I should very much like to give the Turk a clump under the ear. He wants it very badly and is asking for it. I suppose we have been as close to war as is possible. It seemed quite inevitable on several occasions.'[37] His term of command of the Third Cruiser Squadron was now drawing to an end, and during his last weeks at Constantinople the question of where to live in England came to occupy a large share of his attention. Lady Tyrwhitt and her daughters had returned there (and for part of the time to Ireland) a little while earlier, and her temporary ill-health had prevented them from coming out again to Malta as had been intended, so that the choice of a new home had to be made chiefly by correspondence. It was an important decision, since he expected a considerable period on half-pay, and indeed was much looking forward to it as giving him for the first time the settled and uninterrupted home life which he had come to want more and more. 'I shall be jolly glad', he had written in the same letter to Cowan, 'to get home and to have a home at last.' He would have liked to be near the sea, and also near a river in which he could fish, and he confessed to his wife that he had 'always had a hankering for Petersfield or the Meon Valley';[38] but at the same time he declared that he did not mind where they lived 'as long as you like the surroundings and... we have a decent garden and perhaps a paddock', as well as a tennis-court, especially for Bobby. These last requirements were forthcoming in a house called Belle Vale near Haslemere with which Lady Tyrwhitt had fallen in love and which, after some hesitation on his part, they bought and renamed Littlestone House.[39]

CHAPTER NINE

THE FAR EAST

After his return to Britain Tyrwhitt was presently appointed Flag Officer, Coast of Scotland, which post he held for the next two years. A shore appointment and an administrative one, with headquarters at Rosyth, it was no more to his taste than the command at Gibraltar had been a few years earlier, but he discharged its duties conscientiously, again assisted by the invaluable Commander Badcock as his secretary. From time to time he had the task of making a speech thrust upon him, and on these trying occasions he always took the opportunity of emphasizing the need for more cruisers in the now diminished and slowly shrinking Navy.[1]

More congenial were the one or two occasions on which he was invited to Balmoral to stay and shoot with the King; and in September 1924 he received a graceful compliment from Jellicoe, now raised to the peerage and Governor-General of New Zealand, and from the government of that Dominion. Jellicoe wrote that an eminent and scholarly judge of its Supreme Court had drawn his attention to the existence on Lake Wanaka in the South Island of a small island which in turn contained a smaller lake, 400 feet above the level of Wanaka and fed by a spring which kept it full even during a period of prolonged drought. The judge had also informed him that this phenomenon duplicated one found at Syracuse in Sicily, where the island of Ortygia contained a pool fed by what was called the Arethusa Spring, since the myth of the nymph Arethusa being changed into a spring while fleeing from Alpheus had been applied to it. Since, wrote Jellicoe, the name *Arethusa* had become almost legendary in the Navy and had never been more worthily borne than by Tyrwhitt's famous flagship, the judge had suggested giving that name to the small lake, and the New Zealand Government had gone two better and proposed to rename the island on Lake Wanaka Harwich Island and the peak on it which dominated what was now Arethusa Pool Tyrwhitt Peak. 'No one', Jellicoe concluded, 'held the Harwich Force in greater honour than myself.'[2]

On the conclusion of his term of command, just after his promotion to Vice-Admiral in January 1925, Tyrwhitt at last had the opportunity of enjoying eighteen months of peaceful family life at Littlestone House,[3] and then in September 1926 was appointed to the China Command and set off for the Far East in the S.S. *Morea*, accompanied by his wife and daughters, with mixed feelings. 'I confess I was very loth to go back to work again,' he wrote to Keyes during the voyage out:

> 'If I had been left much longer I think I should have chucked it. I am not exactly looking forward to China and never having been there before is unfortunate ... I am taking out my family [but] if only I had known how things were, nothing would have induced me to bring them. However they are very keen to [see the East].'[4]

The situation in China, already complicated and threatening when he sailed, had become even more so before he arrived to take over his new command. During the first four or five years after the Peace Conference of Paris Europe and the Near East had remained the focus of attention and the seed-beds of international crises; but from 1925 onwards the Far East had begun to take an increasingly important place in world affairs. The central factor in the situation was the anarchy and disintegration produced in China by the revolution of 1911, which had replaced the Empire (always marked by a large measure of local independence) overnight by a parliamentary system of government based on western ideas.

Until 1925, this anarchy had been little more than a question of Chinese domestic politics, and no international crisis had arisen serious enough to draw away attention from the problems of Europe. Its chief feature had been the development of a political cleavage between north and south which had already been nascent during the revolution and which reflected the geographical bisection of China by the Yangtse river. The revolutionary movement had drawn its main inspiration from westernized intellectuals in the extreme south, whose leading spirit, Sun Yat-sen, had in due course established at Canton a rival parliamentary government to that of Peking, the former capital. The latter had grown steadily weaker, until in 1922 civil war broke out in the north, which became a bewildering kaleidoscope of constantly changing alliances between rival war-lords. In 1923 Sun Yat-sen acquired an adviser from Soviet Russia, Michael Borodin, and Communist influence began to show itself in an increase of outwardly industrial disputes, which had a political background in the anti-foreign movement created by a growing nationalism. This movement was fed by incidents at Shanghai and Canton, in which the violence of strikers and demonstrators, directed against the International Settlements in these cities, provoked self-defence by arms. The repercussions of these incidents included a widespread boycott, aimed mainly against the British, and a demand for the abolition of foreign privileges which was urged with increasing impatience and vehemence, but which the absence of a government sufficiently responsible to undertake effective negotiations made it difficult for the foreign countries concerned to satisfy. In the south, however, where on Sun Yat-sen's death in 1925 Chiang Kai-shek succeeded to the leadership, there was at least a solid even if obnoxious organisation at the back of the agitation, with an intelligible purpose behind its policy; and though the element of Bolshevism represented by the Russian advisers increased the difficulty of negotiation, since it was definitely bent on embroiling the relations between China and the western powers, a right-wing section presently began to take shape in the southern (now calling itself the National) government which resented Russian tutelage and was opposed to Communism. Chiang Kai-shek himself was the most active opponent of Communist influence, while at the same time his forces were making rapid advances in a campaign against the northern war-lords.[5]

Such were the essentials of the situation when the Tyrwhitts sailed for China, but while they were on their way further developments had followed. In December 1926 the British Government took a new departure in policy by way of an attempt to bring the relations between China and the Western powers on to a new and better footing. In a memorandum to the diplomatic representatives at Peking of the other signatories of the Washington Nine-Power Treaty of 1922,[6] it admitted in principle that the previous system of relations between China and foreign powers had become an anachronism and promised to negotiate a revision of this system as soon as a Chinese government should be forthcoming that could act effectively on behalf of China as a whole. The first steps towards such negotiation were immediately taken when in the same month Mr. Miles Lampson,[7] the British Minister, met Mr. Eugene Chen, the Foreign Secretary of the Canton or 'Kuomintang' (hereafter called the Nationalist) government for talks at the large and important river-port of Hankow, 600 miles up the Yangtse, which had been occupied by that government's forces in September and to which it transferred its capital on New Year's Day. But in spite of this incipient *rapprochement* the successes of the Nationalist government had been accompanied by a good deal of continued agitation against foreigners, and on the eve of Lampson's arrival in Hankow matters took a new turn specifically directed against the British.

In this change of policy the left wing of the Kuomintang, which Borodin and his associates had converted to Bolshevik principles, were the protagonists and the hand of Russia was evident. On 3 January 1927 a large mob attempted to enter the British Concession at Hankow, but was kept out by a cordon of marines and naval ratings without firing a shot. Two days later, however, the defence of the Settlement having been entrusted by agreement to Chinese troops, the mob succeeded in forcing an entrance and most of the women and children in the concession had to be evacuated that same evening. At Kiukiang, lower down the Yangtse, a similar crisis had occurred on January 4, though in this case the women and children were evacuated before the mob broke in. The British Government was thus faced by the very difficult task of trying both to follow up the new policy of conciliatory negotiation and to take the necessary steps to protect British lives and property in China, above all at Shanghai, the focus of international trade with that country and one of the world's principal ports.

To appreciate the steps which were now taken, particularly by Tyrwhitt, certain basic facts must be borne in mind. The Yangtse was navigable as far as Hankow for ocean-going ships, including destroyers, during the summer months when it was swollen by rainfall and by the melting of the snows around its headwaters in Tibet, and for smaller craft at all times. Britain, the United States, Japan and France therefore each maintained a 'mosquito fleet' of such vessels for service on its and other Chinese inland waters, the British force on the Yangtse normally consisting of ten gunboats of the 'Insect' class. The major units of the China Squadron in December 1926 comprised four cruisers and an aircraft-carrier, in addition to which there were nine destroyers, twelve submarines and various auxiliary vessels; but by the middle of January the cruisers had been reinforced to eight, five of which were at Shanghai or on the lower Yangtse while three remained at Hong Kong. Shanghai, one of the five original treaty ports opened to foreign trade in 1842 by the Treaty of Nanking after the First Anglo-Chinese War, contained a population of probably more than two and a quarter millions, of whom all but 40,000 at most were

Chinese, and was divided administratively into three entirely separate areas. These were: an outer zone administered by a purely Chinese authority; an international settlement formed in 1854 out of an original British settlement and successively enlarged, having now a Chinese population of over 800,000 and a foreign population of 22,552; and a French settlement with about 7 000 foreign inhabitants.[8] The International Settlement was administered by a council of nine – five Britons, two Americans and two Japanese – elected by rather less than 2 500 foreigners who possessed the stipulated landowning or household qualification. Besides a police force, it possessed a volunteer corps with a strength of 1 438 commanded by a colonel seconded from the British regular army and equipped with arms – including armoured cars, artillery and machine-guns – lent by the British Government. Although virtually an independent military force, this contingent was of course far too small to deal with the situation now confronting it.[9]

Since the above is rather an over-simplification, or at best a condensation of the essentials, of the situation facing Tyrwhitt on his arrival, it is not surprising that he found it somewhat bewildering. In the letter to Keyes already quoted he had written:

> 'I have been primed with all the various departmental views of China – Foreign Office, Admiralty, War Office, etc. – and I find it difficult to put them all into one bag ... The result is that at present my brain ... is like a badly mixed pudding.
>
> 'It seems [he added] that what we want is not so much more ships but more men,· available for landing ... I think what we want most is a moveable force of Marines like we used to have in the West Indies.'[10]

On arriving at Hong Kong on January 6 he transferred his family to the *Petersfield*, his yacht as commander-in-chief, and lost no time in going north himself two days later to

Shanghai (towards which the Nationalists were now advancing and into which European fugitives from the upper Yangtse were pouring)[11] in the cruiser *Despatch*, accompanied by the *Enterprise*.[12] 'I only wish I knew what I was in for', he wrote to his wife *en route*, 'and I hope someone will be able to tell me'.[13] Nevertheless the (to him unaccustomed) complexity of the situation and the pull of family ties on an increasingly home-loving man did not detract a whit from his former quickness of grasp and action. He arrived at Shanghai on the afternoon of January 11, and by the following day had sent the Admiralty a telegrammed appreciation of the situation there in which he called for a division of troops:-

> 'The conditions since the fall of Hankow and Kiuchiang [he wrote] ... have materially altered all previous appreciations. At the present time there is nothing to stop an advance in force of the Cantonese army ... The Volunteer Force of Shanghai is entirely inadequate for defence purposes and unless it is very materially increased the fall of Shanghai is inevitable ... I consider that a fully equipped division, repeat division, is urgently required ... and ... should be despatched with the least possible delay. Urgency of situation calls for immediate action and delay may be disastrous. Under present conditions the Cantonese army can arrive in vicinity of Shanghai within thirty days. The defence of Shanghai will be purely a military operation; the Volunteer Corps and naval landing parties will be used for maintaining order inside Settlement.
>
> 'I would point out that should this division be forthcoming, in addition to disposing of the present menace to Shanghai it would lead to eventual restoration of concessions at Hankow and Kiuchiang and above all to the re-establishment of British prestige. Moreover the presence of a strong British force in Shanghai would

without doubt encourage our allies to follow suit and thus afford them the opportunity to join with us in dealing with a situation which at present they are inclined to avoid as being a mess of our own making.

'The alternatives to this proposal are:-

(i) The peaceful evacuation of Shanghai at an early date

(ii) Evacuation under similar or worse conditions than existed at Hankow and possibly under fire.

'I have consulted the Consul-General, Shanghai, in this matter and he is in entire agreement, though he adheres to his previously expressed opinion that evacuation would prove physically impossible in practice.'[14]

Tyrwhitt had dined with the Consul-General, Sir Sidney Barton, on the intervening evening and found him 'a very nice man and a great talker'.

> 'What a life this is [he confided to his wife in the same letter] after our lovely and peaceful eighteen months at home! I have several times wished that I had never come, but now that I am beginning to take hold I feel much better. I have never had such problems to deal with before, and the war was child's play to this sort of thing.'[15]

At 6.30 next morning he started up-river in the destroyer *Veteran* in order to size up the position at Hankow, and by half-past six in the evening had reached Nanking, 200 miles up, where he transferred to the river gunboat *Gnat* and pushed on all night. Next day signs of the Nationalist army were visible and some Russian officers in uniform were seen in a junk. At 7 p.m., after darkness had fallen, the *Gnat* reached Kiuchiang and stopped for an hour while Tyrwhitt talked with the British Consul and the captains of a destroyer and a gunboat which by now were stationed there. At 3 p.m. on the third day he reached Hankow, having accomplished in less than sixty hours a journey which he had been told would take four days. Here he found things somewhat better. The violence which had led to the evacuation of the women and children had been instigated and approved only by the left wing of the Kuomintang, during a brief period of ascendancy, and it was already beginning to lose influence again. Meanwhile Chen had taken energetic measures to secure the safety of the British Concessions and their inhabitants, and conversations had already begun in the city between him and Mr. O'Malley, the Counsellor of the British Legation, whom after the riots Lampson had delegated for that purpose. Moreover three British destroyers, a sloop and two gunboats were now lying alongside the Concession, although the British men among the mercantile community of the town were practically prisoners in a large building next door to the Consulate. Tyrwhitt found O'Malley 'a very nice person', with whom he got on well and who was in agreement with all that he had done; and after a stay of thirty hours, the daylight part of which he spent in interviewing people and inspecting the Concession, he set off to return to Shanghai on board a river steamer which he found surprisingly comfortable. During this rapid trip with a small staff he received great assistance from his flag-lieutenant, Clifford ('Kit') Caslon,[16] who had served under him as signal officer in the Mediterranean in 1921–2, and whom he described to his wife as 'splendid ... In fact I don't know what I should do without him'.[17]

The negotiations between Chen and O'Malley were soon afterwards interrupted when the Nationalist government took umbrage at the despatch of British troops to Shanghai in response to Tyrwhitt's urgence, but were soon resumed. On February 19 an agreement was signed which transferred the Hankow and Kiuchiang Concessions to Chinese administration, under regulations to be communicated to the British Minister. Though this agreement caused dismay to the foreign community in other concessions and treaty ports, it was a setback to the Kuomintang left wing, which had hoped to force an unconditional surrender, and was of course in line with the British Government's declared policy of revising the previous relationship. It was not followed immediately, however, by any improvement in the position of foreigners in the Yangtse basin. Indeed, at Hankow this became worse during the next six or seven weeks, though after that it improved considerably when river conditions allowed the arrival of two British cruisers, the *Vindictive* and the *Carlisle*.[18]

Meanwhile between January 17 and 22 the British Cabinet had decided to despatch to China what later became known as the Shanghai Defence Force; and on the 24th the War Office announced that this was to be under the command of Major-General John Duncan, previously G.O.C. of the 54th (East Anglian) Territorial Division, and was to consist of three infantry brigades. Two of these were to be sent from Britain and the Mediterranean and the third, composed of two British and two Punjabi battalions, from India. This was the normal infantry strength of a division, but without the usual divisional artillery apart from an armoured car company. A batallion of marines which had already been ordered to China sailed from Portsmouth on January 26; a Punjabi battalion stationed at Hong Kong was sent provisionally to Shanghai, where it arrived on the 27th;[19] and the First Cruiser Squadron, under the command of Rear-Admiral Boyle,[20] was ordered from the Mediterranean to reinforce Tyrwhitt, arriving at Hong Kong early in February, where for the time being it remained.[21] 'I wish I could have [it] here', wrote Tyrwhitt, 'but at present they would only be in the way, as there is nowhere to put them'.[22] This was perhaps a little disingenuous, since there are grounds for thinking that Tyrwhitt, besides feeling that the need for troops was greater than that for more ships, did not want a second flag-officer at his elbow, and had already signalled Boyle to 'proceed at economical speed'. The enforced stay at Hong Kong angered Boyle and relations between the two were strained for a time, especially as Boyle wanted to bombard the Nationalist stronghold of Canton, which Tyrwhitt vetoed as certain to precipitate war.[23] It is true, however, that before the First Cruiser Squadron arrived on the station, two more cruisers had come up to Shanghai from Hong Kong, one of them being Tyrwhitt's flagship, the *Hawkins*, which had been refitting there and to which he had transferred on his return from Hankow, finding her 'very wet and vibrates like the devil'.[24]

Other powers, and particularly the United States and Japan, were now also taking steps to provide for the security of at least their own nationals at Shanghai, and during February the total of foreign warships in the port rose from twenty-one to thirty-five, representing seven navies – the British, American, Japanese, French, Italian, Dutch and Spanish. Nine of these ships were British, and fourteen in all were cruisers, the rest being destroyers, gunboats and other lighter craft.[25] Co-operation, however, was not all that could be wished. 'Unfortunately', wrote Tyrwhitt on February 2, 'the American admiral[26] is the senior and I suppose naturally wishes to be in the limelight. At the same time he says that in the event of any enemy troops approaching he has orders to embark his men and not to fight.'[27] Little more than a week later, however, 250 U.S. Marines landed in the International Settlement from Manila. The French, for their part, had assumed a separate responsibility for the security of the French Settlement and at first seemed reluctant to commit themselves to any concerted action with the British and other foreign forces for the common defence of the two areas. At a conference of the British, American, French, Japanese and Italian admirals early in the month, Tyrwhitt found that 'they one and all said that they would protect their own interests from mob riot, but if the Nationalist army came in they would retire.'[28]

Another of his worries at that time was lest the troops being sent to China were not going to be allowed to come to Shanghai after all. The Foreign Secretary, Sir Austen Chamberlain, had in fact given a conditional undertaking in a speech that they would be concentrated in Hong Kong and would not proceed to Shanghai unless 'the emergence of fresh or greater danger' required their presence there.[29] This undertaking was not implemented, however, since the victories of the Nationalist army over the northerners and their continued advance towards Shanghai threatened to lead to fighting in and around the city itself; and on February 8 Tyrwhitt wrote delightedly to his wife:

> 'I have done it. I had a wire today from Admiralty giving me an absolutely free hand as to the disposal of the troops, also informing me that I was entirely responsible for the whole show ... Now I have no hesitation in ordering the Indian brigade [which would naturally be the first to arrive] here ... If I had been a real gambler I might have waited for the first British brigade which I would sooner have had, but they are not due until the 27th and the crisis is very near ... Now I feel quite happy ... Nothing worries me so much as waiting for other people to make up their minds ... Lampson ... entirely concurs in all that I have done up to date.'

'The war-clouds seem to be gathering,' he ended: 'I think the next ten days will be the critical period.'[30]

On the 12th – twenty-four hours ahead of time – the first two of the troopships carrying the brigade from India arrived at Shanghai, and Brigadier Sangster, who was in command, came aboard the *Hawkins* and struck Tyrwhitt as 'a very go-ahead fellow and a good sort'. The troops themselves (the two British battalions, the 2nd Gloucesters and 2nd Durham Light Infantry) landed two days later – their billets not having been ready before that – and marched through the town, Tyrwhitt taking the salute, rather to his private gratification. On the same day the senior Italian naval officer called on him and reported that his government were going to send troops and that he had been ordered to co-operate with the British. He was followed by the Japanese admiral, who informed Tyrwhitt that 4,000 Japanese troops were standing by at Sasebo in the extreme south of Japan, its nearest point to Shanghai, ready to join in if necessary.[31] The two Punjabi battalions of the Indian brigade arrived on the 18th and also marched past Tyrwhitt, who was most favourably impressed by these 'very fine brawny people, most of them heavily bearded and with dark gleaming eyes and all looking very fit and businesslike'. Next day he received the Government's approval of his wish to bring on from Hong Kong one of the two other brigades which by now had arrived there, but as accommodation was still limited he sent only for the General and two of its battalions. 'It seems', he wrote to his wife, 'to be a race between the Nationalist army and the *Megantic* [the troopship carrying these battalions].'[32]

Meanwhile as the Nationalists drew steadily nearer the city sporadic strikes, affecting Chinese as well as foreign enterprises and accompanied by intimidation and murder, had been breaking out; and on February 19 these culminated in a general strike, which was fortunately accompanied by surprisingly little disorder. The preparations made beforehand by the municipal councils of the two foreign settlements enabled all utility services to be continued without interruption, and after the first two days a weakening appeared in the ranks of the strikers, while on the fifth the Chinese General Labour Union called off the strike and work was resumed. Nevertheless on the 25th those units of the British Defence Force which were already on the spot were moved out to form a cordon round the International Settlement. A small body of 180 Italian marines, in co-operation, also occupied a sector of the line.[33] Late on the following evening General Duncan arrived with his staff and the two battalions which had been asked for, and came to see Tyrwhitt at 9.30 on the morning of the 27th. The latter liked him personally but was not impressed with him as a soldier. 'He struck me as being anything but a thruster,' he wrote, 'but luckily he has a very fine chief of staff.' This was none other than Colonel Lord Gort, the future Commander-in-Chief of the British Expeditionary Force sent to France in 1939, to whom Tyrwhitt took instantly and whom he was soon describing as 'an extraordinarily able man'.[34] Duncan, on the other hand, he found was inclined to make difficulties, one being his anxiety over the fact that the sixteen-miles-long military cordon which had been drawn trespassed in some sectors outside the settlement boundaries. 'He's quite a nice person, but not a general,' grumbled Tyrwhitt: 'He's a diplomat, and I am sure he will make a mess of it if he tries diplomacy here.'[35]

By March 2 the foreign troops available for the defence of the settlement were as follows: British, three battalions in position and five (including the marine battalion) in reserve; French, none in position, 800 men in reserve and 1,000 arriving; Italian, 180 in position; Japanese, none in position, 1,000 in reserve; American, none in position, 1,300 ashore in billets and more arriving. A few days later two more British battalions, the 2nd Coldstream Guards and the 1st Devons, came on from Hong Kong, and another contingent of American marines landed on March 9.[36] There was still no unified command, however, though an arrangement had been made that the French force in their settlement would act in conjunction with the British if need arose. The Japanese Government, on the other hand, had not yet committed itself in spite of the Japanese admiral's assurances to Tyrwhitt; while the Americans (marines included) seem to have received definite orders not to take part in the common defence of the cordon or to resist Chinese regular forces, but to confine themselves to the protection of American life and property.[37] How far this was a result, and how far a cause, of Tyrwhitt's bad relations with the Anglophobe American admiral is difficult to determine. With the Japanese admiral, on the contrary, his relations steadily improved, especially after the admiral and his flag-lieutenant, while on a visit to the *Hawkins*, had shown great and genuine interest in his hobby of making miniature furniture.[38]

In the event, the retreat of the beaten Chinese northern forces through the area bordering the foreign cordon and its occupation by the Nationalists took place without any serious collision. A fortnight before the occupation the Kuomintang Government, now firmly under right-wing influence, issued a declaration of policy to the effect that it had been decided to re-establish Chinese control over the foreign settlements by negotiation and not by force; and the substitution of its troops for those of the northerners in the Shanghai area was in fact carried out without any clash at all between the former and the foreign forces, the few encounters which these had with Chinese troops during these critical days being all with the northerners. On March 12 a body of 500 of these who tried to enter the International Settlement was turned back by the British. On the 21st the troops already stationed along the cordon were reinforced by naval forces, now including American marines; and at the request of the municipal council of the settlement armed posts were stationed outside the cordon in order to guard foreign properties along the roads beyond the settlement boundaries.[39] According to Tyrwhitt's letters to his wife, it was only with great difficulty that General Duncan could be induced to agree to this:

> 'Old D. stuck his toes in and would not take any steps to safeguard this property ... We were at it for nearly two hours this afternoon and ... at last I said: "Well, if you won't send out troops to protect this property I'll land my sailors and do it with them" ... Eventually I defeated him and he, being a real gentleman, acknowledged the fact and has climbed down ... His staff all wanted to do it but could not persuade him.'[40]

On the 21st northern troops broke through the cordon on the north of the international settlement and began looting, but were driven out by machine-gun fire from two British armoured cars, at the cost of four British wounded and an unrecorded number of Chinese casualties. Next day a brigade of northerners which had been occupying a railway station yard in Chapei, just outside the boundary of the settlement, tried to force their way into it in order to save themselves from being disarmed by the Nationalists. The British troops on the spot were obliged to open fire, and about sixty Chinese were killed and many wounded before the remainder surrendered and were disarmed, partly by the British and partly by Japanese marines outside the cordon.[41]

The Nationalist occupation of the Shanghai area was also effected without any such organised mob violence as had taken place at Hankow and Kiukiang in January, thanks to the grip which the Nationalist right wing speedily took on the situation in and around the Chinese City. For a short time, however, the activities of the Chinese Communist Party and Chinese organised labour caused much anxiety. About the end of the first week of March the General Labour Union had begun to prepare for a fresh attempt at a general strike (timed to coincide with the arrival of the Nationalist army) by a campaign of intimidation against unions or individual workers who opposed their policy, conducted by plain-clothes 'black gunmen' most of whom according to Tyrwhitt had filtered in from outside.[42] By March 18 about twenty murders had been committed, and on the 21st the general strike was duly proclaimed, though it was announced that it was not directed against the foreigners but intended simply to celebrate the Nationalist victory and would last only three days. It was in fact called off on the 24th at the instance of Chiang Kai-shek's lieutenant, General Pai Chung-hsi, who had issued a proclamation on the previous day calling on the population not to insult foreigners or destroy their property. Nevertheless in the meantime sniping by the Communist gunmen had inflicted several casualties on the foreign troops, a Punjabi soldier being shot dead and another seriously wounded on the 21st and two more Punjabis killed and three British soldiers and a Japanese wounded on the 22nd. By the 23rd, however, the tension was already decreasing; on the

25th the first collision between General Pai Chung-hsi's troops and the Communist gunmen occurred in Chapei; by the end of the month the sniping was reported to have ceased; and in the course of April Chiang Kai-shek took the offensive against the Communists at Shanghai and suppressed them.[43]

In contrast to events at Shanghai, serious outrages against foreigners had been committed by Nationalist troops at the relatively unprotected Nanking on March 24, immediately after their entry into that city at the heels of the retreating northerners. Six foreigners, including the British harbour-master, a French and an Italian priest and a seaman on board the British cruiser *Emerald*, were murdered; the British consul-general, an officer of the Shanghai Defence Force, an American and several Japanese were wounded; houses were looted, individuals stripped of their valuables and even their clothes, and a number of foreign women subjected to outrageous treatment, including attempts to rape them. To enable those who escaped with their lives to get away to the warships which were lying in the river, these vessels – the *Emerald* and several American destroyers – opened fire for about seventy minutes, causing Chinese casualties whose number was very variously estimated,[44] but bringing the rioting and shooting to an immediate stop.

The evacuation of the foreigners was completed next day; though it was not until the warships were on the point of opening a second bombardment that the Nationalist commanding general allowed the last of them to be brought down to the waterfront, and the looting of foreign property continued for some days. Similar attacks on property were committed at the next treaty-port down the river, Chinkiang, after its occupation by Nationalist troops on April 3; though here no casualties occurred, since all foreign residents had taken refuge on board ship before the Nationalists arrived. In face of this situation Tyrwhitt showed a restraint and balanced judgement with which some might not have been prepared to credit him.

'I am in the unfortunate position [he wrote to his wife] of having to restrain our people from doing anything violent or stupid, which attitude I must keep up especially on the Lower Yangtse until the Upper Yangtse has been evacuated[45] ... I have been terribly worried by the people at Nanking, who all want to retaliate by another bombardment. I had to be very firm with my man [presumably the captain of the *Emerald*] and I almost got to the point of relieving him by another ship. I quite understand that his feelings were somewhat worked up, but another bombardment would mean war ... I had an admirals' meeting this morning about Nanking and I carried my point. I believe if I had agreed to another bombardment they would have agreed, but we decided to refer to our respective governments.'[46]

To his sister Polly he wrote:

'The Nanking outrage was the climax. I have had much trouble to prevent the three powers [i.e. the British, American and Japanese officers and officials on the spot] from doing anything foolish since the release [by the Nationalist commander at Nanking] of all the nationals. The first bombardment was quite sound and produced the release of practically everyone, but I was adverse [sic] to any more of that sort of punishment ... I put it to the Government that it was up to them now to decide what was to be done.'[47]

On April 11 the American, British, French, Italian and Japanese governments presented identical notes in duplicate: through their consuls-general at Shanghai to General Pai Chung-hsi for his superior General Chiang Kai-shek, and through their consuls-general at Hankow to Chen. In these they demanded

(1) adequate punishment of the commanders of the troops responsible for the outrages and of all persons found to be implicated;
(2) a written apology from the Nationalist Commander-in-Chief, including an undertaking to refrain from all such violence in future; and
(3) complete reparation for personal injuries and material damage.[48]

Meanwhile, Tyrwhitt, having secured promises of co-operation from the American and Japanese admirals, had drawn up plans for action if this ultimatum – as he regarded it – was not accepted and had got provisional approval from the Admiralty and the Government. If the American and Japanese governments did not endorse their admirals' agreement to co-operate, he intended nevertheless to act with the British forces alone. 'The general idea', he wrote, 'is to destroy all the forts in the Yangtse, including the arsenal of Hankow;' and as a preliminary he had obtained air-photographs of them from the aircraft of the carrier *Vindictive*.[49] On April 14 Chen, who had already claimed that the outrages had been committed by northerners and local ruffians, replied to the Powers' notes, expressing regret for what had happened, promising reparation for injuries and damage, and declaring that in future effective measures would be taken to afford proper protection to foreign lives and property. He proposed, however, that bilateral commissions of inquiry should be set up to investigate the circumstances not only of the outrages but of the naval bombardment of Hankow, and suggested that the questions of punishment and apology should wait upon the result of these investigations. He also submitted that the chief danger to foreign lives and property in China lay in the Powers' insistence on maintaining the régime of the 'Unequal Treaties'. The Powers were unanimous in regarding these replies as unsatisfactory, but also in deciding that in view of the growing split in the Nationalist ranks it would be inadvisable to make any attempt to enforce sanctions which might drive the two factions together again.[50]

Tyrwhitt had anticipated this outcome, writing on the 10th:

> 'I feel quite sure that at the very last moment we shall be told to hold off. It reminds me so much of Constantinople, which ended in a washout although we were so very often on the very verge of war.'[51]

Nevertheless, and in spite of his previous efforts to prevent any premature local naval action that might precipitate war, he was bitterly disappointed by the decision not to apply sanctions.

> 'Just as I thought that all was well and arranged [he wrote on the 14th] the Admiralty have put the hat on everything ... I felt inclined to commit hari-kari this morning at breakfast when I got their telegram.'[52]

Instead, after digesting Chen's reply to the Powers' notes he in his turn sent the Admiralty a telegram of protest against inaction, despatched the *Vindictive* and the cruiser *Carlisle* to Hankow, and contemplated following them up the Yangtse himself. By the 26th he had persuaded General Duncan to lend him the Coldstreams and the Devons, and with those and the marine battalion he proposed to go up-river, 'retake' Hankow and 'blow up the Arsenal if they fire a single shot'. To the Admiralty and the Government he argued that this would probably be a bloodless operation, though in his own mind he had doubts about this – 'but we shall have Hankow back at all costs'. By vigorous and prolonged argument he had overcome Ambassador Lampson's misgivings – or at any rate believed that he had – but after some days of anxious expectation there came another telegram of veto.[53]

Some consolation for this second disappointment had been provided by the arrival on the station of his son St. John, now a sub-lieutenant, who on completing his sub-lieutenant's qualifying courses had been posted to the *Carlisle*. After a brief glimpse of his mother and sisters at Hong Kong, he had reached Shanghai on April 4, spent twenty-four hours with his father, and then gone up-river with his ship to Hankow.[54]

Another arrival soon afterwards was Commander 'Turtle' Hamilton,[55] who had been sent out from Britain in the destroyer *Wanderer*, with her sister the *Wolverine* and the gunboats *Aphis* and *Ladybird*. Reaching Hong Kong on April 10, he spent some days there, in the course of which he went to Repulse Bay to see Lady Tyrwhitt, 'who was in great form and very cheerful'. According to a man with whom he lunched, 'everyone swears by Admiral Tyrwhitt out here, and puts the credit of the Shanghai Force entirely down to him.' Arriving at Shanghai on the 30th, he called next day on the Commander-in-Chief, whom he found 'in excellent form and very complimentary about my having produced the gunboats intact'. Since this was a few days before Tyrwhitt received the damping telegram referred to above, he was 'full of war, itching to be at 'em, and cursing the Government for shilly-shallying'. On May 2 Hamilton started off again to Hankow, where he transferred to the destroyer *Wild Swan*.[56] A few days afterwards and just after the heavy blow of the vetoing telegram, Caslon, writing to report to Lady Tyrwhitt on the Admiral's health and spirits, expressed his admiration of his chief:

> 'I really don't know how he's managed to keep going in the cheery way that he has ... though God knows he's had enough to drive the average man crazy ... And yet he goes on and on, struggling to save the situation in spite of everyone – and *he will*, I'll stake everything on it ... [His] mainstays are Gort and Barton – the latter inclined to be a menace at times, being highly strung and apt to go off the deep end, but real value on the whole, as he's very brilliant and very keen and courageous and his views on active action coincide with

> the Admiral's ... He himself is splendidly fit, with the exception of that rotten arm, which has been troubling him a lot lately ... I'm afraid that as long as he goes on wielding squash rackets and so on, there won't be much improvement. But ... to deny him his game of squash ... would be a crime.'[57]

Caslon himself, an excellent player, was Tyrwhitt's chief opponent at the game. The Admiral derived the keenest pleasure from his own rather rare victories in their contests.

The decrease of tension at Shanghai, which had begun to become apparent in the final week of March, had continued steadily till the last serious danger of a catastrophe there was removed by the success of Chiang Kai-shek's local offensive against the Communists in mid-April. On April 4, however, the British Government, though it had vetoed Tyrwhitt's plans for an offensive at Hankow, decided to send another infantry brigade to China as a reinforcement. This Tyrwhitt considered superfluous, and he hastened to assure his wife that it was none of his doing. 'I believe they are to be kept at Hong Kong in reserve,' he added. By May 17 the British military forces at Shanghai already totalled twelve infantry battalions and one marine battalion, with ancillary units, and counting in the foreign contingents there were about 15,000 men in all. At Hong Kong there were, including the fresh brigade then arriving, seven infantry battalions and ancillary troops.[58]

A minor difficulty which by now was arising for Tyrwhitt was that as the tension lessened British people at Shanghai began to ask him whether it would be safe to take their usual summer holidays at the island paradise of Wei-Hai-Wei, which enjoyed a magnificent climate at that time of year and where there were a hotel, a golf-course, tennis-courts and bathing-beaches. Lady Tyrwhitt, too, having the C-in-C's yacht *Petersfield* at her disposal, naturally wanted to know if and when she could go there with her daughters, as she would otherwise have done in the normal course of events. As

Caslon explained the situation to her:

> 'He's in a rotten position. House agents, shore folk of all kinds (even Lady Barton) continually bombard him with "Will Wei-Hai-Wei be all right for this summer?" He doesn't know – maybe thinks it will be – but if he says "Yes" it'll be broadcast far and wide [as] "guaranteed by the Naval C-in-C"; so he just goes on saying "No". If you go there in *Petersfield*, it's tantamount in shore-going eyes to his saying "Yes". They don't or won't realise that you can be evacuated in your ship if necessary at half-an-hour's notice. So each day we hope for the situation to clear.'[59]

In the Yangtse basin the situation reached and passed its most explosive point at some time between the evacuation of British subjects from above Hankow at the end of March and the reopening of the Upper Yangtse to British trade towards the end of the year. During the first four months of this period the British and other Western residents who still remained in the river basin, outside the cordon of Western troops drawn round the foreign settlements at Shanghai, were living virtually in a state of siege. The women and children had been evacuated down river, while such men as remained were concentrated on board ship or else on the river banks with arrangements for taking to their ships at a moment's notice. An unofficial estimate published in the *Times* of April 28 assessed the number of foreign warships in various parts of the river at that time at over a hundred, and it was only where the foreign communities were covered by their guns that they were able to maintain a toehold. Even so, the practice of firing at foreign vessels indiscriminately and without provocation had become habitual since the arrival of the Nationalist forces, and it was now common form for warships to retaliate.[60] 'The Yangtse river', Tyrwhitt wrote to his sister on May 7, 'is in a state of chaos'; and on the 13th he left Shanghai in the *Hawkins* to go up-river to Hankow on a tour of inspection and encouragement, taking Gort with him as his guest. 'He is in great form and thoroughly enjoying a rest,' wrote Tyrwhitt to his wife; and the two first-class fighting-men unbosomed themselves to each other in talks which were as long as Tyrwhitt's leisure moments allowed.[61]

On the eve of his departure he had received two telegrams from the Admiralty, the first of which authorized him, when any of the contending forces in China fired at a British warship or any other vessel flying the British flag, to take retaliatory action with all the forces at his disposal, supplemented if necessary by landing parties to destroy forts and guns guilty of such action. He was also empowered to take immediate punitive action in cases of outrages where the lives of British nationals or British property were endangered. In cases where only the violation of rights was in question punitive action was to be taken only after the sanction of the Government had been obtained. In deciding what action should be taken he was to be guided by the considerations that the purpose was to prevent a recurrence of such hostile acts by forcing the Chinese authorities to assume and carry the responsibility which properly belonged to them for affording adequate protection; that the punishment must not be excessive; that action should preferably be taken against military objectives, such as forts, barracks and military headquarters, and due consideration given to the safety of innocent civilians; that the selected objective should as far as possible be very near the scene of the outrage; and that close touch should be kept with the Minister at Peking and any punitive action reported instantly to the Admiralty. The second telegram amounted to a relay from the Government of the purpose and proposed methods of execution of the policy on which it had determined and which, it declared, was founded on its

> 'desire to maintain as far as possible for the present, and more especially to preserve for the future, the great trade interests which enterprise of British firms ... has

developed throughout China. It was for this interest that they despatched the Shanghai Defence Force ... But [the telegram continued] it was never contemplated that this or any other British force should be used for extended operations in China such as would be required to produce order out of existing chaos or even to hold the various scattered Concessions which it has been found necessary to evacuate. Nor was arrangement for re-occupation of Hankow, as suggested, a measure in itself capable of restoring trade. It was only considered by H.M. Government as a sanction for Nanking outrages. Trade can only flourish in an atmosphere of peace and order where it can develop freely. The re-occupation of Hankow might have enabled British nationals to move freely within the Concession itself as long as occupation continued, but whilst other conditions remained unchanged, it could not have restored trade, which might well have been exposed both there and elsewhere to a more extensive and lasting boycott ...'

After this exposition of the Government's reasons for turning down Tyrwhitt's proposed occupation of Hankow, the telegram went on to answer his subsequent signals of protest:

'... The position appears to be that ... no measures we can take for the present prevent our own or any other trade from suffering from chaos resulting from rapid extension of civil war into Yangtse Valley. H.M. Government cannot, therefore, endorse your view that ... policy they have adopted really ignores these sufferings ... Nor is it a practicable proposition that trade can be irrevocably kept alive and healthy by means of a forcible military and naval protection ...'[62]

Having stopped for a couple of hours at Kiuchiang, where

the British consul, 'a good chap', was 'keeping his end up well', Tyrwhitt went on to discover a storm brewing at Nanking. Here the Nationalists had decided to commandeer the rolling-stock of the Shanghai-Nanking Railway and transport it across the Yangtse in order to use it to facilitate their advance on Peking. Since the whole property of the railway was mortgaged to British interests as security for a loan, Tyrwhitt – in accordance with the instructions he had just received – informed Chen forthwith that if any attempt were made to do this he would take immediate action, and backed his warning by ordering the *Carlisle* to Nanking with instructions to use force if necessary. This being his son's ship, 'I am sure', he wrote, 'he will be delighted at the prospect of a scrap.' The warning sufficed, however, and he went on in the *Hawkins* to Hankow, which he reached on the 16th. Here he 'dined all he could' and did his best to 'buck them all up', with considerable success. In particular, he had 'a most satisfactory interview' with the British consul there and Hamilton, who wrote in his diary:

> 'He was in the very best of form, looking awfully well, and inspired everyone with any amount of confidence. Badcock, his secretary, told me that the Admiral's handling of the whole situation out here was a revelation to him, because he had been afraid he would get fed up with the Chinese and go for them baldheaded as he used to do the Germans, but no-one could possibly have shown more self-restraint in very trying conditions.'

Nevertheless, before he left again Tyrwhitt took Hamilton aside and said: 'I don't want to have an incident before I get back to Shanghai, as I'm going to see the Minister [i.e., Lampson] there and decide on the future policy, but of course if you find it necessary to open fire I shall quite understand.'[63] Moreover, in common with all on board the *Hawkins*, he felt disappointed that she was not fired on during her river cruise, and so was given no opportunity for the retaliation for which everybody was itching. On the day of her arrival at Hankow, however, a British passenger steamer was shot at from Whampoa, near Canton, by cadets of the military college, whereupon Tyrwhitt instantly demanded that the Nationalist authorities should make amends, which they eventually did more or less satisfactorily. He also flung his vehement energy into opposing successfully a proposal to evacuate the British Legation from Peking in face of the Nationalists' continued advance – a move to which Lampson, General Duncan and even (according to Tyrwhitt's own account) the home authorities were inclined.[64]

On his return to Shanghai, which he found 'outwardly quite quiet ... no-one would imagine that anything unusual was taking place here – dinners, dances, etc., every night', his wife and daughters were able to join him, coming from Hong Kong in the *Petersfield* for about ten days, after which they left on June 4 for Wei-Hai-Wei, to which a battalion was being despatched and where they took up their quarters in the Commander-in-Chief's bungalow. 'It was jolly seeing them', he wrote to his sister, 'but I was very glad when they got away, as I am really too busy to attend to families, etc., and to be dining out and dancing night after night ... I escape as often as possible.'[65] His growing nostalgia for a peaceful and unbroken family life emerged in one of his next letters to his wife, in which he wrote (somewhat optimistically):

> 'Thank God this is our last job. I swear I will not go to another, not even the Mediterranean even if I was offered it. I think after two years of this life I shall be glad to say "Finish!" '[66]

At the beginning of July, however, things had quietened sufficiently at Shanghai for him to hand over temporarily to Boyle, join his family at Wei-Hai-Wei, and then take them with him in the *Petersfield* to Peking, where he spent a couple of days conferring with Lampson. After that he returned to Wei-Hai-Wei, where Boyle's presence at Shanghai w]th the First Cruiser Squadron enabled him to concentrate four of his own squadron for a month of much overdue practice. During this he wrote rather ruefully to his old friend Walter Cowan about his twice-frustrated plans for action up the Yangtse River, including 'plastering the Woosung forts with bombs from all the aircraft I could collect and then blowing their guts out by salvoes at close range'.

> 'I wish [he continued] you were here to deal with the conundrums. I have not the brains for that part of it and I expect I am more irritable in consequence ... [but] I have some A1 commanding officers, both in cruisers, destroyers and river gunboats. They always do the right thing and don't want too much telling. I prefer the fellow who acts promptly and says what he's done to the fellow who asks what he is to do.'[67]

At the end of July he returned to Shanghai, where what he described as 'some excitement' had developed again. Friction with the Nationalists had been caused by British military aircraft frequently flying over their territory; protests had been made, but Sir Austen Chamberlain had stated in the Commons in June that Admiral Tyrwhitt had been authorized to use these aircraft in any way he thought desirable for the defence of the Settlement, although this would undoubtedly involve flights over fortified areas and districts where fighting between Chinese forces was in progress. On August 16 a British plane made a forced landing on the Kiangwan golf-course, which lay in Chinese territory about four miles outside the Settlement boundaries. An unarmed party of troops was sent out to retrieve it and succeeded in bringing in the engine and fuselage, but before the wings could be brought away a body of Chinese troops intervened and prevented their removal, as well as detaining the pilot and observer. The British Consul-General requested the local Chinese commissioner for foreign affairs to take the necessary steps to secure their release and the restoration of the wings, but met with a categorical refusal. General Duncan, whom Tyrwhitt described as 'quite hotted up', thereupon conveyed an ultimatum to the Commissioner, expiring at 11 a.m. on the 17th, to the effect that unless satisfaction was given his troops would occupy and cut the loop-line, outside the cordon, which connected the Shanghai-Hangkow and Shanghai-Nanking Railways. This would have the effect of interrupting the Nationalists' main line of military communications at a critical point in their campaign. 'All that is necessary now', wrote Tyrwhitt, 'is to keep the General up to the mark.' But this proved no easy task, since by the next morning Duncan's ire and resolution had cooled considerably, though 'after a long and somewhat heated argument' Tyrwhitt prevailed on him to take the threatened action when the ultimatum expired without response. With the aid of the Japanese admiral's mediation, however, the airmen were released and the wings of the disabled aeroplane restored at 7.30 p.m. on the 18th, in return for a formal assurance that the landing had not been deliberate; and the railway was repaired by British military engineers on the same evening and the troops again withdrawn to the cordon.[68]

The question of reparation for the outrages on Westerners committed at Nanking in March had meanwhile remained unsettled. Soon after Chiang Kai-shek had crushed the Communists in the Shanghai area, a new and right-wing Nationalist government had been set up at Nanking in opposition to the pro-Communist one at Hankow, whose authority then declined, and this Nanking government had several times intimated its intention of accepting responsibility for the outrages and making reparation. But recently both it and the Hankow government (which in its turn had experienced something of an anti-Communist revulsion) had virtually dissolved;[69] and immediately after the successful outcome of the aeroplane incident Tyrwhitt went up-river again in the *Hawkins* to land 150 marines at Nanking to protect the property of the International Export Company, which had been looted by the Nationalists in March and had suffered a great deal of minor damage, though much of this had already been repaired. From there he went on to land for an hour at Kiukiang, where there were 'about 3,000 troops on the bund – a particularly nasty-looking lot, mostly very young, rude and indisciplined' – and then to Hankow, which he found fairly quiet and where he again saw his son.[70]

By now the British forces at Shanghai were being gradually reduced. The two British battalions of the Indian brigade left on July 23, leaving eight battalions which by October had been reduced to six – excluding in each case the marine battalion, which in September was reduced to approximately half strength. The Admiralty also asked Tyrwhitt whether the First Cruiser Squadron could be spared to return to the Mediterranean. As he wrote to Keyes, who was now Commander-in-Chief there, this would be 'awkward if there was trouble in Canton at the same time as the Yangtse', but 'they put it so nicely I could not say no'. By this time, thanks not a little to Flag-Lieutenant Caslon's tactful influence, he had arrived at perfectly harmonious relations with the now departing Boyle, whom he described to Keyes as 'simply splendid... absolutely first-class'.[71]

The trouble which he had envisaged at Canton was the increasing possibility of a new clash between the communist and anti-communist elements in the Kuomintang. This did in fact occur in December, when communist elements attempted a *coup*. They took possession of the city for a couple of days (though without molesting any foreigners), after which it was retaken and they were bloodily suppressed – so completely that when Tyrwhitt, who had just returned to Hong Kong, hastened to take stock of the aftermath he went in the *Petersfield* and took his family with him. At Canton he was motored around to see the damage by the Nationalist Foreign Minister, with a Chinese soldier standing on each running-board of the car and brandishing a revolver, but he found everything quiet again, though many bodies in various stages of buoyancy could be seen in the river.

Afterwards he returned again for Christmas to Hong Kong, where he was able to direct the rescue of an Italian mission who were being held prisoners by Chinese communists at Swabue, a seaport about eighty miles away. On Boxing Day a Chinese convert had brought news to the Roman Catholic Bishop Valtorta that the members of the mission, three priests and seven nuns, had been arrested 'for preaching and practising Christianity', and that one of the priests, a Chinese, was about to be executed by 'the death of a thousand cuts'. The Bishop immediately got into touch with Tyrwhitt, who despatched a destroyer inside an hour. Landing an armed party, the destroyer's captain and the Bishop (who had accompanied him) secured the release of the captives and brought them back 'in a dreadful state of dirt and starvation', as Tyrwhitt wrote his sister. A letter from Polly to the Bishop, conveying the sympathy of the community to which she belonged and telling him how they had all prayed for him and for the mission, evoked a grateful reply which spoke in the warmest terms of 'Sir Reginald's great kindness and prompt action', adding 'a more perfect gentleman and a nobler heart surely cannot be found. God bless him!... The priests and sisters whose lives he has saved and myself will pray for him till the end of our lives.' Subsequently Cardinal Gaspari, the Papal Secretary of State, wrote to Polly (as Sister Mary Clare) to convey the Pope's thanks to Tyrwhitt with his apostolic blessings on him and all his family.

With the situation gradually becoming quieter and more stable and his own activities beginning to approximate more to a peacetime pattern, he then visited Singapore (from which he optimistically reported that the naval base which was being intermittently constructed was 'in good trim'), looked in at Port Swettenham on the east coast of Malaya, and went inland from there for a couple of days at Kuala Lumpur. Next he crossed the South China Sea to Manila in the Philippines, where Lady Tyrwhitt met him and where he had 'quite an *entente*' with the Americans, even finding his *bête noire* the American Commander-in-Chief, Admiral Bristol, 'very pleasant on the surface, but ... I do not trust him a yard'.[72]

From there he returned to Shanghai, where General Duncan had been relieved by a successor whom he found more congenial, though his satisfaction at this was modified by the loss of Gort; and then to Hong Kong in April to receive a visit from a Japanese squadron. 'I like the Japs', he wrote to Keyes, 'and always speak quite openly to them. It is extraordinary how they unbend as soon as they realize you are speaking the truth', adding however, 'I am not sure if they always do so themselves.' 'The last thing the King said to me', he confided, 'was – "Whatever you do, be nice to the Japanese!" '[73] It was not long after this that he received what he described as 'a very charming message' from His Majesty which included the observation that he ought to stay in China until that country was at peace. To this he replied, according to his own account, to the effect that if he did so he feared he would be an octogenarian when he returned.[74] He and his family had already celebrated with enthusiasm the halfway stage of his two years' command in January, and were looking forward to its end; and he had more than once unburdened himself to Keyes to that effect – 'Thank God this is only a two-years' job! Nothing would make me stay on a third year,' and again 'I shall be damned glad when my time is up [though] I shall go with an unsatisfactory feeling that the squadron is not in fighting condition and everything is upside down.'[75] His distaste for continued service on the station, however, was not due entirely to his growing longing for a return to private family life, but owed something to his dissatisfaction with the policy of conciliation being pursued by the British Government, which – though he sought loyally to carry it out and both exercised and imposed on his subordinates restraint in dealings with the Chinese – he failed fully to understand and regarded as a weak betrayal of British interests and a surrender of prestige.

As 1928 wore on matters nevertheless continued slowly to improve on the whole. Despite further internal strife within the Kuomintang its success was maintained; Peking fell to its forces in June, and in July its leading generals attended a ceremony in the nearby Western Hills to announce to the spirit of Sun-Yat-sen the successful end of the civil war. Some defeated and disorderly remnants of the northern troops, however, which had settled down in a no-man's-land just inside the Great Wall, had begun to exact supplies from a local Sino-British mining company, the Kailang Mining Administration; and on June 22 Sir Miles Lampson (as he now was) telegraphed to the Foreign Secretary, Sir Austen Chamberlain, as well as to Tyrwhitt (who had previously pointed out in vain the danger in which the company's situation might place it) and to Duncan's successor General Wardrop, strongly urging the despatch of troops to the area in order to meet this threat. Chamberlain replied favourably, Wardrop ordered the 1st battalion of the Bedfordshire and Hertfordshire Regiment to proceed thither from Wei-Hai-Wei as quickly as the Navy could transport them, and this battalion, with auxiliary detachments, embarked at once in the crusier *Berwick*, landed at Chingwangtao on the morning of the 24th and by the evening of the same day had reached its destination safely and without incident, accompanied by a naval detachment manning two three-pounder guns. Tyrwhitt also ordered the carrier *Hermes* to proceed from Wei-Hai-Wei to Chingwangtao and make her aircraft available if required. For his and the Navy's part in this 'striking demonstration of efficiency' and in the subsequent evacuation of British personnel from the area he afterwards received a signal of appreciation and gratification from the Admiralty.[76]

After the Nationalist advance to Peking the storm-centre of the Chinese Revolution had travelled northwards from the Yangtse basin, where the predominant foreign interests were British, towards the north-eastern provinces, where they were Japanese. The Chinese movement against 'imperialism' thus took a new direction and its brunt began to fall upon the

Japanese, while the British in China experienced a certain relaxation of pressure. Moreover a new and united Nationalist government which had now established itself at Nanking was anxious like all its predecessors to get rid of the 'Unequal Treaties' between China and certain foreign powers, and was well aware that it would have a better chance of gaining these powers' consent to treaty revision if the stumbling-block represented by the still-unsettled controversy over the question of compensation for the Nanking outrages were first removed. Negotiations to that end between Lampson and Hwang Fu, who was now the Nationalist Foreign Minister, broke down in March, but a successful outcome was reached in August by an exchange of notes in which the Nationalists expressed regret and accepted responsibility for the outrages, though declaring that they had been instigated by communists, and undertook to make full compensation; while the British government recognised the essential justice of the Chinese claim to treaty revision and declared that it was prepared to enter into negotiation on this subject in due course.[77]

Meanwhile Tyrwhitt had again gone up the Yangtse to Hankow in the *Hawkins*, taking his family with him, as soon as there was enough water to make this possible. Afterwards, while he remained there, they went on to Ichang in the *Petersfield* and then as far as Wanshien in one of the Asiatic Petroleum Company's steamers. The fact that they were twice under fire from the disbanded soldiers, brigands and bandits with whom the upper Yangtse still abounded and who made a pastime of sniping from behind rocks at every foreign ship that passed merely 'thoroughly thrilled' them. After that he went with them to Chemulpo and Seoul in order to have a look at Korea and the Koreans, whom he found 'rather nice people [though] of course very much under the thumb of the Japanese', returned to Wei-Hai-Wei, and then paid a farewell visit to Lampson at Peking. At the end of August his relief flagship *Kent* arrived from England and the *Hawkins* was sent home.[78] Shortly afterwards

Lieutenant Caslon went to the Mediterranean as Fleet Signal Officer, and Tyrwhitt appointed his son St. John, who had recently been promoted lieutenant, as flag-lieutenant in his place. St. John's great friend at the time was Lieutenant Charles Madden,[79] the son of the then First Sea Lord, who had come out in the *Kent*, and the high spirits of these two, the youngest lieutenants in the flagship, sometimes disquieted the Commander-in-Chief, who in view of his acquaintance with Madden's father was inclined to feel that he stood *in loco parentis* to him also. An attempt which the two made to enliven one of the dinner-parties the giving of which Tyrwhitt regarded resignedly as more of a duty than a pleasure, by donning paper hats at a late stage in the proceedings, earned a subsequent stern rebuke; and on another occasion a request from young Madden to be detached for service up the Yangtse was rebuffed with a brusque 'No, Charles, you are *not* going! If I let you go up-river with that lot I should never be able to face your father and mother again' – which apparently proceeded from a care for his morals rather than for his physical safety.[80]

In late November Tyrwhitt took three of his ships (*Kent*, *Suffolk* and *Berwick*) to Japan to attend the naval review at Yokohoma that followed the recent coronation of the Emperor Hirohito. He had intended to take with him his wife and elder daughter (Patricia having been sent back to school in England), but Lady Tyrwhitt went down with 'flu and 'Bobby' had no choice but to stay behind to look after her. Calling *en route* at several lesser Japanese ports, Tyrwhitt found the country 'delightful' and the people 'charming and all smiles', and was enthusiastically welcomed everywhere. From Shimizu he and St. John drove ten miles inland to call on the provincial governor, who invited them to visit a celebrated shrine on the way back. This they did, only to find that it was on top of a very steep hill and reached by 1159 steps – 'a bit of an effort', commented Tyrwhitt. Next day they went inland again and stayed briefly at a hotel about twenty-five miles from the great snow-clad volcano

Fujiyama, which Tyrwhitt, who had been climbing lesser mountains that were accessible from the ports he visited as he came along, would have liked to tackle, but had not the time. Nevertheless they had some enjoyable walks and wallowed afterwards in huge marble baths fed by an unlimited supply of water so hot that he described it as coming straight from Hell. On December 2 they arrived at Yokohama, finding the whole Japanese navy in review order in the bay, as well as representative American, French, Italian and Dutch warships. A seemingly endless round of salutes and calls followed and then on the 4th the review took place. The Emperor toured the lines of anchored ships in the battle-cruiser *Haruna* escorted by three others, after which all the admirals, diplomats and other distinguished guests repaired on board the *Haruna* for an audience (which merely consisted of making a bow) and a stand-up lunch. For this each guest received a basket wrapped in a silk cloth and containing a large piece of fish, some game pie, an apple, an orange, a piece of cake and a large box of sweets. It was only after Tyrwhitt had made inroads on the contents of his basket that he learned that the correct procedure was to take only a few mouthfuls and then re-wrap the basket and take it away for distribution of the remaining viands among one's friends. Subsequently he was taken below for a long talk with Admiral Togo, the great Japanese naval hero and victor of the battle of Tsushima in the Russo-Japanese War, who was now 83 but 'a very fine old man and very much alive'. In the evening he dined (as did Admiral Bristol) with the Japanese Commander-in-Chief, Admiral Kato – 'an old friend and a very charming man' – on board his flagship. Contrary to his previous experience of Japanese banquets, this proved to be the best dinner he had ever eaten on board ship.[81]

Other functions followed on the subsequent days, including a ball at the British Embassy where Tyrwhitt danced with the Princess Chichebu ('very pretty, talks English perfectly and very jolly') and took her in to supper, and a dinner given by the Mayor of Yokohama where each guest was served by charming little geishas, whose fortunes he – rising to the occasion – pretended to tell by reading their hands with the aid of an interpreter. 'They are all terribly superstitious', he wrote to his wife, 'and when I told them to beware of the man with red hair and a long nose and other things their eyes stood out of their heads. However the promise of a good husband and a fortune soon brought smiles back.' He was also amused and gratified to see them making eyes at his handsome son, who in fact was the object of considerable interest throughout. One Japanese admiral observed to him that the boy's mother must be a very charming woman – which indeed was no more than the truth.[82]

On his departure the Imperial Order of the Sacred Treasure (First Class) was conferred on him by the Emperor; and after visiting the Dutch East Indies, where he encountered 'too much pomp and too many dinners and speeches',[83] he was relieved by Vice-Admiral A.K. Waistell in January 1929 and went home after a tumultuous send-off from a grateful Shanghai. On his return the Lords of the Admiralty expressed their high appreciation of the distinguished services which he had rendered while in command of the China Station, adding:

> 'The tenure of your command coincided with a continuation of the period of chaos in China and presented situations full of uncertainty and difficulty, throwing a severe strain upon all those responsible for upholding British interests in the Far East. H.M. Government have regarded you as their principal military adviser upon broad questions of policy connected with the safety of British lives in China, and in this matter you have been entrusted with a heavy responsibility in respect of both naval and military forces, involving the exhibition of qualities of judgement, tact and decision in a high degree. Their Lordships have pleasure in placing on record their entire approval of the manner in which you

> handled this difficult situation, thereby performing a service... of very great value to the Empire.'[84]

On February 27 he had reached the rank of full admiral, and in July the Grand Cross of the Order of the Bath was conferred on him in recognition of his services in the East.[85]

In the same month he was notified by the Admiralty that, having taken with him a rug from the Commander-in-Chief's apartments in the *Kent*, he would be required to forward to the Accountant-General of the Navy a cheque for £29.10.0.[86] Although it was perhaps typical of him that even at his now exalted level he could still get into a tiny bit of trouble, the feelings which prompted him to preserve this letter among his other papers may probably be guessed.

CHAPTER TEN

THE END OF THE JOURNEY

After his return to England Tyrwhitt again spent some months in happy family life at Littlestone House while the question of his further employment hovered on the horizon. For a flag-officer of his seniority the prospects, other than the command at one of the three principal home ports – Portsmouth, Plymouth and the Nore – which normally marked the close of a distinguished admiral's career, were practically limited to the two main fleets, the Atlantic and the Mediterranean. But these plums of the Service were in practice restricted to the very small number of senior officers who besides their other qualifications possessed the administrative gifts for which Tyrwhitt was not noted and who were regarded as probable or possible candidates for the First Sea Lordship in the near future. His friend Sir Roger Keyes, who was himself about to be disappointed of the latter post, tried in 1930 to secure the Mediterranean Fleet for him, and for this purpose interviewed both Prime Minister Macdonald and the First Lord, A.V. Alexander, but without success. It was then that Alexander's Naval Secretary wrote to Keyes (as quoted at the beginning of this book) that had there been the least chance of war within the next two years there could have been no doubt about Tyrwhitt's pre-eminent suitability for the command, but since there was not it was felt that the appointment ought to go to a younger man. The man chosen, relieving Sir Frederick Field who came home to be First Sea Lord, was Beatty's one-time flag-captain and *fidus Achates*, Sir Ernle Chatfield, who was transferred from the command of the Atlantic Fleet and three years later again succeeded Field, this time at the Admiralty. Expressing his gratitude to

Keyes for his 'fine effort on my behalf', Tyrwhitt wrote: 'I shall never be able to thank you enough... but I am quite resigned, so don't worry about me,' and added 'I am glad Chatfield got the Mediterranean. He's a good man and has some presence.' In another letter he confessed to being disappointed at the prospect of being put on the shelf and revealed that Lady Tyrwhitt, like all loyal and loving wives, was less philosophical than he was: 'If you could have heard what Angey said about your letters to the [retiring] First Sea Lord!... [She] says it's a damned shame and the "Inner Ring" ought to be boiled in oil... Well, it's all over now and I shall rub along somewhat discontentedly.' The consolation prize awarded to him was the command at the Nore; and on moving into Admiralty House at Chatham the Tyrwhitts sold Littlestone House with the intention of finding something 'in a less suburban district' when his tenure of this post came to an end.[1]

The post-war reduction of the Navy had now reached its lowest point with the London Naval Conference and Treaty of 1930. By this Britain agreed with the United States and Japan not to lay down any new battleships during the next five years and to scrap five of her existing capital ships, thus bringing the strength of her battle-fleet down to fifteen. She also surrendered to American pressure for the limitation of total cruiser and destroyer tonnage. It was against the background of the discontent and anxiety this caused in naval circles that Admiral Brock, in proposing Tyrwhitt's health as chairman of the Navy Club at its 1931 dinner, said:

> 'No matter how many disarmament conferences we may have to bear with, what the Government may do, or how the Navy is treated, as long as we have men like Reggie Tyrwhitt, men of such singleness of purpose, such courage and such loyalty, then the Navy can weather any storm.'[2]

But soon there came a blow that in its way was even

heavier – the Invergordon Mutiny. Among the economy measures proposed by the Government to cope with the economic crisis of that year were drastic cuts in the pay of the Services. These would fall particularly hard on the lower deck of the Navy, and especially on all men who had joined it before 5 October 1925 and who according to arrangements that had been made in 1919 to match the inflation of civilian workers' pay-scales were paid at a rate appreciably higher than that subsequently fixed for those joining after that date. There were thus two scales – the '1919 rate' and the '1925 rate' – the latter of which, married men contended, was inadequate to maintain their homes at the level established by custom. The principal naval cut which the Government now proposed would have brought all the lower deck down to this 1925 rate.

Faced by this proposal, the Board of Admiralty, a weak Board further weakened by the ill-health or absence on leave of several of its members, failed either to inform itself sufficiently of the effects the cuts would have and the men's probable reactions or to warn the Government emphatically and persistently enough of the consequences that might be expected; though it did originally state that the measure would be regarded as a breach of faith. It also failed to warn flag and other officers of the impending blow in good time, and gave them no instructions or advice on how to deal with the discontent likely to be caused – which indeed it does not seem to have foreseen. The result of these omissions was all the worse since of late years confidence and communication between officers and men had been decreasing, partly because many of the latter were more politically conscious than their predecessors had been. To cap everything, in the Atlantic Fleet there was an unhappy concatenation of mischances and blunders. The Commander-in-Chief, Sir Michael Hodges, was absent in Haslar Hospital suffering from severe pleurisy. His second-in-command, Rear-Admiral Tomkinson, had taken over only a few days before the cuts were decided on, and the Board bungled the notification of them to him so badly that he did not receive it until after the men had learnt of them from radio programmes and newspapers. Finally it paid no attention to Tomkinson's first signal informing it of unrest – though it is true that he declared that he attached no importance to it – and even when the unrest had developed into a widespread refusal to put to sea for manoeuvres it did not follow the example of its predecessor of 1797 when faced by the Spithead Mutiny and intervene directly and personally. The most it did, in the first place, was to order the ships of the Atlantic Fleet to return to their several home ports pending investigation; an order which the men were fortunately prepared to obey.[3]

Field's predecessor as First Sea Lord, Admiral Sir Charles Madden, who was Jellicoe's brother-in-law and had been his Chief of Staff, is said to have greeted his son when he stepped ashore at this juncture from a continental holiday with the anxious enquiry 'Have they sent for Tyrwhitt?' and followed it with the emphatic assertion that 'The man to sort this out is Tyrwhitt!'[4] The justification of this categorically expressed opinion will soon emerge; but it was Admiral Sir John Kelly who was appointed Commander-in-Chief of the Atlantic Fleet on October 6 for a term of one year and who by his blunt yet sympathetic approach dealt with the situation successfully, while afterwards not sparing the Admiralty in his report.

On the day of Kelly's appointment Tyrwhitt and all other commanders-in-chief received a memorandum from Vice-Admiral Dreyer, the Deputy Chief of the Naval Staff, the aim of which was to exculpate the Admiralty. 'My memorandum', he wrote in his covering letter, 'does not ascribe fault to anyone except the agitators and the foolish men who took their advice... The men should... be taught that the damned agitators have caused them to lose caste and that if they had trusted their officers and given them the evidence of the extent of their private obligations [i.e., the extent of the hire-purchase payments to which many of the married men were committed and which they felt they would be unable to keep up if the cuts were imposed] as soon as the cuts were officially announced, they would have had their pay revised.'[5]

Tyrwhitt, though he would have been less than human if his opinion of the Board had not been somewhat coloured by his recent disappointment, knew better, as his pencilled comments on many passages of Dreyer's memorandum show. His standpoint was that though the Government had been at fault in the first place in the harshness and unfairness of its proposals for the Navy, the Admiralty was greatly to blame for not exhaustively examining their consequences for the men and the men's views, and making these crystal clear to the Cabinet, as well as for its subsequent mishandling of the impact of the news upon the lower deck. In view of this and of the lessened contacts and confidence between the officers in general and the men, of which he showed that he was well aware, he disagreed entirely with Dreyer's assertion that it was not possible to excuse refusal of duty under any circumstances, minuting in the margin that 'in spite of impossibility we will do it this time'.

It was in this spirit that he attended a meeting of the three commanders-in-chief of the home ports on 6 January 1932, called by and presided over by Field to review what had happened, perhaps in the hope or expectation that these elder statesmen of the Navy would help to exonerate the Board.

If that was Field's motive, he was disappointed. As Tyrwhitt wrote a few days later to Kelly:

> '... A good drop of blood was spilt.
>
> 'Field opened the ball by giving us a long *résumé* of what took place at the Admiralty before the cuts. It is quite true they were let down by the Government and as I told him if he had only told the Navy exactly what had happened, he would have cleared his yardarm, more or less.'[6]

The C-in-C. at Plymouth, Admiral Sir Hubert Brand, who had once been a term-mate of Tyrwhitt's in the *Britannia,* then asked leave to read a statement, in which he expressed views very similar to those held by Tyrwhitt, as follows:

> 'That [the discipline of the Fleet] failed clearly shows that there was something amiss and that something was undoubtedly a lack of confidence on the part of the men in their officers and the Admiralty. With perfect confidence they would naturally have turned to their officers, [but] as it was the officers were kept completely in ignorance of what was going on and chief petty officers and petty officers made no effort to inform them... I am afraid that the Admiralty in the mind of the Service will have to shoulder the responsibility of issuing this order without regard for its consequences...
>
> 'To my mind it is the system at the Admiralty which has failed and which requires reorganising.'

With this statement Tyrwhitt expressed his full concurrence, though Admiral Sir Arthur Waistell, the C-in-C. at Portsmouth, made no comment on it. The port admirals then recommended that the Admiralty should issue

> 'an impartial statement accepting some responsibility for events and that Admiral Tomkinson should be relieved of his command, but only if it [was] possible to issue the Admiralty statement sharing the blame.'[7]

As Tyrwhitt put it in his letter to Kelly:

> 'We decided that the Navy should be told what happened. I have not seen the work of art yet, but an apology will, I understand, be included.'

He never did see the 'work of art', however, for it never

materialised; though Tomkinson, despite having originally been complimented on his handling of the mutiny by the First Lord, Austen Chamberlain, in a speech in the Commons, was in due course relieved of the command which by then he was holding, and thus became the scapegoat for it. Meanwhile it had been rather hastily decided to reduce substantially the cuts in the pay of the Services.[8]

Besides making these recommendations the three port admirals went on to give their opinions on future flag appointments in the light of recent events, and especially of the Admiralty's poor showing in them. As a result, heads rolled. Vice-Admiral Dreyer had previously been promised the Atlantic Fleet at the end of his term as Deputy Chief of the Naval Staff, and the question was whether he was now to relieve Sir John Kelly after the latter's year of emergency command. Tyrwhitt 'objected strongly... and had a great scrap but was backed rather half-heartedly by the other two'. Instead, Dreyer was in due course posted to the China Command – though Tyrwhitt at the meeting had proposed only the West Indies for him – which meant the end of any hopes he had of ultimately becoming First Sea Lord. Kelly's appointment was extended for a further year, again on Tyrwhitt's motion, in which he was backed by Waistell, though Brand favoured six months. Admiral Sir Cyril Fuller, the Second Sea Lord, who by virtue of his office was responsible for naval personnel, had been meant to succeed to the honorific Plymouth command; but the three elder statesmen, with Tyrwhitt once more leading, recommended that he should be relieved and not employed again. In the event he was allowed to finish his term but given no further employment. 'I have since', wrote Tyrwhitt to Kelly, 'had a most indignant letter from Fuller... He wrote to all three [port] C-in-Cs and got very straight answers from at least one of them.' Other future appointments, on which the mutiny and its mishandling had less bearing, were discussed, and again Tyrwhitt aired his views forcibly, though with less success. In particular, he fought for Boyle, his former second-in-command in China, as Chatfield's successor in the Mediterranean instead of W.W. Fisher, to whom the appointment eventually went. 'Nothing was settled', he wrote to Kelly,

> 'but I think we have made the Admiralty ring look a bit sideways. Incidentally we discussed your report. Their Lordships were very much upset about it, [for] you did rub it in... [but] I quite agree with you.'[9]

Though the verdict of history has on the whole endorsed Kelly's and Tyrwhitt's criticisms of the Admiralty over the Invergordon affair, it is difficult to avoid the conclusion that the latter's strictures, and indeed the attitude of all three port admirals, were tinged by a very understandable and probably justifiable feeling that they, who at the end of their careers had been passed over for the plums of the Service, could have conducted the whole business much better than at any rate some of those to whom those plums had fallen.

Just before Tyrwhitt hauled down his flag for the last time – the last flag-officer of the 1914–18 war to relinquish active employment – on the conclusion of his three years' tenure of the Nore Command in May 1935, he uttered a grave warning as to Britain's naval position when speaking at the London Press Club's 'Navy Night' dinner.

> 'We used to sing a chorus [he said] that ended up
> "We don't want to fight, but by Jingo if we do,
> We've got the ships, we've got the men, we've got the money too!"
> I'm afraid that now we have not got any of those three vital things. There is no doubt that so far as the Navy is concerned we are down on our uppers. We are short of men, we are short of ships, and there is not a bob in the locker... What we want are cruisers. We have not enough to defend our trade routes... and one-third of our cruisers are obsolete and ought to be scrapped.'

On leaving Chatham he withdrew to Ellerslie House which he had bought at Hawkhurst in Kent. Here there was a delightful garden which Lady Tyrwhitt improved further, as she had done with the gardens of all their homes, and extended considerably. There was a tennis-court, and the Admiral had a squash-court built on which few of the fellow-officers who visited him could beat him, though he still suffered from tennis-elbow. His children also made good use of the courts, and Bobby in particular thought nothing of playing tennis all the afternoon and then squash with him before dinner.[10]

By this time Chatfield had become First Sea Lord and had embarked on what was to be a long and partly successful struggle to build up the strength of the Fleet again. In a speech as guest of honour at the Cutlers' Feast at Sheffield he had emphasised the need to do this, and had received letters of support from several admirals. Tyrwhitt for his part contributed to the *Daily Sketch* an article backing up the speech, in which he again emphasised the need for more cruisers in particular, writing:

> 'I am not advocating an immense expenditure on capital ships, though that question will have to be faced... It is the cruisers and small craft which we lack so terribly... At the present moment the Navy List gives us fifty-two cruisers of all sorts, including [two] of the Australian Navy. Of the British Navy, ten belong to the first series of the well-known C class, and I believe I am right in stating that these are already nominated for the scrap-heap.'

The nostalgic memories that must have crowded upon him as he penned these words and thought of *Centaur* and *Carysfort* and *Cleopatra* and *Conquest* in the old Harwich days were no doubt followed by others more recent as he went on:

> 'The four ships of the *Hawkins* class [his flagship on the China station], splendid vessels in their time, are of the same age. Of the ten D class some were completed before the war, and *Emerald* and *Enterprise* [which had also served him in the Far East] are only slightly younger... I have not mentioned destroyers and submarines, but we are just as short of them as of cruisers.'[11]

A new *Arethusa* was being built, however, and Lady Tyrwhitt had laid her keel-plate in January 1933. A 5200-ton cruiser, she was launched in March of the following year, again by Lady Tyrwhitt. To link her with her famous predecessor and both with the *Arethusa* Training-Ship for Boys, the captain and committee of the latter had presented Tyrwhitt with a silver inkstand to be handed over to the captain of the new cruiser on her commission. This ceremony he performed at Chatham on 18 June 1934, on her quarter-deck and before the whole ship's company.[12]

A link with a more distant past had been provided when in June 1933 a diminished band of fifteen survivors of the thirty-four cadets who had entered the *Britannia* fifty years before met to celebrate the jubilee of that event by a dinner. They included three full admirals – Brand, Sir Richard Webb and Tyrwhitt – two vice-admirals and a rear-admiral. Besides Hood, who had died at Jutland, three others had been killed in action, including Captain H.J. Saville, who had trained in H.M.S. *Worcester* but passed out at the same time and ranked as a thirty-fifth member of the class, and had gone down in command of the cruiser *Hampshire* with Lord Kitchener, whom she was conveying to Russia in 1916. Five others had died while on the active list, and nine had died in retirement or after leaving the Navy. No living member of the class was absent from the dinner.[13]

It was also after hauling down his flag in 1933 that Tyrwhitt took up a cause in which he showed great interest for the rest of his life, by accepting an invitation to become

President of the Ex-Services Mental Welfare Society in succession to its founder, Sir Frederick Milner. This body concerned itself with the care or assistance of ex-servicemen suffering from nervous or mental disorders as a result of their war experiences, of whom there were at the moment 40,000 on its books, 6,000 of them in mental hospitals. It possessed two curative homes (one of which, at Oakshott, is still called Tyrwhitt House) besides an industrial colony where those who had recovered sufficiently could earn an honest wage by their labour. Tyrwhitt and Admiral Gordon Campbell (who had distinguished himself as a Q-boat commander during the war) now co-operated with the Duke of York in arranging a public dinner at the Mansion House in aid of these.[14]

In July 1934 he was appointed an Admiral of the Fleet in succession to his one-time chief in the Mediterranean, Sir Oswald de Beauvoir Brock, who had been removed from the active list in accordance with the rule (abrogated in 1940) that relegated all holders of that rank to the retired list five years after their promotion to it.[15]

At the beginning of the following month, when the twentieth anniversary of the outbreak of the world war was being celebrated in all parts of the world, he and Field-Marshal Lord Allenby (accompanied by their wives) went to Canada in response to an invitation from the Canadian Corps of Ex-Servicemen to represent the British Navy and Army respectively at the commemoration ceremonies taking place at Toronto. Here they received an exuberant welcome which Tyrwhitt in a letter to his younger daughter described as 'a sort of Armistice Night – thousands and thousands of yelling people'. The welcome began in true Canadian style when as Tyrwhitt stepped out of the train an elderly man in a faded and outdated naval uniform slipped in front of the official reception party, seized him by the hand, slapped him on the back and greeted him with 'How's tricks, Reggie?' He then explained that (though he had afterwards reached lieutenant's rank) he had been an able seaman in H.M.S. *Cleopatra* when Tyrwhitt had served in her in North

American waters forty years before. Not in the least taken aback, the Admiral returned the greeting warmly and promised to have 'a good chat' with the veteran before his departure. In the crush that followed Lady Allenby and Lady Tyrwhitt became separated from their husbands and also from two aides-de-camp who had been detailed to guide them, but managed to get by a back way to their hotel, where their menfolk eventually joined them 'with some difficulty', wrote Tyrwhitt, 'though there was no rough play'. His description of the otherwise comfortable hotel as being situated in 'the noisiest street in Europe [sic]' no doubt owed much to the frequently rowdy celebrations which went on day and night and, though always good-humoured, sometimes showed signs of getting out of hand in thelater stages after the more solemn ceremonies were over. War veterans who had been reunited for these made bonfires in the streets of pianos and anything else they could find, though their attempt to send a horse up in the hotel lift failed – fortunately for the horse, as Tyrwhitt wrote.

Throughout the visit his happy and friendly manner and 'kindly, mellow expression, in sharp contrast to the stern features of Lord Allenby' charmed all hearts and might have surprised some of those who had known him only by repute as a commander who did not suffer fools gladly and could be a holy terror on occasion. 'He has been compared to a hawk', a reporter wrote,

> 'but he is now the most amiable hawk that ever looked for prey, a hawk that... is at smiling and slightly amused peace with the world. In appearance he is of middle height slightly stooped, with a face that would look well on a pleasant humoured parson but for a pair of jutting eyebrows that would serve an ordinary warrior for moustaches.'

Interviewing him, the same reporter asked 'Is there any great change coming in the Navy – abolition of the capital ship, for instance?' and got the uncompromising reply of a man whose views were now becoming a little old-fashioned – 'No, we'll always have the capital ship. If they abolish it, it will only mean they will have to build heavier cruisers to take its place.' 'Would you care to speak of the fighting quality of your opponents?' was the next question, to which he replied 'Their gunnery was excellent. They had a wonderful system of fire control. We never got to the secret of that. We don't know it yet.' At the leading question that followed 'Do you think that the Germans should have come out to fight?' Tyrwhitt smiled and answered tactfully 'Well, it was their show and they had to decide what to do.' Pressed more closely with 'If you had been in charge of the German fleet, would you have come out? He smiled again but remained silent until Lady Tyrwhitt broke in with 'Would they have been able to keep you in, Reginald?', at which he ventured, still smiling, 'Well, yes, I think you may say that if the British had been in the position of the Germans they would have come out and made a fight of it.' Asked if he thought there was any danger of another war soon, he answered that things did not look too settled at the moment, but 'with the hesitating, half-questioning look of one who distrusted his own opinion of things political'. When the reporter continued with 'Shall you be in it, if there is?' he said sadly 'No, I'm afraid not. You know, they don't put an admiral in command in wartime after he is sixty-five, and I am sixty-four now.'

On August 4 a great reunion of Canadian ex-servicemen took place, at which 80,000 war veterans paraded with regimental colours held aloft and wreaths were laid at the Cenotaph in the presence of Tyrwhitt and Allenby and leading Canadian political and other distinguished figures. Here again he met a number of old shipmates, including the one-time bugler of the *Arethusa*, and other men who had served in the Harwich Force. A continuous stream of functions followed, involving Tyrwhitt in several speeches which he found hard going, though the only occasion of which he made really heavy weather was one at which, after being told that he need only say a few words, he found himself suddenly called on for a twenty-five minutes' broadcast without having time to read through his notes beforehand. The result, as he put it, was 'some pretty long pauses and a good deal of er-ring'. Meanwhile on the day after the review Allenby had had to go to hospital suffering from a nose haemorrhage and took no further part in the proceedings. Except for a brief moment, that was the last Tyrwhitt saw of him; and indeed they had not hit it off together very well, probably because they were both strong personalities with short tempers.[16]

After a conducted visit to Niagara Falls and a lunch with numerous Canadian cousins, mostly on his father's side, the Tyrwhitts left 'having had a wonderful time but... very glad to get away', and sought a brief rest before returning home. For him this took the form of a few days at a comfortable salmon-fishing club on the Ristagouche River, though his stay was slightly marred by the river being lower than it had ever been in living memory and the salmon consequently 'not at home', so that he caught only two grilse and a trout or two.[17]

In July 1935 he was installed as a Knight Grand Cross of the Order of the Bath in the recently restored Henry VII Chapel in Westminster Abbey.[18] Although this honour had been conferred on him on his return from China in 1929, this was the first installation that had taken place since. A few weeks previously he had attended a sadder ceremony, when with his fellow admirals of the fleet he had marched beside the gun-carriage at Jellicoe's funeral; and in the following March he paid the same last respects at Beatty's.[19] Some of those who saw his hawk-faced figure in the forefront of both *cortèges* may have reflected that, as a newspaper had written a little earlier, 'while the various war-books [had] pulled to pieces the reputations of many of our famous admirals and generals, the fame of "Tyrwhitt of Harwich" still stood firm as a rock.'[20]

In 1924 a Harwich Force Dining Club had been established under his presidency for the purpose of reuniting all officers who had served in the Force at any time during the war at annual dinners to be held during the Easter leave periods of the Home Fleet. These were called the 'Q.O.' dinners after the signal which had been so well known to all the Force and so characteristic of Tyrwhitt, meaning 'Raise steam for full speed with all despatch'.[21] In 1938, chiefly through the energetic activities of Commander C.L.A. Woollard, who had been a lieutenant in the *Undaunted* and since the war had helped to found the Royal Air Force Association and the Royal Navy Old Comrades Association, this was expanded into a society embracing all ranks and known as the Harwich Naval Force Association. On November 5 its first dinner was held, at which the speeches (as on subsequent occasions) were mostly reminiscent, in the vein of 'We happy few, we little band of brothers'. Warm affection was expressed for Tyrwhitt and many of his exploits of leadership were recalled and recounted. Quite a number of the members were of course still serving and others were recalled to service when the second world war broke out less than a year later, so that the reunion dinners presently lapsed for a time, but the Association itself was kept in existence largely by the exertions of the honorary secretary, F.C. Thompson, who had been a 'hostilities only' able seaman in the first war and had not been recalled for the second. At the end of the war he and Commander Woollard made tremendous and successful efforts to establish contact with the surviving and all possible prospective members, and the dinners were resumed. After Tyrwhitt's death in 1951 he was succeeded as President by several flag-officers in turn and then in 1958 by Captain P.L. Gunn, who still (1971) holds that office. As a leading seaman in the *Centaur* when she was Tyrwhitt's flagship, Gunn had been coxswain of his despatch boat. In order to retain a direct link with the Tyrwhitt family St. John, now himself an admiral and Second Sea Lord, was made an honorary member, and after his sadly early death in 1960 his sister Dame Mary Tyrwhitt (as Bobby now was, having attained the rank of brigadier in the A.T.S.) took his place.[22] From an original membership of several hundreds the numbers have by now dwindled to less than three-score septuagenarians and octogenarians at the time of writing, but, in Captain Gunn's own words,

> 'Can there be greater proof of leadership than the fact that fifty-five years after their battle years, and years after the Admiral's death, officers and men whom he led with such indomitable courage meet every year with the prime purpose of honouring the memory of the commander who imbued every one of them with a spirit the equal of which, they contend, it would be difficult to find after Trafalgar?'[23]

On 31 July 1939, when Tyrwhitt had completed five years as an admiral of the fleet, he was transferred from the active to the retired list, with many expressions of the Admiralty's high appreciation of his conspicuously distinguished services.[24] On the following March 3, however, the rule which made this obligatory was abrogated (as has been stated above) and he was restored to the active list together with Keyes, Brock, Field and Sir Henry Oliver, the other surviving holders of this rank.[25]

Nevertheless his prognostication to the Canadian reporter that if there was another war he would not be in it, at least in high command, inevitably proved true, since he was sixty-nine when it broke out. At an early point in it, of which however no record has apparently survived and which his family are unable to pinpoint, he was sent for by Winston Churchill who evidently contemplated finding him some employment, if his age and health allowed, but nothing came of this.[26] When the Local Defence Volunteers, afterwards the Home Guard, were formed in the dark days of May 1940 he was one of the first to join, and he served with them for a couple of years; but with his eyesight beginning to fail he presently found further service beyond him. Nor was the strain only physical, for as a relative rather delicately put it, 'the fact that he was an admiral of the Fleet didn't help much.'[27] The rest of the war he spent raising ducks and rabbits for food, and doing his best to keep up the garden – St. John and Mary being absent on service and Patricia married. He also made an occasional public appearance. In January 1942 he deputised for Lord Chatfield, who was ill, in launching *Ark Royal* Week in Leeds, a special appeal for contributions to the war effort. Here he was greeted by the *Yorkshire Post* with a reminder to its readers that on his mother's side he was descended from Yorkshire dalesmen and an expression of wonder that, with such a man before their eyes, Englishmen still looked back to Elizabethan times for their seafaring ideals. 'He looks out on the world', it wrote, 'from under fierce black eyebrows that turn up in tufts... but their fierceness is only apparent. The Admiral has a gentle humour [and] wears his medal ribbons with becoming modesty.' In his speech at the Civic Hall he mingled frankness with invincible optimism:

> 'In the last war we had a magnificent fleet at least three times as powerful as the Fleet was at the beginning of this. Italy, France and Japan were our allies and we had complete control of the seas of the whole world... I can't sing "Britannia rules the Waves" with the same gusto that I did ten years ago. I am not suggesting that we shan't sing it again very soon, because we shall. But at the moment we are what you call "frightfully down the drain". The Navy has had a rough time and has suffered grievous losses... Luckily we are not easily disheartened.'

He went on to reassure his hearers that the antidote to the acoustic mine with which the Germans had done some damage in the early days of the war had been found, and to speak with the highest praise of our submarine service.[28] At Leicester in the following month he again opened Warship Week and reiterated his message of resolute realism; and at Edinburgh in March he attended a conference under the auspices of the Ex-Services Mental Welfare Society and reviewed its achievements of helping 27,000 officers and men in the course of its career as well as maintaining 6,000 in homes and hospitals at the actual moment and giving frequent help to their wives and children.[29] But his speeches sound like the efforts of an ageing man never at his best on a public platform – not surprisingly, for it was little more than a year later that he and four others of the last nine survivors of the *Britannia* cadets of his term sixty years ago were to meet for their diamond jubilee reunion dinner.

But if he was too old to serve, his children, to his great pride and joy, were doing so with distinction. St. John, who had been in command of the destroyer *Juno* when she was sunk during the doomed Battle of Crete, had afterwards while commanding another destroyer, the *Tartar*, taken part in practically every major operation in the Mediterranean in the later part of the war – convoys to Malta, the North African landings, the Tunisian campaign, the assault and capture of Pantellaria, the Sicilian campaign and the landing at Salerno – as well as a convoy to Russia. For his part in these services he was awarded the Distinguished Service Order and the Distinguished Service Cross and bar. Reaching captain's rank in 1945, he became in 1951 assistant to the Second Sea Lord, whose office he was afterwards to fill himself before his untimely death in 1960.[30] Bobby, having joined the A.T.S. in 1938, had risen rapidly to become Chief Commander in 1942, Controller in 1946 and then Director from that year to 1949, and subsequently Director of the Women's Royal Army Corps for a further twelvemonth, retiring in 1950.[31]

After the war his eyesight, which had been deteriorating for some time, continued to fail, compelling him to give up the presidency of the Ex-Services Mental Welfare Association in 1949.[32]

He died at his home in Hawkhurst, after a short illness, on 30 May 1951 at the age of eighty-one, and his ashes were consigned to the sea off Harwich, the sea which he had kept so well, from the destroyer *Opportune*.[33] A memorial service was held for him in Westminster Abbey, and was attended besides the family by representatives of the King, the Prime Minister, Winston Churchill and the Dominions, and personally by the First Lord of the Admiralty, five admirals of the Fleet including Chatfield and the Earl of Cork and Orrery (to which title Boyle had succeeded), and a long roll of other flag-officers, many of them old friends and comrades such as Sir Hubert Brand, Sir Walter Cowan, Sir William Tennant and Watson and Caslon, both now vice-admirals.[34] Admiral Sir Howard Kelly, brother of Sir John who had died fifteen years before, had already in an appreciation of him contributed to the Press bracketed him with Jellicoe as the two best-loved naval leaders of his own generation, 'both such an essential and personal part of every command they held that they inspired affection and respect in everyone who served with them and so could call without hesitation for the highest endeavour from their subordinates'.[35] In an obituary in the *Times* Watson put it more strongly still from out of his own close association with 'Com. (T)' throughout all the Harwich years:

> 'One of the last and greatest of the old Navy's sea officers, his love was for the sea and for... direct and personal leadership... [He was] supported by some inward flame which was the admiration of all who served with him and loved him and which remained with him till the end undimmed by the passage of the years.
> 'In the words of Drake it can truly be said of him that it is not the beginning of any great matter but the continuing of the same unto the end, until it be thoroughly finished, that yieldeth the true glory.'[36]

Surely the trumpets sounded for him on the other side?

SOURCES

Abbreviations Used

Add. MSS	Additional Manuscripts in the British Museum
Adm.	Admiralty Papers in the Public Record Office
Carr	W.G. Carr: *Brass Hats and Bell-Bottomed Trousers*
Chalmers	Rear-Admiral W.S. Chalmers: *Life and Letters of David Beatty*
Domvile, Diary	Diary of Admiral Sir Barry Domvile in National Maritime Museum
Hamilton	Diary of Lieutenant (later Admiral Sir) Louis Hamilton in National Maritime Museum
Keyes	Admiral of the Fleet Lord Keyes: *Naval Memoirs*
Naval Operations	*Official History of the* (First World) *War: Naval Operations*
Popham	H. Popham: *Into Wind*
Survey	Royal Institute of International Affairs: *Survey of International Affairs*
Taffrail	'Taffrail' (Captain Taprell Dorling): *Endless Story*
Tennant	Diary of Lieutenant (later Admiral Sir) William Tennant in National Maritime Museum
T. Papers	Tyrwhitt Papers
ACT	Alice Catherine Tyrwhitt ('Kitty')
AMT	Angela Mary Tyrwhitt
BT	Beauchamp Tyrwhitt

FMT	Frances Mary Tyrwhitt ('Polly')
MJCT	Mary Jean Catherine Tyrwhitt ('Bobby')
RYT	Reginald Yorke Tyrwhitt
Watson	Diary of Vice-Admiral B.C. Watson
Woollard	Commander C.L.A. Woollard: *With the Harwich Naval Forces, 1914–1918*

SOURCE REFERENCES AND NOTES IN TEXT

CHAPTER ONE: THE FIRST HALF OF THE JOURNEY

1. Keyes Papers: Rear-Admiral Chetwode to Keyes, 2 Mar. 1930. *Times*, 7 May 1933.
2. R.P. Tyrwhitt: *Notices and Remains of the Family of Tyrwhitt*, pp.2–91. T. Papers: A Pedigree of the Ancient Family of Tyrwhitt.
3. *Ibid.*
4. T. Papers: Early Recollections of RYT by FMT
5. *Ibid.* Autobiographical fragment written by RYT about 1946. Where no other source is specifically stated, the account of Tyrwhitt's early career down to the outbreak of the first world war which follows is based on this fragment.
6. The list was headed by the Hon. H.L.A. Hood, who died as a rear-admiral at the Battle of Jutland thirty-three years later when his flagship the *Invincible* was blown up.
7. Another member of the term was H.J. Savill, who was captain of the cruiser *Hampshire* when she struck a mine and sank in 1916 with Lord Kitchener on board.
8. T. Papers: *The Record of a Britannia Term, July 1883–July 1885.* Captain H.W.C. Pack, *History of the Royal Naval College, Dartmouth*, pp.62–3.
9. Chalmers, pp.7–12.
10. T. Papers: RYT to FMT, 18 Oct. 1887.
11. Reports of successive commanding officers of H.M.S. *Alexandra*.
12. *Ibid.*
13. *Ibid.* Report of the Captain of H.M.S. *Calypso*.

14. *Ibid.* Report of the Captain of H.M.S. *Australia*.
15. *Ibid.* RYT to BT, 7 Mar. 1894.
16. In addition to the autobiographical fragment, see M.W. Williams, *Anglo-American Isthmian Diplomacy, 1815–1915,* pp. 286–99.
17. T. Papers: Extract from Admiralty Letter N403, 22 Nov. 1895.
18. *Ibid.* Report of Capt. Curzon Howe, 5 Dec. 1895.
19. *Ibid.* RYT to ACT, 22 Mar. 1896.
20. *Ibid.* Reports of Commander Hugh Tyrwhitt, 1 Oct. 1898, and Commander N.N. Hervey, 23 Nov. 1899.
21. *Ibid.* Letters of RYT to Miss A.M. Corbally, Jan.–Feb. 1902.
22. *Ibid.* Autobiographical fragment and letters of RYT to FMT and ACT, 19 May 1902.
23. *Ibid.* Letters of RYT to Miss Corbally, 20 July, and FMT, 29 July and 26 Sept. 1902.
24. *Ibid.* Letters of RYT to Miss Corbally, 28 Nov.; 2, 8, 12, 15, 18 and 20 Dec. 1902. D.G. Munro, *Intervention and Dollar Diplomacy in the Caribeean, 1900–21,* pp. 66–75.
25. *Ibid.* Report of Capt. N. Grogan, 1 Jan. 1903.
26. *Ibid.* RYT to FMT (undated), enclosing cuttings from *St. James's Gazette*, *Globe* and *Westminster Gazette*.
27. Some of the statements which follow are based on private information from Dame Mary Tyrwhitt.
28. The name given to the four (originally eight) months' course for senior officers in naval history, tactics, strategy and international law which had been started at Greenwich in 1900 and transferred to Portsmouth in 1906.
29. Admiral Gamble's flag-lieutenant was Bertram Ramsay (afterwards the distinguished admiral of Second World War fame) who became a great friend of the Tyrwhitt family.

30. Though later, in the wartime black-out, Sanders knocked down a policeman at Havant cross-roads and involved Mrs. Tyrwhitt in a fine and Tyrwhitt in an epitolary altercation with the chairman of the local bench, who as a retired admiral stood in no awe of him and in which he came off second-best.

CHAPTER TWO: THE BATTLE OF THE BIGHT

1. T. Papers: RYT to AMT, 19 July 1914; and to ACT, 3 Aug. 1914.
2. *Ibid*. Same to same, 22 July 1914.
3. Keyes, I, pp.39, 58–9 and 67.
4. *Ibid*., pp.59–60.
5. The First Flotilla consisted of the *Acheron*, *Archer*, *Attack*, *Ariel*, *Badger*, *Beaver*, *Defender*, *Druid*, *Ferret*, *Forrester*, *Goshawk*, *Hind*, *Hornet*, *Hydra*, *Jackal*, *Lapwing*, *Lizard*, *Phoenix*, *Sandfly*, and *Tigress*; and the Third of the *Laertes*, *Laforey*, *Lance*, *Lark*, *Laurel*, *Landrail*, *Lawford*, *Legion*, *Lennox*, *Leonidas*, *Liberty*, *Linnet*, *Llewellyn*, *Lookout*, *Louis*, *Loyal*, *Lucifer*, *Lydiard*, and *Lysander*. (Carr, p.27).
6. There was also the *Dido*, an old cruiser permanently propping up Parkeston Quay and used as an overflow ship for destroyer crews, about which this ditty was sometimes sung:
   'Don't send away the *Dido*,
   Don't send her out to sea.
   If you send away the *Dido*,
   Then down comes Parkeston Quay!
   (Extracts from the papers of the Harwich Naval Force Association, supplied by Captain P.L. Gunn, R.N.).
7. T. Papers: RYT to BT, 30 July 1914; and to AMT, 31 July 1914.

8. *Ibid*. RYT to AMT, 2 Aug. 1914.
9. Admiral Sir Barry Domvile, *By and Large*, pp.55.
10. Keyes, I, pp.60 and 67.
11. Afterwards Admiral Sir William Tennant. Lieutenant Tennant, incidentally, was contravening orders by keeping a diary while on active service.
12. Tennant, 31 July 1914. Carr, p.28.
13. T. Papers: RYT to AMT, 1 Aug. 1914.
14. Or Sir Richard as portrayed in *The Ballad of the Revenge,* 'Sink me the ship, Master Gunner; sink me her, split her in twain!'
15. T. Papers, RYT to AMT, 2 Aug, 1914.
16. Tennant, 3 Aug. 1914.
17. T. Papers: RYT to AMT, 3 Aug. 1914.
18. *Ibid*. RYT to ACT, 3 Aug. 1914.
19. *Ibid*. Early Recollections of RYT.
20. T. Papers: RYT to AMT and BT, 4 Aug. 1914. Tennant, 4 Aug. 1914.
21. *Ibid*., 5 Aug. 1914. Taffrail, pp.22–4.
22. *Naval Operations*, I, pp.38–9. Woollard, pp.3–4. Tennant, 5 Aug. 1914. T. Papers: RYT to AMT, 9 Aug. 1914.
23. *Ibid*. Keyes, I, pp.69–70.
24. T. Papers: RYT to AMT, 9 Aug. 1914. Tennant, 5–8 Aug. 1914.
25. *Naval Operations*, I, p.79.
26. All unconscious of things to come, he had written to his wife on August 3 apropos of Keyes, admiringly rather than enviously: 'Roger has the *entrée* practically everywhere at the Admiralty. I sometimes wish I had it too.'
27. T. Papers: RYT to AMT, 9 Aug. 1914.
28. Woollard, p.5. Tennant, Aug. 9–14, 1914.
29. T. Papers: RYT to AMT, 15 Aug. 1914. Tennant, 15–17 Aug. 1914.
30. Afterwards Admiral the Hon. Sir Herbert Meade-Featherstonehaugh.

31. Tennant, 18 Aug. 1914.
32. Woollard, pp.6–7. T. Papers: RYT to AMT, 22 Aug. 1914.
33. *Ibid.* RYT to AMT, 25 Aug. 1914. *Naval Operations*, I, pp.99–101. Keyes, I, pp.79–81. Taffrail, pp.24–5.
34. T. Papers: RYT to BT, 26 Aug. 1914.
35. The account of the Battle of the Heligoland Bight which follows is based on *Naval Operations*, I, pp.101–120; Keyes, I, pp.82–97; Taffrail, pp.25–44; Woollard, pp.10–13; Tennant, 27–9 Aug. 1914; and T. Papers: RYT to AMT, 29 and 30 Aug., and to ACT, 2 Sept. 1914.
36. Woollard, p.13.
37. The famous frigate *Arethusa* whose gallant fight against the more powerful French ship *Belle Poule* sparked off France's entry into the War of American Independence in 1778.
38. 'He was absolutely fearless,' the author was told by the officer who was afterwards his flag-captain for the greater part of the war.
39. Woollard, p.14.
40. T. Papers: RYT to AMT, enclosing letter from Sir Raymond Tyrwhitt, 4 Sept. 1914.
41. *Ibid.*, AMT to FMT, Aug. (n.d.) 1914.

CHAPTER THREE: KEEPING THE NARROW SEAS

1. T. Papers: RYT to AMT, 10 Sept. 1914. Domvile, Diary, 7 Sept. 1914.
2. Keyes, I, pp.98–101. Tennant, Sept. 9–10, 1914. T. Papers: RYT to AMT, 2 and 10 Sept. 1914.
3. The late Admiral Sir Barry Domvile.
4. Domvile, Diary, 19 and 29 Aug. 1914.
5. Churchill at that time belonged to the Liberal Party. Tyrwhitt was of course a Conservative.

6. T. Papers: RYT to ACT, 17 Sept. 1914.
7. Keyes, I, pp.102–4.
8. Adm. 137/995: memorandum from Jellicoe to Admiralty, ff.38–41.
9. T. Papers: RYT to ACT, 17 Sept. 1914.
10. Adm. 137/995, ff.38–41.
11. Churchill, Sir W.S., *Thoughts and Adventures*, pp.89–96.
12. T. Papers: RYT to ACT, 17 Sept. 1914.
13. *Naval Operations*, I, pp.172–7. Keyes, I, pp.105–6.
14. The Foreign Office claimed the repatriation of these officers and men, to which the Dutch government agreed, and they were brought back to England on September 26.
15. T. Papers: RYT to ACT, 30 Sept. 1914.
16. Tennant, 7–9 Oct. 1914.
17. Keyes, I, pp.106–8.
18. T. Papers: RYT to AMT, 26 Sept. 1914.
19. *Ibid.*, RYT to ACT, 30 Sept. 1914.
20. *Ibid.*, RYT to AMT, 26 Sept. 1914.
21. *Naval Operations*, I, pp.180–3 and 189–91. T. Papers: RYT to AMT, two undated letters and one of 10 Oct. 1914.
22. Keyes, I, p.111.
23. Tennant, 4 Oct. 1914.
24. It was about this time that when the *Arethusa* left harbour on one occasion the band which had been scraped together by a destroyer not detailed for that particular service played her out with a popular music-hall tune of the day – 'We don't want to lose you, but we think you ought to go!' On her return she entered harbour with her own band playing another popular tune – 'Here we are, here we are, here we are again!' (Carr, p.86).
25. Tennant, 11 Oct. 1914.
26. *Naval Operations*, I, pp.217–8. Woollard, pp.16–20. Tennant, 17 Oct. 1914. T. Papers: RYT to AMT,

17 Oct. 1914.

27. *Ibid.*, same to same, 20 Oct. 1914. *Naval Operations*, I, p.221. Keyes, I, p.121.
28. *Naval Operations*, I, pp.215–7 and 219–225. T. Papers, RYT to AMT, 20 Oct. 1914.
29. The late Duke of Windsor.
30. T. Papers: RYT to AMT, 23 Oct. 1914. 23 Oct. 1914.
31. *Naval Operations*, I, p.238.
32. After the war it was learnt that the submarine, though very badly damaged and losing several of her crew, had nevertheless managed to make port.
33. T. Papers: RYT to AMT, 24 Oct. 1914.
34. Roskill, Capt. S.W. (ed.), *The Naval Air Service*, I, pp.183–4.
35. T. Papers: RYT to AMT, 27 Oct. 1914.
36. *Ibid.*, same to same, three undated letters, on internal evidence at end of Oct. and beginning of Nov. 1914.
37. The story is told of how, when a visiting German eminence reproached Prince Louis for not serving in the navy of Germany, he snapped angrily, 'When I joined the British Navy in 1868, there was no Germany.'
38. T. Papers: RYT to AMT, 8 Oct. 1914.
39. *Ibid.*, same to same, undated.
40. Keyes, I, pp.53–4 and 129–32. Woollard, p.24.
41. Captain Wilmot Nicholson, having been court-martialled for losing the *Hogue* but honourably acquitted, had now been appointed to the command of the *Aurora*, to Tyrwhitt's delight. 'I am so glad to have him with me,' he wrote, 'for he is the right sort and will stick to one for ever' (RYT to AMT, 28 Oct. 1914).
42. A German armoured cruiser, the *Yorck*, fouled a minefield on her way home, and sank with the loss of half her crew.
43. T. Papers: RYT to AMT, 5 Nov. 1914. Tennant, 30

Oct.–3 Nov. 1914.

44. *Ibid.*, 12 Nov. 1914.
45. *Naval Operations*, II, p.11. Woollard, pp.26–7. Popham, p.22. Domvile, Diary, 24 Nov. 1914.
46. i.e., the seaplane raid.
47. T. Papers: RYT to AMT, 18 Nov. 1914.
48. *Naval Operations*, II, pp.12–3. Tennant, 23 Nov. 1914.
49. Domvile, who in view of his previous post had more contacts than most destroyer captains and was also *persona non grata* to Fisher, recorded in his diary that he thought the First Sea Lord had done this to spite Keyes.
50. From an incidental remark in a letter of 14 December from Tyrwhitt to his wife.
51. T. Papers: RYT to AMT, 7 and 11 Dec. 1914.
52. Lieut.-Commander E.K. Arbuthnot, an officer who had reached the rank of lieutenant in 1898 but had retired (as R.N.R.) for a period of some years and then resumed service on the outbreak of war.
53. T. Papers: RYT to AMT, 11 Dec. 1914.
54. The reference is to Von Spee's previous equally annihilating victory over Rear-Admiral Cradock's squadron off Coronel.
55. T. Papers: RYT to AMT, 14 Dec. 1914.
56. In fact three, since the *Princess Royal* had been despatched to the West Indies to cover the possibility that Von Spee might come through the Panama Canal.
57. T. Papers: RYT to AMT, 19 Dec. 1914. *Naval Operations*, II, pp.21–46.
58. These first carriers were strictly that and no more. It was some time before planes could safely be flown off from a carrier; at this stage they still had to be hoisted out to take off from the water.
59. T. Papers: RYT to AMT, 20 Dec. 1914. Tennant, 20–3 Dec. 1914. Woollard, p.28.
60. Now Vice-Admiral B.C. Watson.

61. T. Papers: Lieut. G. Holmes, Christmas 1914 (pamphlet printed for private circulation). Address given by Tyrwhitt to the boys of the Dragon School, Oxford, 2 Feb. 1919.
62. *Ibid*. Holmes, *op cit*. Keyes, I, pp.152–7. Woollard, pp.28–30. Popham, pp.22–4. Tennant, 25 Dec. 1914.
63. Quoted in Roskill, *op. cit*., p.192.
64. T. Papers: RYT to FMT, 31 Dec. 1914.
65. *Ibid*., RYT to AMT, 29 Dec. 1914.
66. *Ibid*., same to same, 4 Jan. 1915.

CHAPTER FOUR: ALARMS AND EXCURSIONS

1. Roskill, *op. cit*., p.188.
2. *Naval Operations*, II, pp.54–6 and 61–6.
3. Add. MSS 48990, ff.175–7.
4. T. Papers: RYT to AMT, 6, 7 and 14 Jan. 1915. Watson, 7 Jan. 1915.
5. T. Papers: RYT to AMT, 16 Jan. 1915.
6. *Ibid*., same to same, 17 Jan. 1915.
7. *Ibid*., same to same, 19 Jan. 1915. *Naval Operations*, II, p.83. Tennant, 18 Jan. 1915. Watson, 18–20 Jan. 1915.
8. Which Domvile and Tennant were of course breaking.
9. This paragraph and the account of the Battle of the Dogger Bank which follows are based on *Naval Operations*, II, pp.83–102; Chalmers, pp.181–193; Domvile, *By and Large*, pp.66–71; Tennant, 23–27 Jan. 1915; Watson, 23–7 Jan; 1915; and T. Papers, RYT to AMT, 27 Jan. 1915.
10. T. Papers, RYT to BT, 28 Jan. 1915.
11. *Ibid.,* same to same, 27 Jan, 1915. I am here much indebted to discussions with Professor Paul G.

Holpern, who is editing the Keyes Papers for the Navy Records Society.

13. Watson, 2, 4, 5, 10 and 14 Jan. 1915.
14. He was certainly suffering at this time from dental and digestive troubles which may have arisen from the strain and contributed to the irritability. (T. Papers: RYT to AMT, 9 Feb. 1915).
15. *Ibid.*, same to same, 13 Jan. 1915. Keyes, I, pp.167–8.
16. *Ibid.*, p.168. T. Papers: RYT to AMT, 13 Feb. 1915.
17. Keyes Papers: RYT to Keyes, undated but evidently Mar. 1915, and 25 April 1915.
18. T. Papers: RYT to AMT, 29 Jan. and 1 Feb. 1915. Tennant, 29 Jan. 1915.
19. Watson, 1 and 2 Feb. 1915.
20. T. Papers, RYT to AMT, 17 and 21 Feb. 1915.
21. Tennant, 7, 9, 15, 16, 22, 25, 28 Feb., and 4 Mar. 1915.
22. Keyes Papers: RYT to Keyes, 25 April 1915.
23. *Ibid.*, RYT to Keyes, Mar. 1915. T. Papers: RYT to AMT, 7, 11, 15 and 22 Mar. 1915.
24. *Ibid.*, same to same, 28 Mar., and to FMT, 28 Mar. 1915. Keyes Papers: RYT to Keyes, 25 April 1915. Taffrail, pp.101–9.
25. T. Papers: RYT to AMT, 31 Mar. 1915.
26. T. Papers: Vice-Admiral Sir D. Gamble to RYT, 23 April 1915.
27. *Ibid.*, RYT to AMT, 13, 19 and 30 April 1915, Watson, 29 Mar., 8, 11–13, 17–8, 21–2 and 29 April 1915.
28. Domvile, *By and Large*, pp.72–3.
29. Woollard, p.53.
30. T. Papers: RYT to AMT, 10 and 11 April 1915. Keyes Papers: RYT to Keyes, 25 April 1915. Watson, 9 and 11 April, 1915.
31. A new device – indicator nets constructed of light material and suspended from steel hawsers strung along a line of floats. Any submarine which fouled them revealed its presence by the disturbance it

caused to the floats.

32. Vice-Admiral H.F. Oliver, previously Director of Naval Intelligence and then Naval Secretary to the First Lord, who had replaced Sturdee as Chief of the Naval War Staff.
33. Watson, 3, 6 and 11–12 May 1915. T. Papers: RYT to AMT, 4, 7 and 13 May 1915.
34. *Ibid*, same to same, 2 and 5 May 1915. Watson, 1 May 1915.
35. T. Papers: RYT to AMT, 14 May 1915.
36. In reply to a letter from Tyrwhitt expressing commiseration and regret Churchill wrote: '... Most of all am I sorry to work no longer with the men I knew and trusted, among whom in the front rank is yourself' (T. Papers: Churchill to RYT, 31 May 1915).
37. T. Papers: RYT to AMT, 26 June 1915.
38. *Ibid.*, same to same, 18, 19 and 31 May and 4 June 1915. Watson, 17–8, 21–4, 29–31 May and 1–4 June 1915. *Naval Operations*, II, pp.135–6.
39. T. Papers: RYT to AMT, 6 June 1915.
40. Watson, 19 June 1915.
41. *Ibid.*, 3 July 1915. T. Papers: RYT to AMT, 8 July 1915.
42. *Ibid.*, same to same, 5 and 8 July 1915. Watson, 4 July 1915.
43. T. Papers: RYT to AMT, 8 July 1915.
44. *Ibid.*, same to same, 13 and 20 July 1915. Watson, 18 July 1915.
45. *Ibid.*, 28–31 July 1915. T. Papers: RYT to AMT, 31 July 1915.
46. As the prisoners were parting company with their captors the German captain asked Lieutenant Atkins, who had rushed from his bunk in his pyjamas when the brief engagement began and was rigged out in borrowed clothing, whether he had any money. Atkins replied that under the circumstances he naturally had none, but did not expect

to need any; whereupon the German pressed an English 'fiver' and other English money on him.

47. T. Papers: RYT to AMT, 5 and 10 Aug. 1915. Watson, 4 and 8 Aug. 1915. *Naval Operations*, III, pp.53. and 122–6.
48. Woollard, pp.62–3.
49. *Ibid.*, p.63.
50. *Naval Operations*, III, p.127. Taffrail, pp.109–110. Watson, Aug. 16–18 1915.
51. The *Nimrod* relieved the *Tipperary*, which went to Plymouth and afterwards to Scapa Flow to become leader of the Fourth Flotilla. Later still she was sunk at Jutland.
52. *Naval Operations*, III, pp.127–8. T. Papers: RYT to AMT, 12 Sept. 1915.
53. *Ibid.*, same to same, 1 and 4 Oct. 1915. *Naval Operations*, III, p.261. Woollard, p.65. Watson, 12–13 and 28–30 Sept. and 1 Oct. 1915.
54. Commander Arbuthnot won the D.S.O. in 1917 during naval operations on the river Tigris.
55. Watson, 11, 14, 16 and 20 Sept; 1, 6, 7 and 12 Nov. 1915. Domvile, Diary, 4, 5 and 6 Nov. 1915. T. Papers: RYT to AMT, 4, 6, 9 and 23 Nov. 1915.
56. The late Captain Taprell Dorling wrote nearly thirty books under this *nom de plume*, mostly naval sketches, novels, reminiscences and history, beginning with *Pincher Martin, O.D.*, in 1916.
57. T. Papers: RYT to AMT, 9 and 11 Nov. 1915. Watson, 8 Nov. 1915. Taffrail, pp.118–123.
58. T. Papers: RYT to FMT, 25 Nov. 1915.
59. *Ibid.*, RYT to AMT, 16 Nov. 1915.
60. From August onwards it was becoming possible, despite many mishaps, to fly aircraft off the decks of carriers.
61. T. Papers: RYT to AMT, 2 Dec. 1915. *Naval Operations*, III, p.273. Popham, p.53. Watson, 4 Dec. 1915.

62. *Ibid.*, 13–4 Dec. 1915.
63. T. Papers: RYT to AMT, 21 Dec. 1915.
64. *Ibid.*, same to same, 30 and 31 Dec. 1915.

CHAPTER FIVE: THE WAR JUST BEYOND THE TENNIS-COURT

1. T. Papers: RYT to AMT, 5 and 6 Jan. 1916. Watson, 1–5 Jan. 1916.
2. *Ibid.*, 10 and 11 Jan. 1916. T. Papers: RYT to AMT, 16 Jan. 1916.
3. He had been promoted Acting Captain on the last day of the old year (Domvile, Diary, 31 Dec. 1915).
4. T. Papers: RYT to AMT, 22 Jan. 1916. Watson, 18 and 28 Jan. 1916. *Naval Operations*, III, pp.273–4. Domvile, *By and Large*, p.75.
5. T. Papers: RYT to AMT, 31 Dec. 1915; 6 and 9 Jan. 1916.
6. *Ibid.*, same to same, 6 Jan. 1916.
7. *Ibid.*, same to same, undated.
8. Keyes Papers: RYT to Keyes, 14 April 1916.
9. T. Papers: RYT to AMT, 3 Mar. 1916. Information supplied by Dame Mary Tyrwhitt.
10. Captain Lynes retired from the Navy after the war in order to devote himself entirely to ornithology, on which he became an authority.
11. T. Papers: Numerous references to his walks ashore in letters to AMT.
12. Information supplied by Dame Mary Tyrwhitt.
13. T. Papers: Various references in letters to AMT.
14. T. Papers: RYT to AMT, 22 July 1915.
15. *Ibid.*, same to same, 14 Feb. 1915. Domvile, Diary, 25 Dec. 1915. On one visit the diversions included puff-football, turning somersaults over Mrs. Cayley's best chair, and skipping, his efforts at which (he recorded) 'nearly made a hole in the floor'. At other times there were charades in which he

figured without distinction.

16. T. Papers: RYT to AMT, 1 Feb. 1915.
17. *Ibid.*, same to same, 4 Feb., 15 Mar. and 6 June 1915.
18. Domvile, *By and Large*, p.74.
19. At a low moment in the war (the spring of 1916) the Fourth Sea Lord, Captain C.F. Lambert, proposed that all admirals should be removed from their posts and Tyrwhitt made Commander-in-Chief! This suggestion was not, of course, taken seriously.
20. T. Papers: RYT to AMT, 18 May and 29 Aug. 1915. Watson, e.g., 20 Jan., 24 Feb., 18 April, 15 July 1915.
21. Domvile, Diary, 7 and 23 Dec. 1914; 7 Jan., 8 Oct. and 19 Nov. 1915.
22. Private information.
23. Domvile Diary, 30. Dec. 1915. Carr, p.220. Tyrwhitt's appearance at an entertainment was generally greeted by spontaneous cheering. It was also at one of these concerts that a civilian entertainer who began to recite 'God gave the sea to England and we must keep it free!' was interrupted by a stentorian voice which bawled from the middle of the audience 'Not 'arf! – 'ow abaht giving us a bloody 'and?'
24. Domvile, Diary, 27 Sept. 1916.
25. *Ibid.*, 27 Nov. and 2 Dec. 1915.
26. Watson was promoted Commander on 30 June 1918. (Watson, 30 June 1915).
27. Domvile, Diary, 5 May and 21 Oct. 1915; 17 May, 21 June, 21 Sept. and 4 Oct. 1916. Tennant, 15 July and Aug. *passim*, 1917. Woollard, p.96. Private information.
28. Tennant, 5 June 1917.
29. See below, p.173
30. Domvile, *By and Large*, p.82.
31. Woollard, p.96.
32. Private information.

33. Private information.
34. T. Papers: RYT to AMT, 11 Nov. 1915.
35. Keyes Papers: RYT to Keyes, 9 Mar. 1916. Watson, 11 Feb. 1916. *Naval Operations*, III, pp.275–6. Woollard, pp.76–9.
36. Tyrwhitt presented her ensign to the Dockyard Church at Chatham, 'where she was born and christened'. Captain Domvile retrieved her masthead steaming light, which was still decorating the porch of his house at the time of his death in 1971.
37. T. Papers: RYT to AMT, 5 Aug. 1915; 16, 18, 22, 23 and 26 Feb. and 5 Mar. 1916.
38. *Ibid.*, same to same, 26 Feb. 1916.
39. *Ibid.*, same to same, 7 Mar. 1916.
40. Keyes Papers: RYT to Keyes, 9 Mar. 1916.
41. T. Papers: RYT to AMT, 9 Mar. 1916.
42. It had been first suggested by Commodore Murray F. Sueter, but Tyrwhitt had elaborated it.
43. By some misunderstanding she was left afloat with an idea of picking her up next day, and was found on April 4 by a Dutch trawler which towed her to Terschelling, where she ran on to a sandbank and became a total loss.
44. *Naval Operations*, II!, pp.290–6. Woollard, p.80. Popham, p.53. Chalmers, pp.212–4. Taffrail, pp.229–37. Keyes Papers, RYT to Keyes, 14 April 1916.
45. T. Papers: RYT to AMT, undated.
46. *Naval Operations*, III, pp.299–300.
47. The Town Council of Lowestoft, however, expressed to the Admiralty the inhabitants' 'high appreciation ... of the splendid way in which during the bombardment ... the enemy ships, though in superior force, were engaged by the British squadron' and their conviction 'that but for this plucky intervention at a critical moment the town would have suffered much greater destruction of property

and loss of life', adding their wish that this expression of appreciation might be conveyed to 'the gallant officer in command and the officers and men under him' (Tyrwhitt Papers: W. Graham Greene, Secretary to the Admiralty, to RYT, 8 May 1916, enclosing letter from Mayor of Lowestoft dated 3 May).

48. *Naval Operations*, III, pp.301–9. T. Papers: RYT to BT, 26 and 29 April 1916.
49. *Ibid.* Copy of letter from Beatty to Jellicoe, 18 May 1916.
50. Presumably the *Cleopatra*. The *Penelope* had been torpedoed in the stern on April 25 – one unfortunate consequence of which was the loss of the MS of Captain Lynes's book on birds, since it was in his cabin, which was destroyed. Luckily, a fellow-ornithologist possessed a photographic copy (Hamilton, 25 April 1916).
51. *Naval Operations*, III, pp.309–11 and 315–7.
52. Domvile, Diary, 19 Mar., 5 and 30 April 1916. Watson, 28–30 April 1916. T. Papers: RYT to BT, 29 April 1916.
53. Domvile, *By and Large*, p.78.
54. See p.174
55. Adm. 137/194, f.70 (20 Aug. 1914).
56. Hamilton, 10 June 1916.
57. Domvile, *By and Large*, p.84.
58. Domvile, Diary, 31 May – 2 June 1916. Watson, 1–2 June 1916. Private information.

CHAPTER SIX: 'THE CONTINUING OF THE SAME...'

1. (Sir Francis Drake).
2. *Naval Operations*, IV, p.25. A. Temple Patterson, *Jellicoe*, p.140. Adm. 137/1937, ff.387–91 and 137/1957, ff.159–63.

3. *Naval Operations*, IV, p.22. Domvile, Diary, 8 June 1916. Watson, 8 June 1916. Hamilton, 8 June 1916.
4. *Ibid.*, 27 and 28 June 1916. De Robeck Papers: RYT to De Robeck, 5 Aug. 1916. Domvile, Diary, 8 June 1916. *Naval Operations*, IV, pp.22–3.
5. *Ibid.*, pp.23 and 27–9. Hamilton, 10, 12, 16 and 19 July 1916. Watson, 21–3 July 1916. T. Papers: RYT to FMT, 5 Aug. 1916.
6. *Naval Operations*, V, pp.29–32. Taffrail, pp.125–30.
7. *Ibid.*, pp.131–3.
8. *Naval Operations*, IV, pp.30–47. Patterson, *op. cit.*, pp.140–2. Watson, 18–20 Aug. 1916. De Robeck Papers: RYT to De Robeck, 22 Aug. 1916.
9. Add. MSS 49032, ff.34–7 (RYT to Jellicoe, 21 Aug. 1916).
10. Patterson, *op. cit.*, p.147. Watson, 18–19 Oct. 1916.
11. See p. 161–2
12. Roskill, *op. cit.*, p.175n. Popham, pp.46 and 49. Domvile, *By and Large*, p.79.
13. After the war Childers embraced fanatically the cause of the Irish rebels, joined the Irish Republican Army, and was shot by the Free State forces.
14. *Ibid.* Woollard, p.34.
15. Domvile, *By and Large*, pp.79–80.
16. Popham, pp.43–4.
17. Watson, 10 and 25 Sept. 1916.
18. *Naval Operations*, IV, pp.53 and 69. Woollard, p.95.
19. De Robeck Papers: RYT to De Robeck, 19 Sept. 1916. Keyes Papers: RYT to Keyes, 29 Dec. 1916.
20. *Naval Operations*, IV, pp.72–3.
21. *Ibid.*, pp.73–9. Domvile, *By and Large*, pp.85–7. Taffrail, pp.110–12 Hamilton, 22–3 Jan. 1917.
22. T. Papers: RYT to FMT, 27 Jan. 1917.
23. *Ibid.*
24. Elias Corbally was his wife's eldest brother.
25. Carson, who took the line as First Lord that he was the admirals' spokesman, but would neither interfere

with them nor let anyone else do so, was much esteemed by many senior naval officers.

26. T. Papers: Beatty to RYT, 16 Jan. 1917.
27. Keyes Papers: RYT to Keyes, 18 Feb. 1917
28. T. Papers: RYT to AMT, 9 and 10 June 1917.
29. The reactions were by no means all on one side. Lieutenant Hamilton's mother, who was living at Rosyth since his father, Vice-Admiral Sir Frederick Hamilton, was now Admiral Superintendent of the dockyard, was 'much impressed with the Commodore' (Hamilton, 16 Feb. 1917). Sir Frederick, who had been Second Sea Lord at the beginning of the war, of course knew him already.
30. Bacon dismissed it, characteristically and caustically, as 'a scheme for the self-glorification of aspiring young naval officers' RYT to BT, 6 May 1918).
31. *Naval Operations*, IV, p.324, and V, pp.36–41.
32. *Ibid.*, V, pp.47–8. Hamilton, 5 June 1917. Watson, 4–5 June 1917. Tennant, 4–5 June 1917.
33. Woollard, p.98. Domvile, *By and Large*, p.87.
34. Hamilton, 12 Mar. and 21 Dec. 1917.
35. Taffrail, pp.133–4. Tennant, 21 Dec. 1917.
36. *Ibid.* Taffrail, p.125.
37. Keyes Papers: RYT to Keyes, 28 July 1917. T. Papers: RYT to FMT, 25 July 1917. Watson, 15–16 July 1917. *Naval Operations*, V, pp.58–61. Domvile, *By and Large*, pp.87–8.
38. *Ibid.*, pp.88–9. Tennant, 24–5 Oct. 1917.
39. *Ibid.*, 15 April 1917.
40. Domvile, *By and Large*, p.87.
41. After all, they were a future Second Sea Lord and a future Officer Commanding, A.T.S.
42. T. Papers: RYT to FMT, 5 July 1917.
43. *Ibid*: Notifications and Patents; also RYT to ACT, 20 July 1917. Domvile, Diary, 3 June 1917. Watson, 4 June 1917.
44. *Ibid.*, 2 Nov. 1916. T. Papers: RYT to FMT, 3 Nov., and

to ACT, 11 Nov. 1916.
45. *Ibid.*, RYT to FMT, 25 July 1917.
46. He resigned his post on the *Times* in January 1918 and became the war correspondent of the *Morning Post*.
47. Colloquially called 'the Street'.
48. These were the Felixstowe F.2A, whose wingspan was actually 100 feet and which was armed with seven Lewis guns, and the 'Porte Baby', respectively.
49. Lt-Col. C.à Court Repington, (Diary of) the First World War, II, pp.38–44.

CHAPTER SEVEN: THE END CROWNS THE WORK

1. *Daily Mail*, 28 Mar. and 31 Oct. 1917. *Morning Post*, 1 Nov. 1917.
2. T. Papers: Secretary of the Admiralty to RYT, 18 Jan. 1918; and RYT to FMT,· 16 Jan. and 27 Feb. 1918.
3. Tennant, Jan. 1918 (which month he describes as a whole, ceasing for some time henceforth to make daily entries in his diary).
4. T. Papers: RYT to ACT, 5 Feb. 1918. Watson, 20–1 Feb. 1918.
5. T. Papers: RYT to AMT, 21 May 1917.
6. *Ibid.* AMT to FMT, 10 April 1918.
7. *Ibid.* RYT to FMT, 16 April 1918. Watson, 4 Mar. and 3 April 1918.
8. *Naval Operations*, V, pp. 223–7.
9. Tennant, Mar. 1918 *passim*. Watson, 18–9 Mar. 1918.
10. Keyes Papers: RYT to Keyes, 25 May 1917.
11. *Ibid.* Same to same, 18 Feb. 1919.
12. *Naval Operations*, V, pp.250 and 253.
13. Woollard, p.101. Tennant, April–May 1918, *passim*. Watson, 4, 6, 12–14, 17, 28–9 and 31 May, 1918.
14. An apparatus for deflecting and cutting the moorings of

submerged mines.
15. Domvile, *By and Large*, p.89. Tennant, 31 May 1918.
16. Watson, 13–4 June 1918.
17. Woollard, p.103. Hamilton, 20 April and 7–10 Aug. 1918. Tennant, 10 Aug. 1918.
18. Roskill, *Naval Policy between the Wars*, I, pp.612 and 686–9. Woollard, p.99. T. Papers: RYT to FMT, 29 Aug. 1918.
19. Woollard, pp.107–8. Hamilton, 15 Aug. 1918. Watson, 15 Aug. 1918.
20. *Ibid*., 29 Sept. 1918. Tennant, 12 Aug. to 30 Sept. 1918, *passim*.
21. *Naval Operations*, V, pp.312–3. Keyes Papers: RYT to Keyes, 1 Oct. 1918. Tennant, 30 Sept. 1918. Hamilton, 1–2 Oct. 1918.
22. *Ibid*., 1–4 Oct. 1918. Watson, 4 Oct. 1918. Tennant, 5 Oct. 1918.
23. *Ibid*., 23 Oct. 1918. Hamilton, 24 Oct. 1918.
24. *Ibid*., 31 Oct. 1918. Tennant, 28 Oct. 1918 *sqq*.
25. *Ibid*., 7–8 Nov. 1918.
26. *Ibid*., 9 Nov. 1918. Watson, 9 Nov. 1918.
27. Hamilton, 11 Nov. 1918, reproduces this in full.
28. The Kaiser had fled to Holland, where he remained for the rest of his life.
29. Domvile, *By and Large*, pp.91–2.
30. Tennant, 11 Nov. 1918.
31. Taffrail, pp.433–9. Carr, p.249.
32. Chalmers, pp.341–7. Tennant (who supplies the anecdote), 14–18 Nov. 1918. Watson, 14–18 Nov. 1918.
33. Several other light cruisers were on detached service, and the *Canterbury* had even left for the Mediterranean a fortnight before the war ended (Watson, 27 Oct. 1918). The *Danae* and the *Dragon* belonged to a new 'D' class of light cruiser, slightly heavier than their predecessors and carrying six 6-inch guns instead of five, but with one knot less

speed.

34. *Times* and *Daily Sketch*, 21 Nov. 1918.
35. Watson, 30 Nov. 1918.
36. Tennant, Nov.–Dec. 1918.
37. Watson, 3, 6, 11 and 16 December 1918; 7 and 19 Jan. 1919.
38. Keyes Papers: RYT to Keyes, 2 Jan. 1919.
39. Watson, 23 Jan. 1919.
40. The ship had what even the hardened Domvile, deputising for Tyrwhitt, described as a really dreadful passage. The sea-sickness to which nearly all the officers and men succumbed was no respecter of Royalty, and the Queen's only companion and solace in her misery was the Admiral's black cat, Nigger.
41. Sir Godfrey Fausset.
42. T. Papers: RYT to AMT, undated.
43. *Ibid.*, RYT to FMT, 12 December 1918.
44. *Oxford Chronicle*, 7 Feb. 1919. T. Papers: Address to the boys of the Dragon School, Oxford, 2 Feb. 1919.
45. T. Papers: Admiralty to RYT, 9 April 1919.
46. St. John became a midshipman in May 1923, joining the *Iron Duke*, which was then the flagship of the Mediterranean Fleet.
47. *South Devon Times*, 22 June 1951. T. Papers: St. John Tyrwhitt to AMT, 20 April 1919.
48. *Ibid.*, RYT to AMT, 23, 25 and 26 April 1919. DoDomvile, *By and Large*, pp.94–5.
49. *Daily Mirror*, 2 May 1919.
50. Obituary by 'B.C.W.' (Vice-Admiral B.C. Watson) in *Times*, 18 June 1951.

CHAPTER EIGHT: GIBRALTAR AND THE MEDITERRANEAN

1. T. Papers: RYT to AMT, 6, 10 and 12 July 1919.

2. *Ibid.*, D. Lloyd George to RYT, 5 Aug. 1919; and Commission as Rear-Admiral, 2 Dec. 1919. Keyes Papers: RYT to Keyes, 26 June 1919.
3. *Ibid*, same to same, 8 Nov. 1919.
4. Cowan Papers: RYT to R/A Sir Walter Cowan, 9 April 1920.
5. The chef had later to be dismissed because of an extravagance amounting to dishonesty.
6. Keyes Papers: RYT to Keyes, 8 Nov. 1919.
7. T. Papers: Walter Long (First Lord) to RYT, 1 Dec. 1920.
8. Cowan Papers: Capt. Maclean to Cowan, 1 Jan. 1921.
9. Private information.
10. T. Papers: RYT to AMT, 9 Feb. 1921.
11. *Ibid.* Same to same, 2, 5, 6 and 13 Mar; and to BT, 7 Mar. 1921.
12. *Ibid.* RYT to AMT, 13 Mar. 1921.
13. *Ibid.* Same to same, 10 Feb. 1921.
14. *Ibid.* Same to same, 21 April 1921.
15. *Ibid.* Same to same, 26 Mar. 1922.
16. *Ibid.* Same to same, 12 April 1921.
17. *Ibid.* Same to same, 13 Mar. 1921.
18. *Ibid.*
19. *Ibid.* Same to same, 26 Mar. 1921.
20. *Ibid.* Same to same, 6 Mar. 1921.
21. *Ibid.* Same to same, 12 April 1919.
22. Tyrwhitt used often to give away to his friends the miniature models which he made of antique bow-fronted chests of drawers, knee-hole writing desks and the like. He made a chest of drawers for Queen Mary's Dolls' House at her request and also presented her with other pieces of his miniature furniture at different times.
23. T. Papers: RYT to AMT, 19 Feb., 2 and 13 Mar. 1921.
24. *Ibid.* Same to same, 19 Feb. 1921.
25. *Ibid.* Same to same, 9 and 19 Feb. and 13 Mar.; and to BT, 7 Mar., 1921.

26. *Ibid.* RYT to AMT, 2 and 13 Mar. 1921.
27. *Ibid.* Same to same, 21 April 1921.
28. *Ibid.* RYT to FMT, 16 Nov. 1921.
29. *Ibid.*
30. *Ibid.* RYT to AMT, 4, 5, 7 and 12 Sept. 1922.
31. *Ibid.* Same to same, 12 Sept. 1922.
32. *Ibid.* Same to same, 14 and 18–22 Sept. and 1 Oct. 1922.
33. It should be borne in mind that the French and Italians could, and did, use the argument that it was the ill-advised encouragement given to the Greeks by the British government which had provoked the Turkish advance.
34. T. Papers: RYT to AMT, 1 and 5 Oct. 1922.
35. *Ibid.* Same to same, 10 Oct. 1922.
36. *Ibid.* Same to same, 14 Oct. and 20 Nov. 1922.
37. Cowan Papers: RYT to Cowan, 10 Dec. 1922.
38. Petersfield lies on the northern side of the South Downs about a dozen miles from Portsmouth along the London road. The river Meon rises near it and flows first west and then south through a series of villages which form probably as attractive a group as any in southern England. During their pre-war life at Waterlooville, which is only a few miles away, the Tyrwhitts (even though he was there for only a little of the time) must have come to know this area well.
39. T. Papers: RYT to AMT, 15 and 17 Oct.; 7, 12, 13, 23 and 24 Nov.; 1, 4, 5 and 7 Dec. 1922; and to ACT, 13 Oct. 1922. Private information.

CHAPTER NINE: THE FAR EAST

1. Private information from Admiral Sir Alan Scott-Moncrieff (who was then Tyrwhitt's flag-lieutenant) and Dame Mary Tyrwhitt.

2. T. Papers: Jellicoe to RYT, 29 Sept. 1924.
3. Private information from Dame Mary Tyrwhitt.
4. Keyes Papers: RYT to Keyes, 14 Dec. 1926.
5. G.M. Gathorne-Hardy, *Short History of International Affairs, 1920–39,* pp.239–46.
6. The United States, Japan, France, Italy, Holland, Portugal, Belgium and China.
7. Afterwards Lord Killearn.
8. The remaining foreigners lived in the Chinese city.
9. *Survey,* 1926, pp.243–4, 302–3, 305–6, 316–7, 348–52, 362–7 and 367n.
10. Keyes Papers: RYT to Keyes, 14 Dec. 1926.
11. Among these fugitives was Lady Moloney, the widow of the Governor of Trinidad at whose house Tyrwhitt had first met his future wife. After her husband's death she had become a nun and embraced missionary work at Hanyang, opposite Hankow. From there she and her sister nuns had escaped disguised as Chinese women and were now working in a Shanghai hospital (RYT to FMT, 13 June 1927).
12. The cruisers *Enterprise* and *Emerald* had been sent from the East Indies Station to the China Station as reinforcements.
13. T. Papers: RYT to AMT, 10 Jan. 1927.
14. *Ibid*: copy of telegram from Commander-in-Chief, China, to Admiralty, 12 Jan. 1927.
15. *Ibid*., RYT to AMT, 10 Jan. 1927.
16. The late Vice-Admiral Caslon.
17. T. Papers: RYT to AMT, 13 Jan. 1927. *Survey*, 1926, pp.352–3.
18. *Ibid*., pp.354–9.
19. This unit was sent back to Hong Kong after the arrival of the Defence Force proper.
20. Afterwards Admiral of the Fleet Lord Cork and Orrery.
21. *Survey*, 1926, p.374. *Times*, 20, 25 and 28 Jan. and 9 Feb. 1927.

22. T. Papers: RYT to AMT, 16 Feb. 1927.
23. Private information.
24. T. Papers: RYT to AMT, 29 Jan. 1927.
25. *Survey*, 1926, p.378.
26. This was Admiral L.M. Bristol, who a few years earlier as American Senior Naval Officer and High Commissioner in Turkey just after the war, had shown strong but not altogether unjustified suspicions of British, French and Italian plans and intentions there (Roskill, Capt. S.W., *Naval Policy between the Wars*, I, p.184).
27. T. Papers: RYT to AMT, 2 Feb. 1927.
28. *Ibid.* Same to same, 4 Feb. 1927. *Survey*, 1926, p.375. *Times*, 12 Feb. 1927.
29. *Survey*, 1926, p.358.
30. T. Papers: RYT to AMT, 8 Feb. 1927.
31. *Ibid.* Same to same, 12 and 14 Feb. 1927.
32. T. Papers: Same to same, 18 and 19 Feb. 1927.
33. *Ibid.* Same to same, 21 Feb. 1927. *Survey*, 1926, pp.376–7.
34. T. Papers: RYT to AMT, 27 Feb. and 2 Mar. 1927.
35. *Ibid.* Same to same, 2 and 5 Mar. 1927.
36. *Ibid.* Same to same, 9 Mar. 1927. *Survey*, 1926, p.377.
37. *Ibid.*, p.378.
38. T. Papers: RYT to AMT, 22 Feb. and 5 Mar. 1927.
39. *Survey*, 1927, pp.370–3.
40. T. Papers: RYT to AMT, 18 Mar. 1927.
41. *Survey*, 1927, p.373.
42. *Ibid.*, p.371. T. Papers: RYT to AMT, 5 and 21 Mar. 1927.
43. *Ibid.* Same to same, 21 and 26 Mar. 1927. *Survey*, 1927, pp.371–2.
44. RYT to FMT, 29 Mar. 1927. According to Tyrwhitt, some Chinese newspapers assessed them at 200,000!
45. i.e. until all British subjects had been evacuated from treaty-ports and mission stations above Hankow,

which was completed by the end of March.

46. *Survey*, 1927, pp.382–91. T. Papers: RYT to AMT, 26 Mar. 1927.
47. *Ibid.* Same to same, 29 Mar. 1927.
48. *Survey*, 1927, pp.391–2.
49. T. Papers: RYT to AMT, 8 April 1927.
50. *Survey*, 1927, pp.392–3.
51. T. Papers: RYT to AMT, 10 April 1927.
52. *Ibid.* Same to same, 14 April 1927.
53. *Ibid.* Same to same, 'Easter Sunday' and 26 and 30 April and 3 May 1927.
54. *Ibid.* Same to same, 12 April 1927.
55. See p.162
56. T. Papers: RYT to AMT, 30 April 1927, Hamilton, 13, 18, 21 and 30 April, 1 and 2 May 1927.
57. T. Papers: Lt. Caslon to AMT, 6 May 1927.
58. *Ibid.*, RYT to AMT, 11 April 1927. *Survey*, 1927, pp.374 and 376.
59. T. Papers: Caslon to AMT, 6 May 1927.
60. *Survey*, 1927, pp.366–8.
61. T. Papers: RYT to FMT, 7 May, and to AMT, 14 May, 1927.
62. *Ibid.* Admiralty Telegrams 812–5 of 11 May and 817–20 of 12 May, 1927.
63. *Ibid.* RYT to AMT, 14 May 1927. Hamilton, 16 April 1927.
64. T. Papers: RYT to AMT, 6, 7 and 10 June, and to FMT, 13 June, 1927.
65. *Ibid.* RYT to FMT, 13 June 1927.
66. *Ibid.* RYT to AMT, 21 June 1927.
67. Cowan Papers: RYT to Cowan, 22 July 1927.
68. *Survey*, 1927, pp.374–5. T. Papers: RYT to AMT, 15–18 Aug. 1927.
69. *Survey* 1927, p.394.
70. *Ibid.* T. Papers: RYT to AMT, 21–6 Aug., and to FMT 4 Sept., 1927.
71. *Survey*, 1927, pp.376–7. Keyes Papers: RYT to Keyes,

28 Oct. 1927.

72. *Ibid.*, RYT to Keyes, 10 Feb. 1928. T. Papers: RYT to FMT, 9 Jan. 1928. Bishop Valtorta to FMT, 20 Feb. 1928. *Survey*, 1927, pp.358–61.
73. Keyes Papers: RYT to Keyes, 10 Feb. 1928.
74. T. Papers: RYT to FMT, 4 July 1928. Tyrwhitt was then fifty-eight.
75. Keyes Papers: RYT to Keyes, 28 Oct. 1927 and 10 Feb. 1928.
76. Gathorne-Hardy, *op. cit.*, p.352. T. Papers: Admiralty to RYT, 21 Jan. and 15 Mar. 1929, with enclosures: RYT to FMT, 4 July 1928.
77. *Survey*, 1928.
78. T. Papers: RYT to FMT, 4 July, 4 Aug. and 6 Sept. 1928.
79. Now Admiral Sir Charles Madden.
80. T. Papers: RYT to FMT, 6 Sept. 1928. Private information.
81. *Ibid.*, RYT to ACT, 13 and 27 Nov.; to FMT, 13 Nov. and 11 Dec.; and to AMT, 26 and 29 Nov. and 3 and 9 Dec. 1928.
82. *Ibid.*, RYT to AMT, 9 Dec. 1928.
83. *Ibid.*, His Imperial Majesty's Secretary to RYT, 7 Feb. 1929: RYT to AMT, 21, 25 and 28 Dec. 1928; 1 and 6 Jan. 1929.
84. *Ibid.* Admiralty to RYT, 12 Mar. 1929.
85. T. Papers: Admiral Sir Charles Madden to RYT, 29 July 1930. Grant of G.C.B., 30 July 1930.
86. *Ibid.*, Admiralty to RYT, 6 July 1929.

CHAPTER TEN: THE END OF THE JOURNEY

1. Keyes Papers: RYT to Keyes, undated and 18 Mar. and 4 April 1930. Private information.
2. T. Papers: 'Cedric' to AMT, 4 May 1931.
3. Divine, D., *Mutiny at Invergordon*, pp.65–177.

Edwards, K., *The Mutiny at Invergordon*, p. 121
4. Private information.
5. T. Papers: Dreyer to RYT, 5 Oct. 1931.
6. *Ibid.*, RYT to Kelly, 12 Jan. 1932.
7. Quoted in Divine, *op. cit.*, pp.233–5.
8. *Ibid.*, pp.238–53.
9. T. Papers: RYT to Kelly, 12 Jan. 1932.
10. Private information from Dame Mary Tyrwhitt.
11. *Daily Sketch*, 21 Oct. 1933.
12. *Ibid.*, 7 Mar. 1934. Log-book of *Arethusa* Training Ship, Mar., June and Sept. 1935.
13. T. Papers: Jubilee Renunion Dinner of *Britannia* Term, July 1883–July 1885.
14. *Daily Sketch,* 14 Mar. 1934. *Daily Telegraph*, 11 Aug. 1933; 14 Mar. and 9 Nov. 1934
15. T. Papers: Notification of appointment, 31 July 1934.
16. *Toronto Evening Telegram*, 4 Aug. 1934. *Globe* (Toronto), 4 Aug. 1934. *Mail and Empire* (Toronto), 4 and 6 Aug. 1934. *Toronto Daily Star*, 4 Aug. 1934.
17. T. Papers: RYT to Mrs. Patricia Lacy, 13 Aug. 1934.
18. *Times*, 3 and 4 July 1935.
19. *Daily Telegraph*, 26 Nov. 1935 and 17 Mar. 1936.
20. *Liverpool Daily Post*, 10 May 1935.
21. T. Papers: Rules and List of Members of the Harwich Force Dining Club.
22. Papers and particulars of the Harwich Naval Force Association supplied by its President, Captain P.L. Gunn, R.N., and by Dame Mary Tyrwhitt.
23. Captain P.L. Gunn to the author, 26 Oct. 1971.
24. T. Papers: Admiralty to RYT, 28 June 1939. *Times*, 31 July 1939.
25. *Daily Telegraph*, 4 Mar. 1940.
26. Private information.
27. Private information.
28. *Yorkshire Post*, 31 Jan. and 1 Feb. 1942.
29. Leicester Mercury, 28 Feb. 1942. *Scotsman*, 7 Mar. 1942.

30. *Bexhill Observer*, 4 Dec. 1943. *Who's Who*, 1959.
31. *Who's Who*, 1953.
32. Commander F. Lipscomb, Hon. Sec., Ex-Servicemen's Welfare Association, to author, 6 Dec. 1971.
33. *Morning Advertiser*, 4 June 1951.
34. *Times*, 23 June 1951.
35. *Ibid.*, 27 June 1951.
36. *Ibid.*, 18 June 1951.

BIBLIOGRAPHY

UNPUBLISHED SOURCES: DOCUMENTS, CORRESPONDENCE, DIARIES, ETC.

Additional Manuscripts in the British Museum
Admiralty Papers in the Public Record Office
The Tyrwhitt Papers
The Keyes Papers
The De Robeck Papers
The Cowan Papers
The Diaries of
  Admiral Sir Barry Domvile
  Admiral Sir Louis Hamilton
  Admiral Sir William Tennant
  Vice-Admiral B.C. Watson
The Papers of the Harwich Naval Force Association

PUBLISHED SOURCES

A. *BOOKS*

Aspinall-Oglander, C.F., *Roger Keyes* (London, 1951).

Bacon, Sir R., *Lord Fisher* (London, 1929).

The Life of John Rushworth, Earl Jellicoe (London, 1936).

Barnett, Corelli, *The Swordbearers: Studies in Supreme Command in the First World War* (London, 1963).

Bennett, Captain G., R.N., *'Charlie B.': The Life of Lord Charles Beresford* (London, 1968).

The Battle of Jutland (London, 1964).

Carr, W.G., *Brass Hats and Bell-Bottomed Trousers* (London, 1929).

Chalmers, Rear-Admiral W.S., *Life and Letters of David Beatty* (London, 1951).

Chatfield, Lord, *The Navy and Defence* (London, 1942).

Churchill, Sir W.S., *The World Crisis, 1911–1918* (London, 1923–9).
Thoughts and Adventures (London, 1932).
Divine, D., *Mutiny at Invergordon* (London, 1970).
Domvile, Admiral Sir Barry, *By and Large* (London, 1936).
Dorling, Captain Tapprell ('Taffrail'), *Endless Story* (London, 1931).
Dreyer, Admiral Sir F., *The Sea Heritage* (London, 1955).
Edwards, K., *The Mutiny at Invergordon* (London, 1937).
Falls, C., *The Great War* (New York, 1961).
Gathorne-Hardy, G.M., *A Short History of International Affairs, 1920–1939* (London, 1950).
Goodenough, Admiral Sir W., *A Rough Record* (London, 1943).
Guinn, P., *British Strategy and Politics, 1914 to 1918* (Oxford, 1965).
Hankey, Lord, *The Supreme Command, 1914–18* (London, 1961).
Hough, R., *First Sea Lord: an authorised Biography of Admiral Lord Fisher* (London, 1969).
Irving, Commander J., *The Smoke-Screen of Jutland* (London, 1966).
Jameson, Rear-Admiral Sir W., *The Most Formidable Thing: The Story of the Submarine to the End of World War I* (London, 1967).
Jellicoe, Admiral of the Fleet Lord, *The Grand Fleet, 1914–16* (London, 1919).
The Crisis of the Naval War (London, 1920).
The Submarine Peril (London, 1934).
Keyes, Admiral of the Fleet Lord, *Naval Memoirs*, Vol.I (London, 1934).
Liddell Hart, Sir Basil, *History of the World War, 1914–18* (London, 1934).
Macintyre, Captain D., R.N., *The Battle of Jutland* (London, 1960).
Marder, Arthur J., *Fear God and Dread Nought: the Correspondence of Admiral of the Fleet Lord Fisher*, 3

vols. (London, 1952–9).
From the Dreadnought to Scapa Flow, 5 vols. (London, 1961–70).

Official History of the War: Naval Operations, 5 vols. (London, 1921–31).

Pack, Captain S.W.C., R.N., *History of the Royal Naval College, Dartmouth* (London, 1959).

Patterson, A. Temple, *Jellicoe* (London, 1969).
(ed.) *The Jellicoe Papers*, 2 vols. (London, 1966–8).

Popham, H., *Into Wind* (London, 1969).

Repington, Lt-Col. C. à Court, *The First World War*, 2 vols. (London, 1920).

Roskill, Captain S.W., R.N., *Naval Policy between the Wars*, Vol.I (London, 1968).
(ed.) *The Naval Air Service: Vol.I, 1908–18* (London, 1969).

Royal Institute of International Affairs, *Survey of International Affairs, 1926* (Oxford, 1928) and *1927* (Oxford, 1929).

Scheer, Admiral R., *Germany's High Seas Fleet in the World War* (London, 1920).

Tyrwhitt, R.P., *Notices and Remains of the Family of Tyrwhitt* (London, 1872).

Wemyss, Lady V. Wester, *Life and Letters of Lord Wester Wemyss* (London, 1935).

Williams, M.W. *Anglo-American Isthmian Diplomacy, 1815–1915* (New York, 1965)

B. *NEWSPAPERS*

Excerpts from:-

The Bexhill Observer
The Daily Mail
The Daily Mirror
The Daily Sketch
The Daily Telegraph
The Globe
The Leicester Mercury

The Liverpool Daily Post
The Morning Advertiser
The Morning Post
The St. James's Gazette
The Scotsman
The South Devon Times
The Times
The (Toronto) Daily Star
The (Toronto) Evening Telegram
The (Toronto) Globe
The (Toronto) Mail and Empire
The Westminster Gazette

INDEX

NOTE: *Since the ranks held by many of the officers who have been referred to changed during the time covered by the references, they have been indexed with the rank held at the period to which the majority of these references apply. The same principle has been followed with regard to the titles of political and other public figures.*